*Rein*
THE HU

Also from Chalice Press:

*Realizing the America of Our Hearts: Theological Voices of Asian Americans,*
Edited by Fumitaka Matsuoka and Eleazar S. Fernandez

# *Reimagining* ᴛʜᴇ HUMAN

## Theological Anthropology in Response to Systemic Evil

## ELEAZAR S. FERNANDEZ

### CHALICE
PRESS

ST. LOUIS, MISSOURI

Biblical quotations, unless otherwise noted, are from the *New Revised Standard Version Bible*, copyright 1989, Division of Christian Education of the National Council of the Churches of Christ in the United States of America. Used by permission. All rights reserved.

Excerpt on pages 224–25 is from "The Woodcarver" by Thomas Merton, from THE WAY OF CHUANG TZU, copyright ©1965 by the Abbey of Gethsemani. Used by permission of New Directions Publishing Corporation.

Excerpt on page 164 is from "Barra and Turtle" by Christine Rowan, in *Earth Revealing, Earth Healing: Ecology and Christian Theology,* edited by Denis Edwards, copyright © 2001. Used by permission of Liturgical Press.

Cover art: "The Ascension," Bagong Kussudiardja, Asian Christian Art Association
Cover and interior design: Elizabeth Wright

This book is printed on acid-free, recycled paper.

Visit Chalice Press on the World Wide Web at
www.chalicepress.com


10  9  8  7  6  5  4  3  2  1          04  05  06  07  08  09


**Library of Congress Cataloging–in–Publication Data**

Fernandez, Eleazar S.
  Reimagining the human : theological anthropology in response to systemic evil / Eleazar S. Fernandez.– 1st ed.
      p. cm.
  ISBN 0-8272-3252-7 (alk. paper)
  1.  Man (Christian theology) 2.  Church and social problems.  I. Title.

BT701.3.F47 2003
233–dc22
                                                            2003018448

Printed in the United States of America

*To Josephine*
*Whose companionship helped me to behold*
*the flower in the bud,*
*the spring in the freezing winter,*
*the butterfly in the chrysalis,*
*the universe in a grain of sand,*
*the sacred in the ordinary,*
*the timeless in the timely.*

# Contents

# Acknowledgments

Writing this book has been a journey of challenges and tremendous blessings. I am aware of those moments when the challenges seemed obstacles and the blessings mere distractions. As authors know, writing a book demands such dedication and focus that it is easy to view as distractions those things that compete with our attention. Writing demands such singular attention that it is easy not to be mindful of our deep and delicate connections. I have been so determined to finish this project that I can only ask forgiveness from those individuals and creatures I may have treated as distractions along the way. I would like to name in particular my family, especially my growing children, Zarine and Joelle, students in my courses, and advisees.

Without doubt, the challenges that I encountered along the way delayed the speedy completion of this project. But they may have saved me from taking wrong turns and heading off in mistaken directions. With the gift of hindsight, I realize that the challenges encountered in writing this book have deepened and broadened my understanding of life and the world. Life's challenges have required me to set my project aside at times, allowing it to gather dust and cobwebs. They have forced me to acknowledge that there is more to life than writing a book and committing it to publication.

Indeed, there is more to life that we need to attend to while writing a book project like this. There are the daily chores, errands, and meetings to attend to as well as delightful moments of celebration: moments to enjoy with friends, moments to listen to uplifting music, moments to watch the changing color of the seasons, and moments to slow down and forget the flow of time. Writing this book has been a growth-producing and life-transforming experience. I feel like I have grown and matured along with this project. Looking back at my files, I realize that this book was not just written yesterday. To my amazement, the notes and research projects I drew on for this work extended as far back as my doctoral studies. As the years passed, I developed this material further while shaping my lecture notes for my course on theological anthropology.

Pondering the long and slow evolution of this writing project, I wonder if I can ever adequately express my deep gratitude to all those who have helped me along the way, whether directly or indirectly. I am sure I cannot remember and name all individuals and events, so it is appropriate that I express my general appreciation to all those who have graced my life. The meeting of our lives has fertilized my thoughts, shaping them in the direction that is now set forth in this book.

More particularly, I want to express my deep gratitude to Nancy Victorin-Vangerud, a longtime friend and colleague who now teaches at Murdoch University, Perth, Australia, for a thorough critique of the whole manuscript and for gentle suggestions. My gratitude goes as well to her husband, Bob, for friendship and hospitality, especially during my visit to Perth. I am also grateful to Fumitaka Matsuoka for his thoughtful comments and for helping me see the limitations of traditional theological categories. Likewise, I am grateful to Kosuke Koyama, who now resides in Minneapolis, for reading the whole manuscript and for his supportive response. Moreover, I want to express my gratitude to Jon L. Berquist of Chalice Press for his enthusiastic support and editorial supervision.

As each of the chapters unfolded over the years, I have been graced by able student assistants. I want to thank Katherine McCurry, Rodney Richards, Matthew Bersagel-Braley, and Kathleen Remund. They served as the first readers of my manuscript and alerted me to some aspects that needed to be clarified or polished. Also worthy of my acknowledgment are individuals who provided me with technical assistance: Dale Dobias, Renee Dougherty, Len Kne, Cindi Beth Johnson, Mary Ann Nelson, and Marcial Vasquez. I remember the times when I stopped them in the hallway to ask for help with research, computer program applications, or copying work.

I also want to express my gratitude to United Theological Seminary of the Twin Cities for two semesters of sabbatical leave that allowed me to focus on writing this book. I am grateful in particular to our dean, Richard Weis, for his encouragement and for his ingenuity in looking for additional financial support in the midst of budgetary constraints. My UTS colleagues deserve my gratitude for giving me the opportunity to present a chapter at one of our faculty gatherings. And to the students in my courses, particularly the course on theological anthropology, I am grateful for your companionship in wrestling with some of the issues I addressed in this book.

As a person who has been blessed by global church connections, I am thankful to many friends and institutions from various countries. My teaching experience at Lisu Theological Seminary in the northern part of Myanmar (Burma), my visit to Fiji and Australia, a theological education seminar in Switzerland, and trips to the U.S.-Mexico border and southern India helped me see the global dimensions of the interlocking systemic evils addressed in this book. I want to thank in particular James Vijayakumar for my trip to southern India in June 2002. My profound thanks go to my host J. Premkumar and his wife Senega of Colachel, Tamil Nadu, for heart-warming hospitality that I will always cherish. And I am deeply thankful to Bishop V. Devasahayam, Diocese of Madras, Church of South India, for helping me see that church ministry can truly make a difference in people's lives.

With deep roots in the Philippine soil, I always look forward to a yearly visit even when the trip is tiring and financially draining. This yearly visit reconnects me to the land of my birth and to the people I know and care about. My appreciation goes to the Global Ministries (common ministry of the United Church of Christ, U.S.A., and Christian Church [Disciples of Christ]) for the mission volunteer opportunity with The College of Maasin in 2002 and to my hosts Miguel Udtohan, Zuriel and Mary Lou Tiempo, and Emmanuel Bascug. My appreciation goes as well to Jaime Moriles, Conference Minister of the Southern-Western Leyte Conference, United Church of Christ in the Philippines, for arranging yearly lecture series for the church workers. I also convey my deep appreciation to Oscar Suarez, Mariano Apilado, Elizabeth Tapia, Noriel and Rebecca Capulong, Bishop Erme and Henie Camba, Bishop Isaias Bingtan, Rebecca Lawson, Carlton "Cobbie" Palm, Ferdinand Corro, Cromwell "Tibo" Rabaya, Edison Lapuz, and Ferdinand Anno, for working me into their busy schedule in some of my Philippine trips, and for making my visits fun and memorable.

The long and cold Minnesota winters, in which daylight time is short and nighttime long, would be cruel to a child of the tropics without a circle of friends and communities with whom to share pain, joy, dreams, and hopes. I am deeply grateful to Karen and Terry Aitkens, Daniel and Sally Mann-Narr, Wendy Trone, Glen Herrington-Hall, Jack Shelton, Carol Chumley, Constancio "Mike" Pineda, Jess de Jesus, Gonzalo and Melita Olojan, and friends in the Philippine Study Group of Minnesota. It is truly a blessing to have friends not only to share the grand moments of living, but to call when I need child care or when my old and tired car refuses to start.

Finally, I could not have gone on without the unfailing love and support of my family in spite of all my failings. I am truly grateful to my wife Jo and to our daughters Zarine and Joelle, for having endured with me throughout these years. When the going gets rough, Jo never fails to remind me that there is more to life that we should cherish; that the days of our lives are fleeting, so we must care for each other and treasure each moment of our togetherness. I cannot say with certainty that I am a better person now, but I can say that I am no longer ashamed to cry in front of my children even as I have learned to share my joys, dreams, and hopes. Thank you, Zarine and Joelle, for walking with me in this life's journey and making it a walk to remember. You have stretched my patience, expanded the boundaries of what it means to care, and given me joy. Our family journey has sharpened my poetic sensibility and creative imagination. God has blessed our journey—and we must not forget to count our blessings!

Eleazar S. Fernandez
Fridley, Minnesota

# Introduction

How can we be human in a world marred by pervasive disregard for the sacred web of life that sustains our whole inhabited world? How can we be human in a society in which the violation of human life is a daily reality? How can we be human when the idols of death continue to inhabit our world and demand daily sacrifices? How can we be human in the midst of the constant assault of systemic evils at both the local and global level? We seem not bereft of good intentions; why is it, then, that we continue to create systems that dehumanize us and ravage the ecosystem? Why do we continue to justify our sinister acts and engage in organized forgetting? Why do we remember "our" Sept. 11, 2001, tragedy and do not remember (or do not want to remember) the tragedy we may have inflicted on others? If "terrorists" can assume the guise of "freedom fighters," is it not equally true that "terrorism can assume the guise of a war against terrorism?"[1]

Are we then condemned to hopelessness? Must we wallow in cynicism and hedonistic play? Must we just wait for apocalypse? Where is that so-called balm of Gilead, to heal our festering wounds? Where will we find the sustenance we need to live a life of integrity in the present? How do we muster courage when the forces of closure are overwhelming? These are some of the painful questions I have wrestled with at various stages in my life, in various contexts, and in various capacities.

I am sure that the above questions are not new, but they have to be asked again and again because they reflect both our painful daily reality and our longings for greater well-being. Many times in my life I tried to run away from the demands that these questions pose in relation to how I live and exercise my vocation. I still remember during my college and seminary years when my parents took steps to shield me from the questions and demands of our ailing society. Even with their humble educational background, they were aware of the high cost when someone truly responds to the haunting questions posed by our broken world.

What my parents feared slowly became a reality. More and more I have been drawn into grappling with the haunting questions of our fractured society. Now that my eyes have been opened, it torments my soul to ignore these questions. The words of the writer of Ecclesiastes resonate with this experience: "For in much wisdom is much vexation, /and those who increase knowledge increase sorrow" (1:18). With years of theological training, I rephrase the text like this: "One who increases in theological wisdom increases in sorrow, and the more one knows theology the more one suffers."

It is not an easy and enjoyable task to name our pains, but name them we must. Our anguished questions must be raised and broadcast from the rooftops. A space must be created where our losses can be mourned and our laments can be raised to the heavens. Silence is not going to protect us. It surely did not protect Carlos Bulosan and the early group of Filipinos who arrived on the shores of the "land of the free and home of the brave." Growing sick and tired of being silent, Bulosan finally found the courage to raise his voice.

"They can't silence me anymore! I'll tell the world what they have done to me!"[2] These were the impassioned words of Bulosan in a letter to his brother Macario after realizing, "like a revelation," that he could "actually write understandable English." It was not only the simple discovery that he could write or articulate "understandable English" that made this occasion momentous, but also because Bulosan had discovered a medium that would give voice to his pain, rage, and dreams. The young Bulosan eventually found a voice that could not be silenced anymore. Writing, Bulosan soon found out, is a political act.

From the day of his arrival on the shores of the United States, Bulosan witnessed and personally experienced the suffering of his "kababayans" (countryfolks) and of other racial minorities. Out of his many painful experiences, he shared a particular moment in his life when he felt extremely "violated and outraged." On this occasion, two policemen invaded a party at a Filipino restaurant, waving their pistols and physically abusing Bulosan and a guest from the Philippines. Hurt and humiliated, Bulosan thought of getting his gun. "I wanted my gun," Bulosan wrote. "With it I could challenge our common enemy bullet for bullet. It seemed my only friend and comfort in this alien country–this smooth little bit of metal."[3] Bulosan went to his hotel room to get the "smooth little bit of metal," but his brother Macario grabbed the gun away from him. Nevertheless, Bulosan vowed to fight back!

He fought back not with bullets, but with his writings. He fought back with words that no tyrant could silence. Bulosan proclaimed to the world the suffering of the laborers in the field and in the fish canneries of America. Through his writings, Bulosan decided to offer his talent in order to give voice to the voiceless. He who had once felt powerless experienced empowerment through his writing. He wrote and wrote even as he was struggling for his own life. "That's it, Carl," Pascal (an editor of a workers' newspaper) would shout with resounding approval to Bulosan. "Write your guts out! Write with thunder and blood!"[4]

It took the right (though painful) confluence of events and circumstances for Bulosan to understand what his brother Luciano had told him during his boyhood years in the Philippines. Luciano had encouraged the young

Carlos "never to stop reading good books...Maybe someday you will become a journalist." At that time Bulosan did not know exactly what it meant to be a journalist. As his life in America unfolded, Bulosan came to know what being a journalist meant. Remembering his parents' hardships and those of the peasants in the Philippines, he sobbed: "Yes, I will be a writer and make all of you live again in my words."[5]

The price of silence is high. Silence is not going to protect us. Silence, to paraphrase José Comblin, is a lie when truth needs to be spoken.[6] We must name our pains no matter how hurtful, for without the courage to name our pains, we are also without words to articulate our deepest joy, soaring hopes, and creative imaginations. There is no route to the humanity we ache and long for that bypasses both the naming and struggle against systemic evils. It is only in confrontation with the systemic evils of our time that our hopes are purged of any easy optimism.

Naming our pains and articulating our soaring hopes are formative to my theology. As a constructive theologian, I consider it an important task to enable faith communities to construct a theology that names their pains and laments their anguish, celebrates their joys, poetically articulates their longings for a better tomorrow, orients their transforming actions to the here and now, and equips them with courage to live as if the future were present. Because we do not do theology *de novo*, out of nothing, the constructive task necessarily involves deconstruction and re-appropriation of what we have received. Recognizing the role that theology has played in perpetuating various forms of dehumanization, theology is an arena of struggle. A theological struggle must be waged by exposing and deconstructing theologies that are hurtful and constructing theologies that promote greater well-being.

The constructive task of a theologian is not an easy one, but I have accepted this challenge. More particularly, I have accepted the challenge of constructing a theological anthropology that names our pains and articulates our longings for a better tomorrow. While it is true that there are other valid approaches in dealing with the questions posed by our fractured society, the area of theological anthropology remains critical and strategic. I say this based on my understanding that if there is one concern—among many—that people of varied ideological persuasions agree on in spite of their passionate disagreement, it is that our construal of anthropology bears upon how we live, organize our societal dwelling, and relate to other creatures. Specific to theological anthropology, it is a discourse about us human beings as we seek to interpret our identity, plight, and destiny in light of our religious understanding and practice. Put differently, it raises profound questions about our own humanity, namely: Who are we, where are we, what do we hope for, and how do we get there?

In pursuit of this constructive theological project, the questions borne out of anguish and longings that I raised in opening this project have given way to questions for anthropological construction: How would I reimagine and construct a theological anthropology that articulates our longings and struggles to forge a new human being in the fullness of God's shalom? What sensibilities would I advocate and nurture that may lead us to greater well-being? What is the place of human beings in the cosmic web of life? How would I name the radical evils of our time? What is the basis of hope in our struggle to find a new humanity?

More specific to this project is my interest in constructing a theological anthropology in response to systemic evils of our time, particularly the four radical evils: classism, sexism, racism, and naturism.[7] Of course we can add to the list, but I have chosen to deal with the four as a test case for anthropological construction. With our deepening awareness of the complex and sophisticated ways of dehumanization, I am sure that new forms of systemic evil will become part of our daily vocabulary. It remains true, however, that the four systemic evils that are the focus of this study are among the major and pervasive evils that have beleaguered our world.

These four systemic evils that have plagued our society have been challenged and breakthroughs have been made. But with every inch of "progress," new expressions appear or new realizations happen that offset the "progress," so that "progress," it seems to me, has only occurred against the measure of older forms. While every inch of victory needs to be celebrated to sustain us in the long and arduous journey, self-satisfaction can be self-delusion. Gloria Yamato's comment about racism can be applied to other forms of systemic evils as well: "Like a virus, it's hard to beat racism, because by the time you come up with a cure, it's mutated to a 'new cure-resistant' form. One shot just won't get it."[8] Francis Garchitonera's words also can be appropriated here: "If you build a better mousetrap today, it doesn't mean you'll have fewer [mice] tomorrow. What you will have [are] smarter mice."[9]

As in other forms of systemic evil, there is something properly theological in classism, sexism, racism, and naturism that make them proper subjects for theological investigation. I say properly theological because at the heart of classism, sexism, racism, and naturism are matters of faith and idolatry–the elevation of something finite to the status of ultimacy. These four forms of systemic evil are prime instances of idolatry: worshiping human constructs and living under false securities.

Idolatry strikes so deep because it addresses our need for security. Do we not desire to close all possible windows of vulnerability? Because finite and mundane goods fill the gaping void and our deep craving for security, we become attached to them and we are possessed by them. Eventually, we give them the status of eternal securers–idols. Idolatry is living under false securities; it is sin defined as "living a lie."[10] Living under this lie may become so deep-seated as to lead individuals and communities to believe in Mark Twain's sage observation that "one of the most startling differences between a cat and a lie is that a cat has only nine lives."[11]

I agree with Pablo Richard in saying that in an oppressive world, the fundamental enemy of evangelization is not atheism but idolatry.[12] Idolatry, not atheism, is the fundamental enemy of life. Atheism does not demand sacrifice, idolatry does. Idols demand the sacrifice of our souls, bodies, time, and anything that we cherish most. Even those who proclaim themselves atheists have their idols of death. In the face of these idols of death, we need to say with Ernst Bloch that "only an atheist can be a good Christian."[13] This is no mere atheism of the modern secular person, but Christian prophetic atheism. Prophetic atheism was the stance of the early Christians against the idols of the Roman Empire. They faced persecution and death rather than worship the idols of the Empire. Likewise, prophetic atheism must be our stance against the idols of death that claim ultimate allegiance. In the face of the idols of death of our time, prophetic atheism is a mark of our Christian faithfulness.

Having come to the point of stating the main focus of this theological project, more specific questions tied to the constructive work have come to the fore: What is the shape and content of a theological anthropology that seeks to respond to the evils of classism, sexism, racism, and naturism? How do I give theological voice not only to human pain in general, but to the pain of those who have been crushed by systemic evils of our society and who are dying before their time? What framework would be helpful in integrating the distinctive but interlocking structures of systemic evil? What images and metaphors would I use to articulate my vision of a human being liberated from the clutches of classism, sexism, racism, and naturism?

To carry out this constructive work, I divided this project into nine chapters. Chapter 1 presents my hermeneutic lens for constructing theological anthropology. Any adequate reconstructive or imaginative work cannot proceed without engaging in deconstruction as well; thus, along with my proposed hermeneutic lens is my deconstruction of some of the prevailing conceptual traps such as: disembodied knowing, totalizing discourse, essentialist thinking, dualistic and atomistic thinking, and the myth of original uniformity that preceded diversity. Against these conceptual traps, I advance some hermeneutic lenses that, in my judgment, would help us not only to avoid some of the conceptual traps but also to move beyond "reactive" and binary oppositional ways of thinking. These hermeneutic lenses provide the epistemological undergirding for my reading of contexts and texts, as well as for theological reconstruction.

Chapter 2 proceeds with my presentation of the interlocking structure of classism, sexism, racism, and naturism. Here I take the position that they are not isolable from one another. I also make the assertion that the configuration of one's experience of a specific form of oppression is influenced by the extent to which one is affected by other forms of oppression. In other words, one's experience of any of the four systemic forms of oppression is always circumscribed by the other forms. When a person shifts social and geographical location, her or his experience of the systemic evils also takes a different configuration. I want to establish in this chapter that though the various forms of systemic evils are distinct, they intertwine in an interlocking demonic structure.

Following my account of the interlocking structure of the various systemic evils is my theological rendering of this phenomenon (chapter 3). In this chapter I re-center the notion of sin from one primarily understood as a rebellion against God to that of violation against creation's well-being. Still, sin is violation against God, but only by way of our violation of creation's well-being or only because we human beings encounter God through the created world. Focus is also given to my social construction of sin and the role social institutions play in the perpetuation of sin and evil. Additionally, I point out in this chapter that the systemic character of sin sheds light on the notion of "original sin" and the necessity of systemic change.

Chapters 4–7 focus on my specific treatment of each of the four systemic evils. Each chapter includes a critique of the systemic evil in question, a brief exposition and deconstruction of theological anthropologies that undergird it, and my anthropological reconstruction. With this format, each chapter (4–7) can stand on its own as a work of reconstruction, even as each is an integral part of the overall constructive project. I would like to highlight for the readers that each of the chapters (4–7) model my constructive work, even as the broader constructive theological integration is still to come in chapter 8. In other words, chapter 8 is an integration of my constructive work, not the beginning.

My treatment of the four systemic evils follows this order: classism (chapter 4), sexism (chapter 5), racism (chapter 6), and naturism (chapter 7). There is nothing sacrosanct with this order. The order in my treatment of these evils does not mean the primacy of one over the others, but it reflects my expanding awareness and intentional wrestling with their presence at various points in my life. Also, only in the recent part of my life, especially as a professor teaching in the United States, did I come to see with greater clarity the interlocking structure of the various evils.

I start my critique of systemic evils, and reconstruction of an alternative theological anthropology, by dealing with classism (chapter 4). Again, I emphasize, there is no claim being made here that classism is the fundamental "ism." I start with it because of its pivotal role in my experience. Still vivid in my memory are those events in my boyhood years in the Philippines when my family of origin was treated condescendingly because of my parents' economic and social status. I still live with the memory of my parents being threatened with eviction from our dwelling place. Classism is a glaring and brutal reality in the country of my birth, and those in the higher social echelons will make a point to remind the underdogs of this. Thus, I start with classism in my separate treatment of the four systemic evils because it has played a pivotal role in the development of my personality, social consciousness, and current theological concerns.

Chapter 4 situates classism within the wider global market system and explores its theological undergirding as well as its various expressions. In this chapter I articulate the various expressions of sin in relation to classism. I also explore the connections between classism and elitism; classism, consumerism, and identity; classism, powerlessness, and fatalism; classism, contempt, and the fear of falling into the lower status. The other portion of the chapter is my attempt to reconfigure theologically the human face that has been shattered by classism. In this reconfiguring task I have found the concept of God the economist and *imago Dei* as an economic commission to be insightful.[14] This concept provides the orienting vision in which I judge our economic system and its reason for being.

The next chapter (chapter 5) tackles the evil of sexism, exposes patriarchal and sexist theologies, and attempts to reconstruct a theological anthropology. Sexism follows my treatment of classism because it was the next systemic evil that made a claim on the way I live and do theology. As in the previous chapter, an important portion of this chapter is devoted to a reinterpretation of sin in light of sexism. The rest of the chapter presents my alternative reconstruction of anthropology in which I advocate a theology of vulnerability, embodiment, and connections. Also in this chapter is my attempt to reinterpret *imago Dei* and christology as they bear on my alternative theological anthropology.

Sexism is followed by the chapter on racism (chapter 6). Even while in the Philippines I was aware of the evil of racism, but racism did not define my day-to-day experience. I took the issue of race for granted because my race was not an issue. This situation, however, changed dramatically when I settled in the U.S. Every time I look in the mirror, white America reminds me that I belong to the "other" race. In white America I could not take my race for granted anymore: My race in a white racist America has become an issue of contestation. It has become a source of pain. White America has brought the evil of racism to the forefront of my social consciousness and to the way I do theology.

Chapter 6 confronts the evil of racism, exposes its theological undergirdings, and explores an anthropology that aspires to move beyond racism. As in the chapter on sexism, I reinterpret sin in light of racism. This focus lends to an interpretation of sin that is particular to the systemic evil that is addressed. Sin even assumes different expressions between the dominating race and the subjugated race. This reinterpretation of sin is followed by my attempt to articulate a new humanity redeemed from the thrall of racism and a vision of a colorful society. I envision this colorful future not as mere pluralism or a multi-colored world, but as a world in which image representations, difference, and power dynamics serve to secure the well-being of all.

The anthropological challenge of naturism is addressed in chapter 7. This chapter critiques the ideology of naturism and exposes its devastating consequences for the ecosystem. In order to make sure that my reading of naturism takes into consideration the interplay of other systemic evils, I devote a significant portion of this chapter relating ecology to the issue of social justice. As in my chapters on classism, sexism, and racism, I critique the devastation of the whole ecosystem and the role human beings have played in such a crisis. In this chapter I argue that the move beyond naturism requires not simply a call to an ethical responsibility but a call to a new sensibility—a new way of thinking and dwelling.

Chapter 8 culminates my reconstructive enterprise with a multi-dimensional and integrated approach to anthropology. If the various systemic evils interlock, theological construction must take an integrated approach so as to address in multiple ways the various aspects of our dehumanization. This approach does not adopt a binary view of male and female natures, nor does it abbreviate human nature into a single ideal to which everything and everybody must conform. Rather, it sees the various elements that constitute human existence within our cosmic home in an integrated and holistic way.

Whereas I started with classism and ended with naturism, in chapter 8 I synthesize the various constructive points by starting with ecological insights. There is a valid reason for doing this. Ecology deals with the worldview or the overall structure through which we see ourselves in relation to the whole scheme of things. Ecological sensibility helps us to de-center and situate ourselves within the cosmic web of life. It is within this wider framework that I situate the insights garnered from my critique of classism, sexism, and racism.

The final chapter (chapter 9) takes account of eschatology and its bearings on human agency, especially in relation to our struggle for full humanity. As much as we think about eschatology in relation to the future, it is really more about the future as its power is experienced in the present. In other words, the humanity of the future that I am trying to paint theologically is not simply out there waiting for our arrival, but is in the journey. While we look forward and anticipate the fullness of our liberation, the struggle itself is an experience of liberation. We see this new humanity coming into being among those who have struggled and continued to hope in spite of the durability of the forces of closure. This chapter is an expression of my defiant hope and eschatological imagination.

I offer to you the invitation to journey with me in this quest for an alternative anthropology because I believe that you are as passionately concerned as I am. Let this passion propel us to ache for an anthropology that is nonanthropocentric; an anthropology that seeks connections while respecting the integrity of the individual; an anthropology that moves beyond patriarchy and makes possible the development of an integrated self; an anthropology that transgresses class privileges and restores the humanity of all; an anthropology that is not "color-blind" nor indifferent to difference, but sees difference as a principle of interdependence and life.[15]

Reconstructing theological anthropology with a vision of moving beyond classism, racism, sexism, and naturism is not a simple discursive and nondiscursive task. The reconstructive move is complex, fraught with danger, and, indeed, daunting. I pursue this project not to offer the master discourse that would provide closure to our common search for the human, but to continue the quest and conversation. The task is complex and enormous, but it need not be paralyzing. Rabbi Tarfon's words have been a source of inspiration for me and I hope they are to you as well: "It is not upon [us] to finish the work. Neither are [we] free to desist from it."[16]

So far as this specific project is concerned, it is finished. However, much remains to be done, and this project is only a moment in our common struggle to forge a new humanity. The poem *Sleep My Child*, written by a Taiwanese girl, speaks deeply of a resolute hope and a commitment to forge a better tomorrow in our trying times.

> To bed now, my child!
> It is already very late.
> Tomorrow, we still have work to do,
> Tomorrow, we still have to go to school.
> Child! Why are you not yet asleep?
> I know:
> You still have much to say.
> I know:
> You still have many things you want to do.
> But,
> Tomorrow…
> I know when you all grow up,
> You will surely know what it is that I want to say.
> Sleep then, my child![17]

What is tomorrow in the heart of a girl? Small or big, she believes that there is a tomorrow and that there must be a tomorrow. But this tomorrow does not come by itself. The mother in the poem reminds her child of the work that must be carried out. I say, blessed are those who dream dreams, but we also need blessed people who are willing to help make our common dreams come true. I release this project to the world of readers knowing full well that "tomorrow, we still have work to do." Tomorrow's work is waiting, for our dreams of a new humanity and a new world are still unfinished.

The chapters that follow unfold my struggle in the quest for an alternative theological anthropology. Though the focus of my theological construction is in response to just four systemic evils–classism, sexism, racism, and naturism–I believe that the framework and insights in this work are "extensible."[18] As I said earlier, each chapter can stand on its own. However, in order to see the whole picture of my constructive enterprise, reading the work in its entirety is advised. I hope that you will be engaged by my deconstructive critique and reconstructive theological proposals. May this work inspire us to explore alternative ways of being human that promote the web of life in which we all are woven.

## Notes

[1]Lee Griffith, *The War on Terrorism and the Terror of God* (Grand Rapids, Mich., and Cambridge, U.K.: William B. Eerdmans, 2002), x.

[2]Carlos Bulosan, cited in Ronald Takaki, *In the Heart of Filipino America: Immigrants from the Pacific Isles* (New York and Philadelphia: Chelsea House Publishers, 1995), 90.

[3]Ibid., 88.

[4]Ibid., 91.

[5]Ibid., 90.

[6]José Comblin, *The Church and National Security State* (Maryknoll, N.Y.: Orbis Books, 1979), 15.

[7]I use the term "naturism" to name the ideology that undergirds destructive practices against the ecosystem.

[8]Gloria Yamato, "Something About the Subject Makes It Hard to Name," *Experiencing Race, Class, and Gender in the United States*, ed. Virginia Cyrus (California, London, and Toronto: Mayfield Publishing Company, 1993), 207.

[9]Francis Garchitonera, Presiding Justice of the Sandigan Bayan of the Philippines (anti-graft court), on curbing corruption within the government, in *Filipinas* (August 1998): 37.

[10]Sallie McFague, *The Body of God: An Ecological Theology* (Minneapolis: Fortress Press, 1993), 110.

[11]Mark Twain, cited in Donald Messer, *Christian Ethics and Political Action* (Valley Forge, Pa.: Judson Press, 1984), 129.

[12]Pablo Richard, *Our Struggle Against the Idols* (Ozamis City, Philippines: Community Formation Center, 1984).

[13]Ernst Bloch, cited in José Miguez Bonino, *Room to Be People: An Interpretation of the Message of the Bible in Today's World*, trans. Vickie Leach (Philadelphia: Fortress Press, 1979), 9–25.

[14]See M. Douglas Meeks, *God the Economist: The Doctrine of God and Political Economy* (Minneapolis: Fortress Press, 1989).

[15]I am reluctant to use the term "color blind" even for metaphorical reason, but it is a precise language that conveys my point well. See Kathy Black, *A Healing Homiletic: Preaching and Disability* (Nashville: Abingdon Press, 1996).

[16]Rabbi Tarfon, cited in Paul Kivel, *Uprooting Racism: How White People Can Work for Racial Justice* (Gabriola Island, British Columbia: New Society Publishers, 1996), xii.

[17]A poem by Lin Lin in *Li Poetry Magazine*, no. 93, 43, cited in C. S. Song, *Theology from the Womb of Asia* (Maryknoll, N.Y.: Orbis Books, 1986), 106–7.

[18]"Extensible" or capable of extension. See Ian Barbour, *Religion in an Age of Science* (New York: HarperCollins Publishers, 1990), 45.

# CHAPTER 1

# *Exploring Hermeneutic Lenses for Reconstructing the Human*

Out of the pain of those who have experienced life at the margins new voices have emerged challenging our usual ways of thinking and doing. These voices are not simply content to give "new" answers to "old" questions (answers that, as it is argued, continue to operate within the old parameters); rather, they attempt to raise "new" questions that often jar the parameters of the old questions.[1] This questioning of the old parameters is an expression of a crisis simmering at the heart of our society, a crisis that I would characterize as a crisis of sensibility. I am taking these new voices seriously and this chapter reflects my own struggle to find a different hermeneutic lens for constructing theological anthropology. What follows is a simultaneous double move of deconstruction of some conceptual traps and an articulation of a hermeneutic lens.

## From Hermeneutic Manicheanism to Embodied Knowing

The term "hermeneutic Manicheanism" is my reappropriation of William Lloyd Newell's notion of "methodological Manicheanism."[2] Newell characterizes this as a methodology that has forgotten its own historicity. What Newell calls methodological Manicheanism resonates with what others call "disembodied knowing," a knowing that has forgotten its own embodiedness.[3] It is a knowing that has severed the head from the body, as if it were possible to think without our bodies or as if we do not think through our bodies. If I am who I am only through my body, it is inconceivable to imagine a form of thinking that has forgotten the body. But this form of thinking is a pervasive one.

I am aware that with the advent of modernity there has been a greater realization of our conditionedness or a greater awareness that we understand

11

as we do because we "exist" as we do and, conversely, we exist as we do because we interpret as we do. This hermeneutic move toward humans' historical conditionedness points in the proper direction, but the move has been aborted and left hanging before it has touched the ground. By remaining at the ontological level, this move has abbreviated "history" into "historicity."[4]

Karl Marx and Friedrich Engels launched a similar criticism against Ludwig Feuerbach at the turn of modernity.[5] Feuerbach vigorously challenged speculative thoughts and identified his stand: "I differ *toto coelo* from those philosophers who pluck out their eyes that they may see better; for *my* thought I require the senses, especially sight; I found my ideas on materials which can be appropriated only through the activity of the senses."[6]

But Marx and Engels found the Feuerbachian-turn-to-the-self or to the realm of the senses unable to touch the ground completely. Engels could only say of Feuerbach that "the lower half of him is materialist; the upper half is idealist."[7] Feuerbach remained bourgeois materialist and stopped short in general psychology and anthropology without grounding his subjects in embodied history. In a similar way, many hermeneutic theories stop short in ontology and historicity or in the linguisticality of understanding and interpretation.

Cornel West continues the criticism launched against disembodied knowing. For him, any talk about historicity that does not deal with our embodied sociality (geographical location, class, race, gender, etc.) is "thin" history. In West's lines:

> To tell a tale about the historical character of philosophy while eschewing the political content, role, and function of philosophies in various historical periods is to promote an ahistorical approach in the name of history. To undermine the privileged philosophic notions of necessity, universality, rationality, objectivity, and transcendentality without acknowledging and accenting the oppressive deeds done under the ideological aegis of these notions is to write an intellectual and homogeneous history, a history which fervently attacks epistemological privilege but remains relatively silent about forms of political, economic, racial, and sexual privilege.[8]

Feminists and womanist writers have launched a sustained critique against various expressions of disembodied knowing and its oppressive consequences.[9] Disembodied knowing usually portrays itself as pure and value-free (pristine logic), and is associated with male rationality: detachment and objectivity. Such a view, feminist thinkers argue, is opposed to embodiedness and subjectivity, which are ways of knowing traditionally identified with women. Disembodied knowing, which is masquerading itself as objective and universal, must be exposed for what it is: "concrete, situated, particular, and limited."[10]

There is, I believe, a need to move away from the view that denigrates our embodiedness toward an embodied knowing: a way of knowing that celebrates our embodiedness.[11] Embodied knowing sees reality through the configuration of our bodiliness and seriously considers the effects of ideas as they bear on bodies and vice versa, especially the disfigured bodies of the marginalized. As a form of knowing, it demands that one does not remain content with mere assertions of historicity that mute differences; instead, it pays attention to radical plurality, particularity, and the differences between human beings and other living beings.

Pursuing historical embodiment seriously requires that we take the "who" of our discourse in such a way that introduces into hermeneutics the rich detail of social location, which is crucial to any interpretive enterprise.[12] When we take the "who" of our discourse beyond the ontological level into the rich details of geography and social location, we come to the realization that our interpretations are not separate from, but are tied to, who we are. Not only do we interpret texts, the interpreted texts interpret us. Moreover, *our identities* also interpret the texts.[13]

Embodied knowing calls us to a different way of seeing, opening up new and rich dimensions for constructing theological anthropology. Contrary to the understanding that an embodied hermeneutic is myopic and exclusivist, it is broad and responsive to the particularities of a given context. Embodied knowing opens up novel ways of interpreting various theological concepts, such as transcendence and immanence. In embodied knowing, transcendence and immanence are two sides of the same reality. Transcendence is not moving away from embodiment, but being thoroughly embodied in multifarious specificity. Instead of running away from embodiment, the transcendent is, in fact, experienced in concrete embodiments.

### Beyond Totalizing Discourse

Disembodied knowing works along with universalizing and totalizing discourse. Oftentimes without knowing it, we elevate a particular perspective to the level of universality; thereby, we impose it on others under the mask of objectivity and neutrality. "I am increasingly aware," writes Sharon Welch, "that to speak of the universal is all too often, and perhaps even necessarily, to elevate as universal and normative a particular aspect of human being."[14] Similarly, James Cone points out that many white theologians "do not recognize the narrowness of their experience and the particularity of their theological expressions. They like to think of themselves as universal people."[15] Our tortuous history testifies that universalizing and totalizing discourse has undergirded many projects of conquest, colonization, and exploitation. Thus, the subversion of totalizing discourse is not only an epistemological, but also a political, necessity.

Subversion of universalizing and totalizing discourse has been central in the struggle of counter-hegemonic movements. This is certainly true in the case of theological movements identified with the Third World and, more specifically, in a theological current known as contextualization. By contextualization I mean something beyond translation or adaptation of the unchangeable deposits of faith to specific contexts. It is not simply a mode of communication or finding cultural media as vehicles to communicate some eternal truths, but a mode of apprehension that recognizes that context shapes the perception of reality, the way theology is done, and the content that may emerge.

Contextualization has become a common theological term both in the Third World and the wealthy countries of Europe and North America. Nevertheless, there is still that pervasive understanding of the normativity of Western theologies. Many of the dominant theologies of the West readily acknowledge the contextuality of Third World theologies, but they are often forgetful of their own location. Robert McAfee Brown helps to clarify this point in noting a remark made by a Latin American theologian during a conference of North and South American theologians: "Why is it that when you talk about *our* position you always describe it as 'Latin American theology,' but when you talk about *your* position you always describe it as 'theology'?"[16] This is not a simple matter of forgetting; it is deeply grounded in the understanding that Western theology is "normative" and universal, whereas other theologies are "derivative" and particular.

The contextual character of theology has been emphasized for several years now, but it has been the Third World theologians, feminists, womanists, and other marginalized groups who have pursued the contextual thrust with passion. That these groups have pursued the contextual character of theology is not surprising, because to insist on the contextual character of theology is to subvert the normativity of the dominant theological views and create a space for other theological voices. In other words, contextualization is not only made on epistemological and theological grounds, but also because of its extreme political implications. When theology listens to the once submerged voices, it is going to experience dramatic change.

My critique of universalizing and totalizing discourse does not mean that we are forbidden from making claims that have universal validity, otherwise we become imprisoned in our individual boxes of particular assertions that do not take seriously the challenge that others make about who we are, how we constitute ourselves, and what we can be together. What I am targeting is the kind of discourse that elevates a particular perspective to the level of absolute universality, but has forgotten its own particularity and has failed to return to the particular.[17] Critique of universalizing and totalizing discourse as well as master narratives does not mean the abandonment of any meta-narratives or meta-theories.

Meta-narrative is not the problem as such, rather those narratives that employ a sole standard and claim to embody a universal experience while muting other narratives. Counter-hegemonic voices need meta-theories and meta-narratives because of their explanatory power and ability to relate the specific into the broader context. To reject meta-narratives, following the lines of Henry Giroux, "is to risk being trapped in particularistic theories that cannot explain how the various diverse relations that constitute larger social, political, and global systems interrelate and mutually determine or constrain one another."[18]

### Power-Knowledge Nexus: Avoiding New Hegemonies

In spite of the many disavowals, various counter-hegemonic movements have not always been vigilant in rooting out their own hegemonic tendencies. As much as we hear about "hermeneutics of suspicion" in counter-hegemonic discourses, the suspicion has not always been carried out with rigor internally. It has not been carried out sufficiently in the choice of tools to destroy the master's house. At times, in the name of some noble goals, democratic processes are not allowed full latitude. Leaders of people's movements often become guardians of orthodoxy as new generations challenge the reigning ways of thinking and doing. Cases are commonplace enough that I do not feel compelled to provide a litany of them. In spite of the fact that the ultra-leftists stand in opposition to the ultra-rightists, they have one thing in common: "they both suffer from the absence of doubt."[19]

For a time, liberation theologies (Latin, Asian, black, and others) have been oblivious to the plight of women. Feminists are saying that what has often been referred to as "human experience" is, in actuality, a "male experience" raised to the level of universality. Feminism (especially at its early stage) has also fallen into the trap when speaking of "women's experience," while muting the experience of women who suffer because of their color. In fact, white feminism, as womanists argued, has perpetuated "white racism" in the name of "universal sisterhood" and in making "sexism" or "patriarchy" the primary category of analysis. Patriarchy is an inadequate category, Delores Williams contends, because it is silent as to women's oppression of women. Audre Lorde has expressed this aptly:

> If white american feminist theory need not deal with the differences between us, and the resulting difference in our oppressions, then how do you deal with the fact that the women who clean your houses and tend your children while you attend conferences on feminist theory are, for the most part, poor women and women of Color? What is the theory behind racist feminism?[20]

Counter-hegemonic movements can, I believe, maintain their counter-hegemonic posture if they remain acutely vigilant of the specific contextual loci of their own discourses and, following Michel Foucault, the "regime of truth" in which they operate.[21] The notion of regime of truth helps us to understand that the relationship between truth and power is not simply a relationship of cause and effect respectively. It is not simply that truth is power or that might is right, but truth and power coproduce each other. In *Discipline and Punish* Foucault contends:

> Perhaps we should abandon the belief that power makes mad and that, by the same token, the renunciation of power is one of the conditions of knowledge. We should admit rather that power produces knowledge (and not simply by encouraging it because it serves power or by applying it because it is useful); that power and knowledge directly imply one another; that there is no power relation without the correlative constitution of a field of knowledge, nor any knowledge that does not presuppose and constitute at the same time power relations.[22]

Using the notion of the regime of truth to critique feminism, Jennifer Gore contends that it "allows us to posit that feminism may have its own power-knowledge nexus which, in particular contexts and in particular historical moments, will operate in ways that are oppressive and repressive to people within and/or outside of the constituency of feminism."[23] Counter-hegemonic movements, like feminism, do create their own regimes of truth; hence, they must be vigilant of the regimes of truth they establish. "Feminists committed to the articulation of what was 'other' in relation to masculine thought," say Kathleen Lennon and Margaret Whitford, must "confront the challenge of other 'others' for whom they constituted a *new hegemony* and in relation to whom they themselves stood in positions of power and domination."[24]

An alternative hermeneutic framework must incorporate this power-knowledge nexus. The traditional clear-cut division between power and knowledge needs radical overhauling. This division often serves as a mask: It does not expose the productive role of power (i.e., its power to create knowledge and to legislate "truth") and it allows knowledge to present itself as truly immaculate, unstained or unspoiled by power. "It hides," in the words of Kyle Pasewark, "the involvement of power with knowledge, allowing knowledge a reign of its own, a royal dress so dangerous precisely because it presents itself as uninterested in power."[25] Counter-hegemonic discourse does not escape from becoming a new hegemony by claiming that it is beyond the power-knowledge nexus, but only by exposing the power-knowledge nexus of all forms of discourse and critiquing them in light of the plight of the most vulnerable. The task is not to soar beyond power-knowledge but, following Foucault, of "detaching the power of truth from the powers of hegemony."[26] Foucault's point that power is constitutive of any truth or scientific claims or an aspect of the will to knowledge is a way to dispossess the established truths of their mystifying power.

The notion of the regime of truth is a powerful ally in the struggle of liberation theologies to unmask the misuse of the gospel by the dominating classes, which is often "abetted by a good part of exegesis that is thought of as 'scientific.'"[27] Dwight Hopkins sees Foucault's "micro-physics of power" as complementing Cone's piercing critique of the macro-structures of domination.[28] While regimes of truth are present in various localities, it does not require volumes of writings to show that macro-structures of domination and power-differentials operate in favor of the dominant class and to the detriment of those in the margins.

## From Dualistic Thinking to Holistic Thinking

Dualistic thinking relates to disembodied and totalistic knowing. During the Middle Ages dualistic categories were employed between soul and body, spirit and matter, and between the perfect eternal forms and their imperfect embodiment in the world. The second category in each pair serves the first: the body for the soul, matter for the spirit, and the goal of the present life is to prepare for the next. This dualistic thinking did not die with the advent of the modern period but assumed different categories. In fact, John Cobb considers dualistic thinking a hallmark of the modern culture.[29] Isaac Newton accepted the Cartesian dualism of mind and body, with human rationality as the mark of human uniqueness.

As in other forms of dualism, the dualized categories are also hierarchized. Karen Warren noted this point: "Oftentimes,...hierarchial thinking is applied to conceptual dualisms, so that one side of the dualism is valued 'up' and the other 'down.'"[30] That which is valued up or that which is at the higher scale of the hierarchy establishes itself as the norm in relation to that which is at the bottom of the hierarchy. This norm has the "power to oppress," Elizabeth Dodson Gray rightly points out, "because it is an expression of a social hierarchy or pyramid of status or *power*."[31] The norm is a creation of power; power produces norm. It is a creation of the power-knowledge nexus. The "valuing up" and "valuing down" also acquires the status of sacrality because it is seen as part of the natural order created by God; thus it becomes more resistant to change. Anyone who attempts to change this hierarchical dualism or holy order is going against the natural order and is, therefore, an enemy of the Creator.[32]

Dualistic thinking has been challenged seriously in various fields. The dualism of mind and body has been undermined by contemporary science and in various fields such as psychology and medicine. The human being is a psychosomatic unity. If at the microscopic level matter does not consist of tiny substances called atoms but relations of energy, then at the very basic level mind and body dualism does not exist. Mind and body, matter and spirit are expressions of one and indivisible relations of energy. The fundamental category is not entities or separate substances, but relationship.[33]

I am aware that there are many approaches that claim to have overcome dualism, but they often fail to live up to their claims, for the reason that they simply equate holistic thinking with putting the separate components together: body, mind, emotion, and so on. A unified epistemology must start with the basic presupposition of the nonisolability of an entity from the whole, or that an entity is only as such in relation to the whole. Or, to put it differently, it is the whole that defines the part. The parts derive their being from the whole, even as the parts constitute the whole.

## Moving beyond Generic Essentialism

Disembodied knowledge, because it forgets its social embodiment and specificity, not only dovetails with totalizing and dualistic discourse, but also with essentialism. This means that a critique of disembodied and totalistic knowing must also involve a critique of essentialist or foundationalist discourse. What I mean by essentialism is that mode of thinking that seeks to isolate an essence or kernel from the husk. It presupposes an understanding that one can get into the essence of things that is free from interpretation or the noninterpreted essence. This essentialist thinking comes in many forms and disguises. It comes in the classroom when students ask the professor to give the essence of something that would settle once and for all the conflict of interpretations. Likewise, it is present in the students' strong reaction when the professor says that interpretation builds on other interpretations all the way down (much like some concepts of the world that sits on the back of a big turtle, which sits on the back of another turtle, with more turtles upon turtles all the way down). And it comes in the duality asserted between gospel and culture.

Serious questions are now raised against the essentialist mode of thinking. Basic to the challenge against the essentialist mode of thinking is the idea that there is no point of departure or beginning point that is a sanitized, interpretation-free space. Put differently, there is no ground, foundation, or essence free from interpretation to anchor one's interpretation. In fact, the ground on which we want to stand on does not stand by itself. Ludwig Wittgenstein's inversion of one of Descartes' favorite images is helpful here: "I have arrived at the rock bottom of my convictions. And one might almost say that these foundation-walls are carried by the house."[34] The noninterpreted ground is not available to us because, in Jean-François Lyotard's words, "we always start in the middle."[35] It is not even a clean middle but a "messy middle." This is a version, notes Vincent Leitch, of Jacques Derrida's poststructuralist aphorism: "What happens is always some *contamination.*"[36] We are born in the middle of interpretation. If the gospel of John could say that in the beginning was the Word, I also could say that in the beginning was interpretation.

This is not to say that there is no "ground" at all, but only to say that there is no "noninterpreted ground" to provide a norm across socio-cultural boundaries that stands outside of the communicative encounter. This ground that I am talking about is made of fragile materials we call interpretations, always shifting and shaky, but it is nevertheless a ground for us to stand on.[37] The shaky ground matters to us, for interpretations are not just interpretations. We live by our interpretations, according to our constructed world; so we also let others die by our interpretations.[38] Interpretations promote life as well as kill! In this regard, then, I do not take interpretation in the mode of hedonistic play but with all seriousness, even as I take this task with joy and excitement.

In contrast to the image of foundation or to the metaphor of knowledge as a pyramid in which one stone is laid upon another to build a firm foundation, the imagery of a raft or ship would aptly characterize this hermeneutic stance.[39] Theological scholars must realize that their construals are made on board a moving ship amidst the waves of the open sea. Though they are trained in the basics of theological navigation to sail into the open sea with some degree of safety and direction, the elemental forces of nature that drive the ship are beyond their full control.

It should be noted, however, that though no interpretation can claim grounding outside of the interpretive arena, the playing field is convoluted by power differentials. In the conflict of interpretations, new participants are not only challenged to advance alternative interpretations, but have to face the reality that those in privileged locations have the advantage to make their interpretations "stick."[40] More than that, they also have the means to make those who challenge the dominant interpretations "stink."

Our notion or interpretation of human nature is a case that is of direct relevance here. Human nature, as understood in essentialist discourse, is that which is essentially human regardless of culture, class, gender, or race. Not only is this discourse oblivious to its universalization of what is particular–"male nature" elevated to the status of "human nature"–but the general notion of "human nature" as well as the more specific "male nature" are themselves social constructs or interpretations.

Counter-hegemonic discourse has also fallen into essentialist epistemology. In relation to women of color, white feminist discourse has, for some time, assumed the privileged position of defining the woman, even as it challenged the dominant white male discourse. White feminists fell into this trap because, unlike women of color, they do not have to qualify their being women in a white racist society. It is a different story for a person of color or, specifically, for a woman of color. A black woman is not simply a woman in a white society, but she has to and is asked to qualify "woman" with "black." Such is the case with Hispanics and Asian Americans. They are the nonnormative, nongeneric Americans. Essentialist epistemology necessarily seeks to isolate the essence from the "trappings" or "additions." This comes, for example, in the effort to identify one's identity. In this way of thinking, Patricia Hill Collins says:

One must be either Black or white...—persons of ambiguous racial and ethnic identity constantly battle with questions such as 'what are you, anyway?' This emphasis on quantification and categorization occurs in conjunction with the belief that either/or categories must be ranked.[41]

"What are you, anyway?" presupposes a definitive essence of who one really is, forcing the one being questioned to identify who she or he is, and to make a stand as to which one is given primacy or priority. Racial minorities often get this form of questioning from European Americans, and women get this kind of questioning from men. Many black men ask a similar question to African American women: Are you "black first" or "women first"? Their answer hits the bullseye: "We cannot be black from Monday to Thursday, then women from Friday to Sunday. We are black women seven days a week."[42]

A "nonadditive" framework is what is called for here. This move stresses the point that one's vision of humanity and society cannot take for granted the once-considered "attachments" or "additions" to the self: gender, age, race, nationality, and so forth. And, if class, gender, race, age, and so on are constitutive of who we are and must be seen in nonadditive terms, so is our experience and encounter of various life-negating "isms." Though I still find value in talking about "triple" or "multiple" oppression, as women of color have done, I do not approach the interconnections of various forms of oppression as if one were simply put on top of another. The configuration of one's experience of a specific form of oppression is influenced by the extent to which one is affected by other forms of oppression. A woman of color, for example, does not experience sexism as a woman—like any white women—and then experience racism like any woman of color. Instead she experiences sexism as a *woman of color*. Her experience of sexism is not isolable from her color, unless one spins the idea of *generic* woman—a colorless woman, and also an odorless woman, a woman who does not burp, who does not have any of the attributes or actions of living people.

### Moving Away from Atomistic Thinking: We Are, Therefore I Am

Working in tandem with other conceptual traps is the atomistic way of thinking. The person who is stripped of historical specificities and reduced to a generic person is also viewed as an atom or a billiard ball that collides with other balls. In what Iris Marion Young calls the "aggregate model," an individual is viewed as ontologically prior to the collective because group attributes are mere attachments to the individual self—not something constitutive.[43] Moreover, consciousness here is conceived as "outside of and prior to language and the context of social interaction, which the subject enters."[44]

A variety of postmodern thoughts have exposed as illusory the ontology of a "unified self-making subjectivity," an ontology that postulates a subject of autonomous origin, or a subject with an underlying essence to which attributes of gender, class, family role, nationality, and others might be attached to the generic and atomized human being.[45] This is the ontology of the many contemporary theories of justice; it is individualist and atomist in its methodology.

Over against atomistic ontology and an essentialist approach, the position I hold, following a host of contemporary thinkers, is that the "self is a product of social processes, not their origin."[46] The self is socially constituted and one's gender, nationality, family role, and so forth are constitutive of one's very self. In this way of thinking, sociality and relationship are fundamental categories. To use an analogy, it is not the musical note that makes music, but relationship: relationship makes music. At the heart of an entity is sociality, or at the heart of individuality is sociality, which is always a product of social interaction.

This move away from essentialist and atomistic ontology—a way of thinking that puts the individual as ontologically prior to the social and conceives of the self as prior to the linguistic and practical interaction—to the ontology that views the self as totally embedded in and as a product of the social as well as the linguistic and practical interaction, is politically, ethically, and theologically crucial. Subjectivity is no longer assigned to the "apolitical wasteland of essences and essentialism"; rather, it is constructed as an ideological terrain of conflict and struggle.[47] It is a site of conflict and struggle because, as Teresa Ebert says, subjectivity is the "effect of a set of ideologically signifying practices through which the individual is situated in the world and in terms of which the world and one's self are made intelligible."[48]

### The Myth of Original Uniformity That Preceded Diversity: Thinking about Difference

Complementary to essentialism is the "myth of original uniformity that preceded diversity."[49] This myth seeks to establish the inviolability, singularity, and undiluted identity of the original moment, which is that stage before the fall.[50] In other words, origin precedes the fall. In the beginning was singularity and uniformity. Not only does uniformity have a historical precedence, it also has ontological precedence. From the point of view of those who are mesmerized and hypnotized by the myth of original uniformity, the "original blessing," contrary to the message advanced in Matthew Fox's work, is uniformity.[51] The fall is that time when the singular has been diluted, when the singular has become plural. Diversity is an aberration, a falling away from the original blessing; it is "missing the mark" (sin). Because the original is the uniform and the original is the normal, the solution is not in the exploration of an alternative future that takes account of diversity, but to go back to the past, to the founding origin when there was, as it is mistakenly believed, mellifluous uniformity. Diversity has its future or salvation only when it surrenders to the bosom of the original uniformity.

Painful as it sounds, following Foucault, this search or effort to return to the origin is an infantile longing and dreaming of a "pure" stage before the fall.[52] But there never was such a pure beginning in the history of humanity. The so-called origin may just be a stage in the hazardous play of domination and exploitation. This notion of return to original uniformity has found expression in the "postmodernism of reaction," which is the temptation to turn the clock back; to stay in the comfort of our old beliefs.[53] This return to the comforts of the old beliefs, as expressed in the heightening of Third World immigrant-bashing in the United States (and Western Europe), means a return to the "original whiteness." But the reality is that there was no such thing as "original whiteness," and this claim is not even congruent with a society whose *arche* or constitutive self-identity is "from many, one" (*e pluribus unum*).[54] "Postmodernism of reaction" suffers from what Alvin Toffler calls "future shock," that is, "maladjustment with the present because of the longed-for-past," rather than what Letty Russell names "advent shock"–"maladjustment with the present because of the longed-for future of God."[55] Because the postmodernist reactors dwell in the glory of the past, they need a medicine or transportation that must take them, to use the title of a well-known movie, "back to the future."

In contrast to the understanding that diversity is an aberration from the so-called original uniformity, I make the claim that diversity and difference are at the heart of things. Our "original blessing" is not uniformity but diversity and difference. We should not be scared of our rich diversity and difference, because that is who we are. Difference is a critical category not only to counter hegemonic practices but also for seeing the world.[56] Difference is not the problem, but it is our attitude toward these differences. Audre Lorde puts it rather succinctly: the main problem "is rather our refusal to recognize those differences, and to examine the distortions which result from our misnaming them and their effects upon human behavior and expectation."[57]

The notion of difference is an asset: it helps us in understanding better who we are and our rich possibilities of being together as a society; it helps us see that equality is not predicated on *sameness* or *identity*.[58] It is an asset because those who are different, claims María Lugones, "are mirrors in which you can see yourselves as no other mirror shows you...It is not that we are the only faithful mirrors," she continues, "but I think we *are* faithful mirrors. Not that we show you as you *really* are; we just show you as one of the people who you are."[59] In a similar vein, argues Sharon Welch, we arrive at a better understanding of the world and who we are not by denial of our differences or through the acceptance of one universally valid truth, but by learning "from and with those shaped by other equally partial traditions."[60]

However, for difference to truly become an asset, it must be allowed to present itself for what it is and not be tamed to suit our interests. When difference is muted, the "others" do not become faithful mirrors. Difference must not only not be muted, if it is to serve as a faithful mirror; it must be recognized that to see difference from a contextually-embodied hermeneutic is to see difference in the plural. Difference annihilates itself when it does not see differenc*es*. A notion of difference that does not see differences among the different produces a "boomerang gaze," in which one's image is reflected back unto oneself.[61] In this case, difference fails to deliver its promise.

We must be vigilant of the notion of difference that verges on indifference, especially since "difference in the postmodern sense often slips into a theoretically harmless and politically deracinated notion of pastiche."[62] I am seeing this notion of difference even among those who are trying hard to be "politically correct," in nonengaging liberal "niceness," and in postures of "exoticism" as well as "tokenism." In many instances, "marginalized groups are told they can celebrate their 'difference,' but this difference won't be allowed to make a difference to those who are in power."[63] The other (different), who brings a "unique" and "special" form of expertise, may be invited to share his or her expertise (exotic subjects like Third World voices), but only in a way that puts her or his discourse in the category of the harmless exotic.[64] When one steps beyond the confines of the exotic, the response, following Trinh Minh-Ha's lines: "We did not come to hear a Third World member speak about the First(?) World, We came to listen to that voice of difference likely to bring us *what we can't have* and to divert us from the monotony of sameness."[65]

A response by feminists of color to homogenization, especially as it happens in feminist discourse, is, I think, insightful to us all. Instead of conceptualizing gender subordination from the sole point of women's experience, which homogenizes all women's experiences, Aida Hortado, along with Patricia Zavella and others, propose that "social structure should be the analytical focus, which allows for profound differences."[66] When gender subordination is seen vis-à-vis social structure, there are profound differences in women's experience. No woman experiences as a woman per se, but always in relation to other factors that constitute who she is.

Diversity and difference as analytical categories need to be extended to the whole ecosystem, a dimension absent in common discourses on diversity and difference. Though we are not mindful of it, biodiversity is a fact of life. Without it, the earth dies; it sustains life on our planet.[67] Embracing a hermeneutical viewpoint in which diversity is at the heart of our cosmos is crucial in helping us to value our diversity and differences.

Diversity is not an aberration but the norm. We should not be threatened by diversity because it promotes life and sustains our cosmos.

When we see diversity as a fact of life, we also see the intrinsic value of each being. Intrinsic value, however, needs to be qualified in a world so driven by individualism, for it can easily be construed as promoting an intrinsic monad. Intrinsic worth must be construed within the context of what I call "intrinsic relationality." Holmes Rolston III strengthens this point when he argues that intrinsic worth must always be seen "in a role, in a whole."[68] Nature has a value apart from its usefulness for human beings, but not in isolation from the rest of the biotic community.

### Standpoint Epistemology: Viewing Reality from the Plight of Those Who Are Dying before Their Time

We see reality only from specific standpoints. Standpoint epistemology does not claim to view reality from everywhere (*sub specie aeternitatis*), which is tantamount to viewing reality from nowhere, but reads texts and social texts acutely aware of its own social insertion and point of departure. We do not see reality from God's eyeview, but only as embodied beings who are shaped by the context in which we are located. Context is not merely that space that is the recipient of my actions; it is also that which shapes who we are and how we see things around us.

I hope I am not giving the impression that there is a one-directional straight line connecting location and viewpoint, a weakness in the case of certain forms of Marxism.[69] While our standpoint is certainly shaped by our context, it is not determined completely by it. If it is determined completely by the context, then there is no point in doing what Paulo Freire calls *conscientizacão*.[70] This means that standpoint is not automatically given by location; it is also an "achieved standpoint," specifically a "critical standpoint."[71]

In this work I have opted to privilege the standpoint of the marginalized and have claimed marginality as a "site of resistance." I am privileging the standpoint that comes out of the experience of the marginalized not for the reason that this is an "innocent standpoint," but because the bearers of this standpoint are dying before their time. Scholars who advocate standpoint epistemology have no illusion of an innocent standpoint; rather, they call for the acknowledgement of the "deadly innocence" or the "skeletons in the closets," as an indispensable component of any liberating hermeneutic.[72] Donna Haraway's articulation of the importance of the standpoints of the subjugated contributes to my point:

> The standpoints of the subjugated are not "innocent" positions. On the contrary, they are preferred because in principle they are least likely to allow denial of the critical and interpretive core of all knowledge. They are savvy to modes of denial through

repression, forgetting, and disappearing acts–ways of being nowhere while claiming to see comprehensively.[73]

Subaltern scholarship does not privilege the experience of the subjugated because of its innocence, but because their plight is a nagging reminder that things are not right, and that it is not all right. Subaltern scholarship seeks to expose the other side of life that the powerful of this world want to push under the rug: that every age of civilization is also an age of barbarism; that the age of reason is also the age of conquest and colonization; that the age of progress is also the age of the exploitation of the most vulnerable.

There is more, however, to exposing the other side of the myth of progress. I privilege the standpoint that comes out of the experience of the marginalized not because of innocence but because of its openness to the not yet. When we see reality from the experience of the marginalized, we are prevented from equating the present reality with the final *telos* (end) of history. The cry of the marginalized not only tells us that there is something wrong with the system, but it is also an expression of openness to the future. There is no doubt that marginalized people have internalized colonization, but their laments reflect an openness to a new social arrangement. Unlike those who occupy the top echelons of power and privilege, they have nothing to lose when the status quo is changed. It is not necessarily that the marginalized have a prophetic consciousness, but their experience is a ground for prophetic criticism and imagination. God is not finished yet with history. The cry of the marginalized obliges the whole of society to search, to innovate, to create something new, and to break down barriers: It is an ongoing ferment of destabilization and invention.

With this unequivocal affirmation of the reality of standpoint and the privileging of the experience of those who are dying before their time, it is clear that I am advocating a kind of scholar who is no longer the "rhapsodist of the eternal," to use Foucault's lines, but is organically situated in specific communities of resistance and hope.[74] Situatedness in specific communities does not mean, however, that one's attention and action are confined to that locality; rather, it is a base for global imagination and engagement.

### Cumulative Voices: Community of Interpreters

The subversion of totalizing discourse is a necessary step in the constructive process, but it may leave us with a disparate cacophony of voices, each struggling to establish its regime of truth. One does not have to be a sagacious observer to notice that balkanization follows in the wake of the disintegration of hegemonic power. While I lament the festering conflicts and our seeming inability to come together, return to hegemonic practices is not the solution. Neither would I entertain the idea of a return to the once upon a time pristine beginning or to the "good old days," as if the origin were pure and homogenous. There is no retreat from the challenges of competing interpretations, but we must find our present and our future in the cacophony of interpretations.

How do we find a liberating hermeneutic in the midst of competing interpretations? How do we find a liberating hermeneutic when counter-hegemonic movements are also subject to the temptation of totalizing discourse? How can we arrive at a liberating hermeneutic when counter-hegemonic movements are not beyond the power-knowledge nexus? Standpoint epistemology's acute awareness of the embodied, contextual, interpretive, perspectival, and power-laden character of knowledge and any truth claims indicates an openness to the presence of hermeneutic companions who are equally committed to the formulation of a liberating hermeneutic. As embodied knowers or concrete knowers our views are limited, but through the aid of a community of interpreters the limited views are exposed to the possibility of expansion. It is only in relation to, or in interaction with, hermeneutic others, and in allowing our "safe" enclaves of hermeneutic privilege to be challenged, that we can move beyond reactive and binary oppositional hermeneutic lenses.

Our hermeneutic companions must not be limited to those within our regimes of truth. Neither should our domain of experience be closed to the contributions of other interpreters, though constant vigilance must be maintained. While it is true, for example, that men should not speak for women, or whites should not speak for people of color, the basic question is: Does one's hermeneutic framework allow for the experience of women or people of color to speak through us? What I am suggesting here is that we should not run away from our responsibility to participate in the formulation of a common discourse that would be healing for all. I agree with the idea of Sandra Harding that "men must not be permitted to refuse to try to produce fully feminist analyses on the grounds that they are not women."[75] Men should not speak for women, or theorize for women, but they can be pro-feminist men: men accountable for their role in the perpetuation of patriarchy and participants in the formulation of a feminist discourse, a discourse that includes men's liberation and healing. Doing this does not mean speaking for or exercising responsibility for others. What is more proper, to follow the lead of Barbara Harlow and Sharon Welch, is not that we are "responsible for" the "other," but primarily for ourselves, "for seeing the limits of our own vision and for rectifying the damages caused by the arrogant violation of those limits."[76]

It is in the context of our involvement in a community of interpreters that the search for the "common" is explored. If the concept of difference is an important category, so is the notion of the common. What is this common? This search for the common is not motivated by the nostalgic loss of a universalizing norm or an attempt to counter the mushrooming of new voices. Its motivation is predicated on our shared life and, more particularly, it is pursued because it is crucial in challenging discursive and nondiscursive practices that are hurtful, and in calling into accountability all members of this shared life. The notion of the common demands that various interpretations need to be woven. This weaving of interpretations is what Sara Ruddick calls "cumulative analyses" and "cumulative universality," in contrast to "absolute universality." The scattered interpretations must be woven, for it is the cumulative interpretations that have the power to challenge totalizing discourse.[77]

Counter-hegemonic movements must engage in a "conspiracy," that is, following its root, "breathe together."[78] To conspire is to share breath: share life-affirming ways of thinking, dwelling, and acting. The term "companion" (*cum+panis* [bread]) complements the term "conspiracy."[79] The conspirators are companions sharing the life-giving breath as well as the nourishing bread of the journey. Breathing together and sharing bread by conspirators and companions are necessary to sustain oneself in the long struggle. Conspiracy and companionship are epistemologically and politically necessary: They are necessary because it is only through the frail instrumentality of another that we can be liberated from the regimes of truth that we create, and necessary because it is only through conspiracy and companionship that we gain the power to dismantle and construct alternative ways of thinking and dwelling.

## Notes

[1]Ada María Isasi-Díaz, *En La Lucha: A Hispanic Women's Liberation Theology* (Minneapolis: Fortress Press, 1993), 73–74.

[2]William Lloyd Newell, *Truth Is Our Mask: An Essay on Theological Method* (Lanham, Md.: Univ. Press of America, 1990), ix.

[3]Sallie McFague, *The Body of God: An Ecological Theology* (Minneapolis: Fortress Press, 1993), 47–54.

[4]Johann Baptist Metz, *Faith in History and Society: Toward a Practical Fundamental Theology*, trans. David Smith (New York: The Seabury Press, 1980), 131.

[5]Frederick Engels, *Ludwig Feuerbach and the Outcome of Classical German Philosophy* (London: Lawrence and Wishart, 1947), 6.

[6]Ludwig Feuerbach, *The Essence of Christianity* (New York: Harper and Row, 1957), xxxiv.

[7]Engels, *Ludwig Feuerbach and the Outcome of Classical German Philosophy*, 49.

[8]Cornel West, review of *Philosophy and the Mirror of Nature*, by Richard Rorty, in *Union Seminary Quarterly Review* 37 (Fall/Winter 1981–1982): 184; also, see his book, *The American Evasion of Philosophy: A Genealogy of Pragmatism* (Madison, Wis.: The University of Wisconsin Press, 1989), 208.

[9]Mary Field Belenky, et al., *Women's Ways of Knowing: The Development of Self, Voice, and Mind* (New York: Basic Books, 1986); Elaine Graham, *Making the Difference: Gender, Personhood and Theology* (Minneapolis: Fortress Press, 1996), 192–213.

[10]McFague, *The Body of God: An Ecological Theology*, 52.

[11]Newell, *Truth Is Our Mask: An Essay on Theological Method*, ix.

[12]Mark Kline Taylor, *Remembering Esperanza: A Cultural-Political Theology for North American Praxis* (Maryknoll, N.Y.: Orbis Books, 1990), 58.

[13]See my essay "Confronting the White Noise: Mission from the Experience of the Marginalized," in Tom Montgomery-Fate, *Beyond the White Noise: Mission in a Multicultural World* (St. Louis: Chalice Press, 1997), 97–98.

[14]Sharon Welch, *Communities of Resistance and Solidarity* (Maryknoll, N.Y.: Orbis Books, 1985), 51.

[15]James Cone, *God of the Oppressed* (New York: Seabury Press, 1975), 15.

[16]Robert McAfee Brown, *Theology in a New Key: Responding to Liberation Themes* (Philadelphia: The Westminster Press, 1978), 77.

[17]Peter Hodgson, *Winds of the Spirit: A Constructive Christian Theology* (Louisville: Westminster John Knox Press, 1994), 201.

[18]Henry Giroux, *Pedagogy and the Politics of Hope* (Boulder, Colo.: Westview Press, 1997), 211–212.

[19]Marcio Moreira Alves, cited in Paulo Freire, *Pedagogy of the Oppressed*, trans. Myra Bergman Ramos (New York: Herder and Herder, 1972), 23.

[20]Audre Lorde, *Sister Outsider: Essays and Speeches* (Freedom, Calif.: The Crossing Press, 1984), 112.

[21]Michel Foucault, *The Foucault Reader*, ed. Paul Rabinow (New York: Pantheon Books, 1984), 51–75.

[22]Michel Foucault, *Discipline and Punish: The Birth of the Prison*, trans. Alan Sheridan (New York: Vintage Books, 1979), 27.

[23]Jennifer M. Gore, *The Struggle for Pedagogies: Critical and Feminist Discourses as Regimes of Truth* (New York and London: Routledge, 1993), 61.

[24]Kathleen Lennon and Margaret Whitford, eds., *Knowing the Difference: Feminist Perspectives in Epistemology* (New York and London: Routledge, 1994), 3. Emphasis added.

[25]Kyle Pasewark, *A Theology of Power: Being Beyond Domination* (Minneapolis: Fortress Press, 1993), 9.

[26]Foucault, *The Foucault Reader*, 75.

[27]Gustavo Gutiérrez, *The Power of the Poor in History*, trans. Robert Barr (Maryknoll, N.Y.: Orbis Books, 1983), 18.

[28]Dwight Hopkins, "Postmodernity, Black Theology of Liberation and the U.S.A.: Michel Foucault and James Cone," in *Liberation Theologies, Postmodernity, and the Americas*, ed. David Batstone, Eduardo Mendieta, Lois Ann Lorentzen, and Dwight Hopkins (New York: Routledge, 1997), 205–221. See Foucault, *Discipline and Punish: The Birth of the Prison*, particularly pages 3–31.

[29]John Cobb, Jr., "Postmodern Christianity in Quest of Eco-Justice," in *After Nature's Revolt: Eco-Justice and Theology*, ed. Dieter Hessel (Minneapolis: Fortress Press, 1992), 22.

[30]Karen Warren, "Feminism and Ecology: Making Connections," *Environmental Ethics* 9 (1987):3–20, cited in J.B. McDaniel's *Of God and the Pelicans: A Theology of Reverence for Life* (Louisville: Westminster/John Knox Press, 1989), 116.

[31]Elizabeth Dodson Gray, *Green Paradise Lost* (Wellesley, Mass.: Roundtable Press, 1981), 131. Emphasis added.

[32]Ibid., 7.

[33]Hodgson, *Winds of the Spirit: A Constructive Christian Theology*, 87–88.

[34]Ludwig Wittgenstein, *On Certainty*, #248, ed. G. E. M. Anscombe and G. H. von Wright and trans. Denis Paul and G.E.M. Anscombe (New York: Harper & Row, 1969), 33, cited in William Placher, *Unapologetic Theology: A Christian Voice in a Pluralistic Conversation* (Louisville: Westminster/John Knox Press, 1989), 26.

[35]The quotation from Jean-Francois Lyotard is Vincent Leitch's translation from Lyotard's *Le postmoderne expliqué aux enfans: Correspondance 1982–1985* (Paris: Galilée, 1986), 157. See Vincent B. Leitch, *Postmodernism: Local Effects, Global Flows* (Albany, N.Y.: State Univ. of New York Press, 1996), x.

[36]Ibid., x.

[37]M. K. Taylor, "In Praise of Shaky Ground: The Liminal Christ and Cultural Pluralism," in *Theology Today* 43:36–51; also cited in Paul Knitter, *One Earth, Many Religions* (Maryknoll, N.Y.: Orbis Books, 1995), 76.

[38]See Sallie McFague, *Models of God: Theology for an Ecological, Nuclear Age* (Philadelphia: Fortress Press, 1988), 28.

[39]Hodgson, *Winds of the Spirit: A Constructive Christian Theology*, 13–18. Also, see Francis Schüssler Fiorenza, *Foundational Theology: Jesus and the Church* (New York: Crossroad, 1986), 288.

[40]See Sidonie Smith and Julia Watson, eds., *De/Colonizing the Subject: The Politics of Gender in Women's Autobiography* (Minneapolis: Univ. of Minnesota Press, 1992), xvii; John B.

Thompson, *Studies in the Theory of Ideology* (Cambridge, Mass.: Polity, 1984), 132.

[41]Patricia Hill Collins, *Black Feminist Thought: Knowledge, Consciousness, and the Politics of Empowerment* (Boston, MA: Unwin Hyman, 1990), 225.

[42]See James Cone and Gayraud Wilmore, *Black Theology: A Documentary History, 1980–1992*, vol. 2 (Maryknoll, N.Y.: Orbis, 1993), 257.

[43]Iris Marion Young, *Justice and the Politics of Difference* (Princeton, N.J.: Princeton Univ. Press, 1990), 44.

[44]Ibid., 45.

[45]See, for example, David Kelsey's essay, "Human Being," in *Christian Theology: An Introduction to Its Traditions and Tasks*, ed. Peter C. Hodgson and Robert King (Philadelphia: Fortress Press, 1985), particularly pages 185–188 for a discussion of this concept.

[46]Young, *Justice and Politics of Difference*, 45; see Rosalind Coward and John Ellis, *Language and Materialism* (London: Routledge and Kegan Paul, 1977).

[47]Giroux, *Pedagogy and the Politics of Hope*, 203.

[48]Teresa Ebert, "The Romance of Patriarchy: Ideology, Subjectivity, and Postmodern Feminist Cultural Theory," *Cultural Critique 10* (1988): 22–23, cited in Giroux, *Pedagogy and the Politics of Hope*, 203.

[49]See Dawn de Vries, "Creation, Handicappism, and the Community of Differing Abilities," in *Reconstructing Christian Theology*, ed. Rebecca Chopp and Mark Lewis Taylor (Minneapolis: Fortress Press, 1994), 129.

[50]Foucault, *The Foucault Reader*, 79.

[51]Matthew Fox, *Original Blessing: A Primer in Creation Spirituality* (Santa Fe: Bear & Company, Inc., 1983).

[52]Foucault, *The Foucault Reader*, 79.

[53]Hal Foster, ed., *The Anti-Aesthetic: Essays on Postmodern Culture* (Port Townsend, Wash.: Bay Press, 1983), xii.

[54]Fumitaka Matsuoka, *Out of Silence: Emerging Themes in Asian American Churches* (Cleveland: United Church Press, 1995), 13–52.

[55]Letty Russell, *Becoming Human* (Philadelphia: Westminster Press, 1982), 41–42.

[56]Katherine E. Zappone, "'Women's Special Nature': A Different Horizon for Theological Anthropology" in *The Special Nature of Women*, ed. Anne Carr and Elisabeth Schüssler Fiorenza (Philadelphia: Trinity Press International, 1991), 92.

[57]Lorde, *Sister Outsider*, 115.

[58]Giroux, *Pedagogy and the Politics of Hope*, 213, citing Joan Wallach Scott, *Gender and the Politics of History* (New York: Columbia Univ. Press, 1988), 176–77.

[59]María Lugones, "On the Logic of Pluralist Feminism," cited in Isasi-Diaz, *En La Lucha*, 189.

[60]Sharon D. Welch, *A Feminist Ethic of Risk*, revised edition (Minneapolis: Fortress Press, 2000), 138.

[61]Ann Kirkus Wetherilt, *That They May Be Many: Voices of Women, Echoes of God* (New York: Continuum, 1994), 21.

[62]Giroux, *Pedagogy and the Politics of Hope*, 212.

[63]Lennon and Whitford, *Knowing the Difference*, 270.

[64]Wetherilt, *That They May Be Many*, 23.

[65]Trinh Minh-Ha, cited by Wetherilt, ibid.

[66]Aida Hortado, *The Color of Privilege: Three Blasphemies on Race and Feminism* (Ann Arbor, Mich.: The Univ. of Michigan Press, 1996), 42; Patricia Zavella, "The Problematic Relationship of Feminism and Chicana Studies," *Women's Studies* 17 (1978):123–34.

[67]See Edward Wilson, *The Diversity of Life* (Cambridge, Mass.: Belknap Press of Harvard Univ. Press, 1992), 15, cited in Anne Primavesi, "Biodiversity and Responsibility: A Basis for a Non-Violent Environmental Ethic," in *Faith and Praxis in a Postmodern Age*, ed. Ursula King (New York: Cassell, 1998), 47–59.

[68]Holmes Rolston III, cited in Jay B. McDaniel, *Of God and Pelicans: A Theology of Reverence for Life* (Louisville: Westminster/John Knox Press, 1989), 57.

[69]See Cornel West, *Prophesy Deliverance: An Afro-American Revolutionary Christianity* (Philadelphia: Westminster Press, 1982), 49.

[70]See Freire, *Pedagogy of the Oppressed*, 17–22.

[71]Wetherilt, *That They May Be Many*, 117.

[72]Angela West, *Deadly Innocence: Feminism and the Mythology of Sin* (London and New York: Mowbray, 1995); Justo González, *Mañana: Christian Theology from a Hispanic Perspective* (Nashville: Abingdon Press, 1990), 38–40, 75–80.

[73]Donna Haraway, "Situated Knowledges," in *Simians, Cyborgs, and Women: The Reinvention of Nature* (New York: Routledge, 1991), 191.

[74]Foucault, *Foucault Reader*, 23.

[75]Sandra G. Harding, *Whose Science? Whose Knowledge? Thinking from Women's Lives* (Ithaca, N.Y.: Cornell University Press, 1991), 284–85, cited in Wetherilt, *That They May Be Many*, 122.

[76]Welch, *Feminist Ethic of Risk*, 139.

[77]Sara Ruddick, cited in Zappone, "'Women's Special Nature': A Different Horizon for Theological Anthropology," in *The Special Nature of Women*, 95.

[78]Donald Messer, *A Conspiracy of Goodness: Contemporary Images of Christian Mission* (Nashville: Abingdon Press, 1992), 148.

[79]Robert McAfee Brown, *Persuade Us To Rejoice: The Liberating Power of Fiction* (Louisville: Westminster/John Knox Press, 1992), 67.

# CHAPTER 2

# *The Interlocking Structures of Forms of Oppression*

In this chapter I am going to deal with what I have identified as forms of oppression (classism, sexism, racism, and naturism) and their interlocking structures. I take the position that these systemic forces of oppression and exploitation cannot be isolated from each other even as they are distinct. As nonisolable, they affect each other; as distinct, the elimination of one does not necessarily mean the elimination of the other. The elimination of classism, for example, does not necessarily mean the elimination of racism.[1]

Neither do I think of these forms of oppression in additive terms, as if one were external to the other. I follow the nonadditive framework in which one form of oppression is not simply piled upon another, nor experienced as separate from another. As I argued in the previous chapter, the configuration of one's experience of a specific form of oppression and exploitation is influenced by the extent to which one is affected by other forms of oppression.

## Is There a Paradigmatic Form of Oppression?

It took me some time to figure out the approach to take in articulating the interlocking structure of forms of oppression. Reading Mark Kline Taylor's *Remembering Esperanza* helped me to arrive at a decision.[2] Taylor begins his analysis and presentation of the interlocking structure with sexism for two reasons: personal and social location, and because, as he puts it, "sexism has a certain ubiquity demanding immediate and constant, if not first, attention." Taylor says: "There is something inauthentic for me, a white, heterosexual, relatively affluent male in North America, to reflect on systemic distortion, or a theology of liberation from it, out of someone else's situation of pain." This is considered by Taylor as "voyeurism with regard to other's pain." Instead, he argues for the importance of starting in those regions of pain (sexism) that are more accessible to white, heterosexual, and affluent males. Beyond personal reason and accessibility, Taylor, after qualifications, suggests that sexism "may be seen as a paradigmatic form of oppression."[3] He is not suggesting, however, that sexism should be the starting point for everyone.

While Taylor starts with sexism, I start with classism. My reason for starting with classism rests primarily on the first reason that Taylor suggested: it is based on my personal and social location. Unlike Taylor, who is entertaining the idea that sexism may be seen as paradigmatic, I am not suggesting that one form of oppression is paradigmatic or more fundamental than others. My reason for starting with classism is based solely on personal and social location and not on any claim that classism is the fundamental alienation.

The claim that there is one fundamental or paradigmatic form of oppression, is, for Elizabeth Spelman, ambiguous and problematic; it is fruitless, argues Iris Marion Young.[4] I agree with their criticism and argue further that the claim is theoretically flawed and practically dangerous. It does not take into full account the interplay of various factors, and it reduces other forms of oppression as expressions or consequences that have their underlying basis in the paradigmatic or fundamental "ism," whatever that may be. In a subtle way, it perpetuates experiential imperialism and totalizing discourse.

For some time, classism was the unchallenged paradigmatic form of oppression of Latin American liberation theology. It was effective in unmasking classism not only in Latin America but also at the global level. However, it was silent for a long time regarding the plight of blacks in Latin America. Its reliance on a certain form of Marxist analysis, with the superstructure being determined by the economic base, made it prone to subordinate the role of "discursive practices" (e.g., popular religions and culture in Latin America) to "nondiscursive structures" (e.g., economic structure). In this case, Latin American theology has made race an adjunct to class, having no distinct identity of its own, which made black theologians suspect that it unconsciously acquiesced to the sin of white supremacy.[5] Like its European Marxist intellectual base, Latin American liberation theology suffered from reductionism. It took a period of time before Latin American theologians admitted this pitfall. "One of our social lies," Gustavo Gutiérrez later acknowledged, "has been the claim that there is no racism in Latin America."[6]

Black theology challenged the primacy of classism in Latin American liberation theology by presenting racism as a paradigmatic form of oppression. But it, too, with the exception of a few black scholars, was long silent as to the presence of classism in black experience. There was this failure to understand that classism was operative in the blacks' experience of racism, a failure that led to an inaccurate understanding of the more subtle but pervasive systemic form of racism that hides its ghastly face in the form of "capitalist racism."[7] With Latin American theology emphasizing classism (yet silent with regard to racism), black theologians' early encounters with Latin American liberation theologians were, to say the least, not pleasant ones. James Cone, a first generation black theologian, was more comfortable conversing with Asian theologians and endorsing their theological works than with their Latin American counterparts.[8]

Like Gutiérrez, Cone was eventually to acknowledge the category of class as crucial to understanding the black situation in North America. In the twentieth anniversary edition of his *A Black Theology of Liberation*, Cone has these words to say:

> Anyone who claims to be fighting against the problem of oppression and does not analyze the exploitative role of capitalism is either naive or an agent of the enemies of freedom. I was naive and did not have at my disposal sufficient tools for analyzing the complexity of human oppression. My strong negative reaction to the racism of many white socialists in the United States distorted my vision and prevented me from analyzing racism in relation to capitalism.[9]

Feminism followed suit and it, too, for some time, reduced other systemic forms of oppression to peripheral status while brandishing sexism as the paradigmatic form of oppression. Because it considered sexism as the paradigmatic oppression, it also leveled the experience of sexism of all women regardless of their class and race. This privileging of sexism, according to Gayatri Chakravorty Spivak, "erases the complex and often contradictory positionings of the subject."[10] The idea that sexism is the most fundamental form of oppression that unites all women does not take into serious consideration the fact that sexism is experienced differently by women of the Third World.

It is not even the case that because women are women, they must all start with the issue of sexism. Oftentimes, women of the Third World present their struggle not first and foremost as a struggle against sexism, but a struggle for women's rights under the much broader umbrella of social rights. Third World women intellectuals put their struggles (including sexism) within a much broader frame because they have known what it means to work side by side with their male counterparts in various counter-hegemonic movements against other systemic evils: imperialism, classism, feudalism, and global apartheid. What is true with Third World feminists' struggle around the world is also generally the case with feminists of color in the U.S. Their struggle focuses on general public issues such as affirmative action, school desegregation, racism, immigration issues, prison reform, voter registration and ethnic empowerment.[11]

Although, in general, women have been subordinated to the lower economic status, women themselves are not of equal economic status in relation to one another both within and outside of their race, nor in relation to males both within and outside of their race. Women assume a subordinate position within the overall sexist structure, yet some assume the dominant position in relation to class and continue to perpetuate classism.

Does this diminish the experience of sexism among women who are in the upper economic echelons? No, their experience of sexism is real and painful. Peel away the cosmetics and accessories, the luxurious mansions, the expensive cars, and much more, and you may well have an upper-class woman who is suffocated daily by a sexist relationship with a spouse. Despite the high level of prestige and wealth, in cases where a wife does not have an outside job, she becomes a perennial dependent and has no identity except as someone's wife or mother.[12] She has to bend her life to fit her husband's, and basically finds her *raison d'être* in performing the "stroking" function: "showing solidarity, giving help, agreeing, listening, understanding, and passively accepting."[13] The upper-class wife is a concierge deluxe. She may not actually cook the dinner, care for children, or do the laundry, but she has to attend to a lot of things and make sure that her husband's energies get focused on "manly" affairs.

As real and painful as upper class white women's experience of the confluence of sexism and classism may be, they are also in a situation of privilege. Women are victims of sexism, but class position makes this experience of sexism different. In relation to men and women of her race who are economically underprivileged, the upper class white woman has the advantage. Though she is a victim of sexism, and her class status is often an adjunct to that of her husband who controls the money, she has the luxury that lower-class women—also victims of sexism—do not have. Even at a time in our history when full-time mothering was the normative route for married women, their being full-time mothers was a privilege in relation to poor women who had to work outside the home and still were expected to be good mothers. In our era when women are liberating themselves from the domestic confines and are pursuing careers, who will take care of the domestic chores? The "liberated" women need exploited women in order to be "liberated." In this case, women's "liberation" simply shifts the weight of domestic chores "from one group of exploited women—mothers—to another group—the babysitter, housekeeper, cleaning woman, day-care staff, teacher."[14]

## Interlocking Structures in a Broad Framework

The notion of an interlocking structure seems to convey well the theoretical framework in which I approach the relationship of the various systemic evils. Class, race, gender, and the ecosystem are so interlocked that it would be imprecise to isolate one dimension as if it was free from contamination by the others. As long as we continue to isolate one dimension, or to think in additive terms, or to argue that one dimension is more fundamental than the other, I do not believe that it is possible for us to truly understand the interlocking structures of the four forms of oppression. It may sound like an exercise in rhetorical overkill (see chapter 1), but I believe that we cannot reach a proper understanding of the interlocking structures if we remain captive to essentialist premises.

How is the essentialist presupposition related to an additive way of thinking and, thus, related to our failure to see properly the interlocking structures? Essentialist presuppositions, I argue, maintain an essential, generic human being who can be isolated from class, race, nationality, and so forth. Because of such essentialist presuppositions, it has been possible to speak of womanhood or manhood with a universal flair. But the essential and generic woman or man does not exist; it is not an existing, breathing human being. A real human being has gender, class, race, and particular geographical-ecological location. My manhood, for example, cannot be isolated from my being a Filipino who is now living in the United States. To the question raised by Spelman, "Are there elements of race and class in notions of masculinity and femininity?" my answer is an unequivocal yes.[15]

As I said in the previous chapter, counter-hegemonic thoughts have also fallen into essentialist epistemology and, along with it, additive thinking. White feminist discourse, in relation to women of color, assumed the privileged position of defining the woman, even as it challenged the dominant white male discourse. White feminists have fallen into a similar trap because, unlike women of color, they do not have to qualify their being women. Whites tend to forget their color, because their color is normative (in a white racist society), but people of color do not, because they always have to take account of their color in a white society. It is a different story for a person of color or, specifically, for a woman of color. A woman of color is not simply a woman (because this refers to the normative white woman), but is pressured by society to fully qualify her identity.

I underscore "white racist society" because white is not necessarily normative, but it is only so in the context of a white racist society. In a context where people of color are not the minority and, with further qualification, not marginalized (they can also be the majority but marginalized, e.g., apartheid South Africa), they also tend to forget their color. Considering, however, the pervasiveness and grip of white culture all over the world, it is difficult to imagine a race that has not struggled against the white race's assumed normativity and superiority.

The interlocking structures of various forms of oppression cut across lines; thus, a person has several levels and dimensions of relationship. The argument that all women are inferior to men is a gross generalization and an inaccurate representation. There is not one universal patriarchy, but various patriarchies, and there are various positions of men in relation to patriarchy. And, men's differences in relation to patriarchy have bearing on the specific relationship of women to those men.[16] We need to explore various contexts  and levels of relationship. As a male person I share the privilege of being a male, but I am not a generic male person. As a male person of color from a Third World country, I often experience the category of whiteness overshadowing my maleness, even the whiteness of females. The dominant shadow of whiteness even extends to the shores of the country of my birth–the Philippines. With centuries of history of colonization, whiteness is so pervasive in my country of origin that it is formative of the way Filipinos think of themselves and deal with others. It is true, indeed, that the colonizers (Spaniards and European Americans) are long gone, but they left their marks by "whitening" the Filipino psyche, not to mention the new face colonization has assumed in the form of globalization.

Even before coming to the "land of the free and home of the brave," Filipino Americans know, following Eric Gamalinda's words, that "America is a presence as huge as God."[17] During my boyhood years on the island of Leyte (the landing site of General Douglas MacArthur's "liberation" forces during World War II), I encountered the association of hugeness with Americanness in the literal physical sense through objects, plants, and animals. The largest frog that I came to know was what the barrio inhabitants called the "American frog," and the largest bread that I dreamed of eating someday *hanggang sawa* (eat until I drop) was the "American bread" (rectangular loaf bread). I learned that when something is huge, it must be American. But the hugeness of America, I realized later on, was more than what was incarnated in that huge American frog. "America is a presence as huge as God" because every Filipino is expected to acquire an exhaustive understanding of America the beautiful and is expected to love America with all their hearts and to denounce with all their might those that smell Filipino.

Early in their education, Filipinos are trained to think and see things from the perspective of our colonial and neocolonial masters. In my elementary education I had to memorize the names of U.S. presidents and the various states that comprise the U.S. Abraham Lincoln often was cited by my teachers as a person to be emulated, and students were told that in America even a poor boy has a chance to become president. The recipe is hard work and determination. The colonial education that I learned at school also was reinforced at home. I remember, for example, those Christmas holidays when my mother had to make white Christmas trees by using white paint or white soap. Soon I was dreaming of a white Christmas even in the tropical Philippines.

I have experienced this pervasiveness of whiteness still more in my years in the U.S. Within the confines of my household (and to an extent in the wider society), I am privileged as a male, but my kingdom is, in a sense, small, and my maleness is qualified (diminished) by my race. Every time I go out of the house into the wider white world my skin color dictates how I am perceived and received by people. In situations of conflict, the white society does not protect me because of my maleness; it protects whiteness, including the whiteness of females, even the whiteness of gays and lesbians, especially if they stay in their closets. Spelman, a white feminist, strengthens the point I am making here. She says:

> If a poor Black boy in the United States thinks that being "masculine" entitles him to dominate white women, since he's male and they are female, he's not been prepared well for the society into which he's been born…This is not to say that he may not wish to dominate white women (along with Black women), but rather to remind us that if Emmet Till had been white, he wouldn't have been murdered by white men for talking to a white woman, nor would his murderers have been acquitted.[18]

Thus, I suggest that we view the four systemic forms of oppression in dynamic interaction, and recognize that the predominance of one over the other shifts in different contexts along with the interaction of several factors. I suspect that the failure of some white feminists to see the impact of race in relation to sexism is an indication of the pervasiveness of the ideology of racism.

What follows is my attempt to spell out the interweaving of the four systemic forms of oppression. It is not my intention to explain in detail each in this chapter (this will come in the next chapters); rather, I am going to focus more on their connections. Since classism is my entry point, I am going to allot more space in relating classism to each of the other evils. However, I am going to take the longer route of giving each the chance to be the springboard in which others are viewed, for this brings perspectives that are not available when one sticks to a single springboard, such as classism.

### Classism as a Starting Point into the Interlocking Structure: Journey into a Deepening Awareness of the Systemic Forms of Oppression

My starting point in dealing with some of the radical evils of our time is my first conscious struggle against classism. I start with classism because my awareness of classism came at a young age. I am aware that there are feminists who would contend that our consciousness of our gender identity comes first.[19] It is not my main intention to argue for or against this idea, but simply to say that I came to feel the pain of classism at an early age. It was traumatic and painful enough that it has become formative in the development of my self-consciousness, and it has become my springboard in responding to the rest of systemic evils that I have come to recognize later in my life.

Classism is a systematic oppression and exploitation of people that results in their economic and political marginalization. (More of this will follow in chapter 4.) It is a system of prejudice that belongs in a category by itself, say Susan Brooks Thistlethwaite and Peter Hodgson.[20] While ethnic, gender, and sexual difference are good in themselves, class is not. Thistlethwaite and Hodgson argue that "class carries with it *necessarily* its ideological legitimation in the form of *classism*–the belief that social stratification or class division is justified on the basis of inherent human inequality, or the will of God, or accommodation to the fallen condition, or productive efficiency, or some other reason."[21]

### The Collusion of Classism and Racism

The violence of classism, Christine Smith points out, cannot be separated from all other forms of oppression.[22] Race, gender, age, disability, and sexuality form a constellation of factors that complicate and contribute to class distinction and economic oppression. The racial others–whether minority (U.S.) or majority (apartheid South Africa)–in a racist society are also, most often, the underclass. There are of course racialized others who have "made it" in any system, but this does not erase the plight of common racialized minorities or marginalized racial majorities.

Classism has an international as well as a domestic face, and the international face might be called imperialism. I am not sure if I would say that imperialism is a global "repercussion" of classism, as others have done, since imperialism has other dimensions (e.g., racism), but there is certainly a connection between the two.[23] There is the centrality of economic exploitation and the maintenance of class distinctions in order to secure a world of privilege for both domestic and international elites. With the increasing phenomenon of globalization, perhaps there is a strong reason to speak of classism at a global level in the way scholars have now started to speak of "global apartheid."[24]

At the international level, especially where there is an encounter with another race, classism takes on a different texture. The subjugated race becomes the target of "racialized classism" or "colored classism." The subjugated race is readily relegated to the lower rung of society and the dominating race assumes the higher echelons of society. Society does not, however, function in a bald division between the dominating class and the dominated. For the system to continue, local elites arise and act as conduits in the exploitation of the inhabitants, even against their own race. As society evolves into greater complexity, the middle-class and the professional-managerial stratum come to play the role of conduits in the exploitation. We, the readers of this work, whom I assume are educated professionals, may like to believe our positions of privilege readily benefit those in the lower rung, but this is "sheer self-delusion," argues Edna Bonacich. More often than not, she continues, we professionals are "sergeants of the system" paid by the wealthy and the powerful, to "keep things in order" and maintain the "system of inequality."[25] We need to take account of this if we want to be agents of transformation rather than "sergeants of the system."

The connection between international and local classism is very illuminating for the U.S. scene. Robert Blauner argues, in his article "Colonized and Immigrant Minorities," that there is a strong connection between the plight of Third World people and the plight of racial minorities in the U.S. The economic, social, and political marginalization of people of color in the U.S., what Blauner calls the "Third World within," is a

> microcosm of the position of all peoples of color in the world order of stratification. This is neither an accident nor the result of some essential racial genius. Racial domination in the United States is part of a world historical drama in which the culture, economic system, and political power of the white West has spread throughout virtually the entire globe…The oppression of racial colonies within our national borders cannot be understood without considering worldwide patterns of white European hegemony.[26]

Many Asian Americans, for example, came to the shores of America because of political turmoil, economic devastation, and exploitation of their countries of origin, and the pull from the U.S. to provide a labor force to advance the "progress of civilization" of the continent. White America ordered laborers in alphabetical order right along with other commodities: bone meal, canvas, chinamen, fertilizer, filipinos, japanese, macaroni, and so on.[27] But the importation of foreign laborers also had another motivation. White America wanted laborers from foreign lands to "elevate white workers in the stratified racial/occupational structure." In the words of a white American, "I think that every white man who is intelligent and able to work, who is more than a digger in a ditch…who has the capacity of being something else, can get to be something else by the presence of Chinese labor easier than he could without it."[28] The "menial labor" that white society would rather assign to racial minorities has served to perpetuate "colored classism."

As it is true in other colonized countries, classism in the U.S. co-opts people of color as conduits, while maintaining their racial status. This cooptation serves to conceal the workings of the system by pitting one racially subjugated group against another. We can cite as an example the phenomenon in South Central Los Angeles. Acting as "middle-agent minorities" or "immigrant entrepreneurs," Korean Americans were perceived by frustrated and depressed African Americans as representing the face of the dominant race in the U.S. In the racialized classism of the U.S., Korean Americans functioned as a "buffer zone" that protected the white establishment.[29]

The U.S. census helps us see the intertwining of classism and racism. While it is true that most of the poor are whites, (shattering the commonly held assumption that the poor are African Americans, Hispanics, etc.), there is a far larger percentage of poor nonwhites than whites.[30] Instead of the economic gap between whites and racial minorities getting narrower, it, in fact, has widened since 1965.[31] Let me take the case of Hispanics:

> According to information gathered by the U.S. Census Bureau, in 1972 11.9 percent of all U.S. persons were poor. But the percentage of persons of Hispanic origin who were poor was twice that: 22.8 percent. In 1989 26.2 percent of Hispanics were poor compared with 12.8 percent of all U.S. persons; in 1990 28.1 percent of all Hispanics were poor while only 12.1 percent of all non-Hispanics were poor. By 1991 28.7 percent of all Hispanics were poor. It is important to notice that in 1978 the poverty rate of Hispanics was 2.5 times that of whites; by 1987, the poverty rate went up to 2.8 times that of whites.[32]

The classist system, nevertheless, is not completely impervious to marginalized racial groups. From time to time it shows its benign face by letting a few climb up the ladder of social stratification. The trial of O. J. Simpson shows that class was a contributory factor in his defense. Without his wealth, Simpson could have easily landed behind bars, but race played an important part (though many white "color-blind" people may not see it) in the overall trial and the general public mood. After the "not guilty" verdict, Stephanie Wildman and Margalynne Armstrong, both professors of law, took note of how "the media constructed reactions to the verdict along a racial divide and portrayed the mostly female, African American jury as emotional and incompetent. Implicit in this portrayal was the privileging of white reaction to the verdict as rational, objective, and nonbiased."[33] The general public reaction of whites was, however, different upon Simpson's conviction in the civil suit.

Class may play a dominant role while race takes a back seat or vice versa, but they surely interplay. A person of color in a racist society may have acquired a comfortable class status, but that person is still a person of color in the eyes of white society. A poor white person may be low in class position, but you can still hear him or her say: "I may be poor, but I'm not black" (or Hispanic or Asian).

### Classism and Sexism: The Capitalist Patriarchy

An unholy collusion not only exists between classism and racism, it is also present between classism and sexism. Most of the poor of the world are women. There is what is called the "feminization of poverty." This phenomenon cannot simply be explained in terms of bare economic figures, but is undergirded by a matriphobic way of seeing reality or what has been called "capitalist patriarchy."

Women contribute to the economic well-being of society in what are traditionally called domestic chores and mothering, but within the mindset shaped by capitalist patriarchy, such activities are considered "nonwork." "Oh, she does not work. She just stays at home," is a common answer that husbands give when asked about the work of their spouses. One may not hear this remark among sophisticated men anymore, but the domestic tasks that women do continue to be treated as nonwork and do not count as a factor in standard economic analysis. All recent talks about family values amount to lip service in a capitalist economy that does not view women's household work and raising children as part of production.

In recent years we have witnessed the growing number of women working outside the confines of the home, but they continue to reap a small portion of the economic benefits. A 1980 United Nations report shows that women throughout the world perform two-thirds of the world's labor, but receive 10 percent of the pay and own one percent of the property.[34] They also continue to assume positions that are paid less in comparison to men. Men are still predominant in managerial positions. In the U.S. economic scene, for example, the proportion of women working in secretarial/clerical jobs has not changed since 1950. Ninety-eight percent of all secretaries remain females.[35] In the 1990 Congressional Research Service Report, Linda Levine wrote that "not only are women concentrated in low paying industries, but they also earn less than men regardless of industry." Women's pay averages only 70 percent of that of men even though they hold a 42 percent share of industry's jobs.[36]

When we look into the situation of the elderly, we can see a continuing pattern. Not only is there a feminization of poverty, there is also the feminization of poverty among the elderly. It is true that women live longer than men and in every age category women are economically poorer than men, but the ratio gets wider especially in the later years. Statistics show that women are only 58.7 percent of all elderly, while 72.4 percent of the elderly poor are women. Or, to put it in another way, 15.2 percent of women sixty-five years or over live below the poverty threshold (two and a half million women) compared to 8.5 percent of elderly men. The poverty rate increases to 19.7 percent for women over the age of eighty-five.[37]

If one is also a woman of color, there is certainly the phenomenon of triple jeopardy. There is not only the feminization of poverty, but also, as Ronald Takaki rightly pointed out, the "racial" feminization of poverty.[38] Taylor resonates this point: "Perhaps nowhere is the coalescence of misogyny and classism more manifest than in the diverse plights of third-world women."[39] If we include (and we should) people of color who are elderly, we have the racial feminization of poverty among the elderly. What we have here is a fourfold jeopardy: classism, racism, sexism, and ageism.

## The Coalescence of Classism and Naturism

While ecological hazard is generally felt by the whole populace, especially when its effect has reached to climacteric proportion, it is in the daily life of the underclass that the coalescence of classism and naturism shows its ugly face. The body of the poor bears the marks of classism and naturism, of injustice and ecological crisis. It is possible for the upper class to be suffering from toxic hazards without being a victim of injustice, but the poor have suffered both. Most often, it is only when the environmental degradation has reached an alarming proportion that the upper class starts to worry. But the poor have suffered the impact of ecological devastation long before its effects are felt by the social elites. Poverty has forced them to live in places that are environmentally hazardous because those are the only places they can afford. It is also true that these places are often the choice of legislators and businesses for dump sites.

The coalescence of classism and naturism, especially as it is experienced in the daily life of the poor, means that ecological well-being is part of the struggle against unjust domestic and global structures. In many instances the poor have contributed to the destruction of the ecosystem. But in every major destruction of the ecosystem the right to life of the poor has been violated.

It has been the experience of Third World people that the advent of the foreign invaders on their sacred shores is synonymous with the rapacious destruction of their countries' ecosystems. It has been their experience that in their economic, political, and cultural subjugation, their fertile lands, lush and bountiful forests, and ocean teeming with marine life have likewise been raped and plundered. The poor have come to the awareness that the corporations that have exploited their labor—the same with capital and technology—are often the very same corporations that are environmentally destructive. In an effort to respond to the gigantic appetite of North Americans for hamburger, virgin forests in the Amazon and in countries like Costa Rica have been cleared to give way to pasture lands. The result is the hamburgerization of Costa Rica's rain forests. What is economic "growth" for transnational corporations (e.g., hamburgers for fast-food operations) is resource depletion for Costa Rica: degraded land, washed-away topsoil, destroyed forests, and so on.[40] The alliance of the local ruling elite and the foreign invaders has made this exploitation of people and nature possible.

From the point of view of the poor, passion for the ecosystem is a protest against the "toxic terrorism" or "environmental imperialism" of wealthy nations and their local counterparts. Rosemary Radford Ruether supports this perception of the struggling poor in the following words:

Converting our minds to the earth cannot happen without converting our minds to each other, since the distorted and ecologically dysfunctional relationships appear necessary, yet they actually support the profits of the few against the many...Any ecological ethic must always take into account the structures of social domination and exploitation that mediate domination of nature.[41]

Within the present industrial and economic system, the protection of the earth and its ecosystem will always remain frustrated. For, as Alan S. Miller emphatically puts it, "A healthy environment will emerge only from a healthy and non-exploitative economic system."[42] It is for this reason that ecology has to be interpreted in relation to the struggle against domestic and global structures of injustice and exploitation.

### Racism in Relation to Classism, Sexism, and Naturism

Using racism as a springboard to analyze the interlocking structure of systemic oppression brings some dimensions that are obscured in classism. I am not going to be detailed in expounding its relationship with other systemic oppression, as I did with classism, but will only establish broad connections.

As I said earlier, my coming to the United States has put my race in the forefront of my identity and experience. The prominence of one systemic evil in relation to one's experience is not constant. With a change in geographical location, what was for me at the forefront (class) became intertwined with the question of race. As a professor, I did not feel much personal agony over the class division (there are those, many of whom are whites, who are in a much lower economic strata than myself), but the challenge of racism was more vexing. What happens when race occupies the forefront of one's daily life? How does it relate to classism, sexism, and naturism?

Like classism, racism has both a global and a domestic face, and it operates most effectively and deceptively in collusion with other forms of oppression. Racial domination went along with the "voyages of discovery" and racist discourse served to justify conquest and exploitation. Racist discourse portrayed the conquerors as benefactors and saviors to the conquered "savages" that needed to be civilized and Christianized. With inferior racial status being conferred upon conquered people, it was easier for the conquerors to relegate them to the lower class status. The words by a spokesman for U.S. imperialism portray this relationship of the benefactor and the uncivilized beneficiary:

American imperialism, in its essence...is American valor, American manhood, American sense of justice and right, American conscience, American character at its best, listening to the voice of God, and His command nobly assuming this republic's rightful place in the grand forward movement for the civilizing and Christianizing of all continents and all races.[43]

Race and class coalesce, and the painful drama of this coalescence can be discerned in the lives of racial minorities in the U.S. Racial/ethnic groups, in spite of the "success" stories of some, have to overcome difficult hurdles in order to climb the ladder of social stratification. Underemployment and unemployment rates in inner-city communities of color have skyrocketed—from 50 percent to 70 percent—in spite of assertions that the general unemployment rates have dropped.[44]

Media pundits have exaggerated the Asian American "success" story. The well-advertised success story of Asian Americans has earned them the title "model minority." This does not, however, take into account the plight of many of them. The use of "family income" as an economic index has been misleading, for Asian American families have more persons working per family than white families. They work long hours in several low-paying jobs, often without complaining. (That's a model!) Many Chinese American women, because they do not speak English, are limited to being seamstresses, while the men work in restaurants. As seamstresses, Asian American women are "paid by the piece and only a few can make good money. They don't protest because they don't know how to talk back and they don't know the law."[45]

Asian Americans take the idea of "model minority" with much caution. Not only does it not portray accurately the plight of Asian Americans, but it also encourages invidious comparison among racial minorities. Furthermore, it makes them a visible target of whites' frustration, especially when the country is undergoing an economic downturn. So, Asian American reception of the "model minority" status has been circumspect.

Racism is not only worsened by classism but gets exacerbated when we incorporate the dimension of sexism, especially as it is seen in the lives of women of color. Women of color not only suffer sexism from men of their own race and those of others, but they also suffer racism from their white sisters. An analysis of patriarchy or of sexism without the element of racism leaves too much out of the picture that is important to those who suffer from racism and sexism. The notion of patriarchy, says Dolores Williams, "is silent about white men and white women working together to maintain white supremacy and white privilege. It is silent about the positive boons patriarchy has bestowed upon many white women."[46]

Compounding and interweaving with racism is naturism. If we can speak of "environmental classism," we certainly can speak of "environmental racism" and "radioactive racism." Eighty to ninety percent of uranium mining and milling in the U.S., for example, has taken place in or adjacent to American Indian reservations, with serious consequences to the health of American Indians.[47] "As long as there are…minority areas to dump on," argues Leon White, "corporate America won't be serious about finding alternatives to the way toxic materials are produced and managed."[48] The struggling racial communities have discovered that there is a functional relationship between racism and the industry's assault on the environment.

### Sexism in Relation to Classism, Racism, and Naturism

At a point when my ammunition against racism was increasing, I was challenged to grapple with another form of oppression that was at the heart of my home and my relationship with women: sexism. Like others in a patriarchal society, I did not grasp the extent of the destructive power of sexism until the feminist movement made headway in making the wider public aware of its reality. I am going to attempt a cursory critical exposition of this form of oppression in this section.

As with other systemic forms of oppression, sexism interlocks with classism, racism, and naturism. In the unholy alliance of patriarchy and capitalism (patriarchal capitalism), women, in general, are pushed to the bottom of the economic ladder. In the previous section (classism in relation to sexism) I provided concrete figures to show the unholy alliance of classism and sexism. Thus, there is a common cause among women all over the world.

When we traverse the dimension of race, the confluence of sexism, classism, and racism finds its concrete manifestation in women of color. Again, like the upper class white women, we have to be reminded that there is no one straight line of subordination and marginalization. There are wealthy women of color; thus, privileged in terms of their class status. A woman of color experiences the interlocking forms of oppression in different levels in relation to others, both male and female within and outside of her racial identity. When we link sexism and classism to racism, we see that a high number of the poor women who take care of the children and chores of upper and middle class white women are women of color. Whether it was in the old way, when women were confined to the mothering role, or in the move toward greater opportunity for outside pursuits, poor women of color are there as servants.

The relationship of subordination and abuse, which are expressions of the confluence of the various forms of systemic oppression, can be gleaned from the lives of women of color who have come to the U.S. in various capacities as professionals, domestic helpers, tourists, refugees, and mail-order brides. Aside from getting a higher education, marrying a U.S. citizen is, for many women, a passport to a better life. Women seek relationships with U.S. citizens regardless of personal character and appearance, for the sole purpose of coming to the U.S. Various means are usually employed to establish the relationship. An overstaying Filipina tourist who worked illegally–a former teacher, married and with children–was forced to marry in order to change her immigration status. She even paid the man with her hard earned money to become her husband. It turned out that the man was sexually and physically abusive, and he constantly harassed her for more money with the threat of being reported to the immigration officials.[49] This is not an isolated case. I have come to know some of those in similar situations. They endure the abusive relationship and do not report it to the proper authorities for fear that their bid for a "green card" or citizenship may be jeopardized.

There are of course those who are legally and happily married to U.S. citizens and, as I mentioned earlier, they are generally women. One can easily perceive a relationship of equality when both spouses are highly educated. But in cases of mail-order brides, where the bride is most often of lower academic and professional status, a relationship of subordination is not uncommon. I know of some cases in which wives are denied opportunities for outside exposure, confined to the house, not taught how to drive a car, and not allowed a say in matters regarding the rearing of children.

The confluence of sexism and racism does not only take the form of economic exploitation and domestic abuse, but it also takes the form of the demonization of the sexuality of the racialized other. If we can speak about "racialized classism," we can also speak of "racialized sexism" (conversely, "sexualized racism"). Sexual harassment of women of color, says Catherine MacKinnon, can be the perpetrators' "sexist way to express racism and a racist way to express sexism."[50] Intertwined with white racist ideology is the negative construction of the sexuality of people of color. Sexuality of people of color is seen as chaotic and animalistic. European Americans, as pointed out by black scholars, have been fearful of black sexuality.[51] A similar case can be observed with regard to European Americans' portrayal of Filipino American sexuality: their love-making is "primitive," "heathenish," and more "elaborate." "The Filipinos are hot little rabbits, and many of these white women like them for this reason," a California businessman put it bluntly.[52]

While white racism pedestaled (also disempowered) white women's sexuality as spiritually superior to the male and more fitted to operate away from the "dirty" world of public life, women of color are identified with the sensuous and the bodily. When raped, women of color are seen as naturally promiscuous; thus, they are less worthy of protection. Racism also distorts the responses to the victimizers. "If the offender is a white male," says Marie Marshall Fortune, the "assumption is that he can take what he wants. If the offender is a male of color, it's assumed that 'that's the way those people behave normally.'"[53]

The identification of women—particularly women of color—with the earthly, bodily, and the sensual illustrates the interweaving of sexism and naturism. "Yet we cannot in my opinion," says Elizabeth Dodson Gray, "separate the rape of the earth from our culture in the United States where a woman is violently assaulted every eight seconds. These two cannot be separated."[54] The "naturization" of women's experience of menstruation, childbearing, and childrearing in a patriarchal-sexist culture that puts nature at the lowest rung to be exploited, has led to the subordination and exploitation of women by those who transcend nature—the men. Along with this, women's sexuality, construed as more natural and sensual, needs to be tamed and controlled by the "rational" mind (men). Only men, capable of transcending nature, can control and decide the "appropriate use" of women.

### Naturism in Relation to Classism, Racism, and Sexism

Naturism interweaves with classism, racism, and sexism. In this interlocking structure, naturism brings a dimension that broadens one's concern beyond economic justice and the plight of the poor to the whole ecological system, of which human beings are a part. In fact, it is not really beyond justice, but a reinterpretation of justice in a much wider sense. The interaction of various species within the whole web of life is a matter of justice. The vision is not only toward a democratic society but also toward a "biocratic" cosmos.

Naturism also takes a wider meaning when viewed in relation to racism. If we speak of the "naturization" of women, there is also the naturization of people of color, which justifies their subordination and exploitation. Naturism is an ideology that reduces people of color to nature that is not given value as such, but only as it serves the interest of those who are in the upper echelons of power and race differentials.

If we can speak of the naturization of women, the converse is also true. There is the phenomenon of the "feminization of nature." In this interweaving, nature, being identified with the feminine, suffers a similar fate with women. Since women in Western culture are identified with nature, and nature, in turn, is an object of domination by men (males), then, Ruether argues, "it would seem almost a truism that the mentality that regarded the natural environment as an object of domination drew upon imagery and attitudes based on male domination of women."[55] Our language reveals this interweaving. "Virgin" forests are raped (de-virginized) and exploited as women are raped and exploited. The ideology that subjugates women is also the same ideology that subjugates and rapes nature. This suggests that the struggle against naturism is simultaneously a struggle against sexism.

### Multiple Strategic Responses to Forms of Oppression

My attempt to explicate the interlocking structures only shows how forms of oppression are deeply intertwined and how they exacerbate one another. Only a nonadditive framework and only a plural explication of the concept of oppression can capture the interlocking structures of the various forms of systemic oppression. Short of that, the power and grip of one form of systemic oppression is only partially understood and the multiple locations we experience do not come into the analysis.

Moreover, the interlocking structure of systemic oppression calls for multiple strategies of action. "We must work with many fronts at once," says Charlotte Bunch, because people are oppressed by multi-dimensions of issues in different degrees. "While we may say at any given moment," Bunch continues, "that one issue is particularly crucial, it is important that work be done on other aspects of the changes we need at the same time."[56]

Aida Hortado states a similar point: "[A]ll forms of oppression afflicting... groups have to be taken into account simultaneously."[57] We have much to learn, argues Hortado, from feminists of color with regard to this issue of simultaneous, multiple-strategic response. By virtue of their own experience of multiple levels of oppression, they know by heart that other forms of oppression and exploitation cannot be postponed or pushed aside. In response to the homogenizing focus on generic women's experience by white feminists, their discourse on difference points to the necessity of dealing with forms of oppression that are particular to certain groups. Instead of conceptualizing gender subordination from the sole point of view of women's experience, which homogenizes and imperializes, Hortado, along with Patricia Zavella and other feminists of color, proposes that "social structure should be the analytical focus, which allows for profound differences among women."[58]

Within the framework of interlocking structures and the need for multiple responses, many of the Third World movements (revolutionary movements, human rights movements, and so forth), for example, cannot continue to justify pushing under the rug feminist struggle on the basis that it diverts the movement's attention from the main problem (e.g., imperialism and classism), or that it is internally divisive. Struggle against other forms of oppression and exploitation cannot be postponed in the name of unity of a particular social movement. The interlocking structure of forms of oppression, indeed, calls for a multiple strategic response.

The multiple strategic response cannot, however, be carried by one group; thus, it calls for networking and coalition building. Considering the global extent of the interlocking structures of domination and exploitation, networking and coalition building must not only be carried on within domestic confines but at the global level as well. As the forces of closure are "glocal" (globalized and localized),[59] people's struggles against them must also be global in their reach, yet particular enough to address differences. This is certainly so in the era of globalization.

Our isolation from one another has made us vulnerable to the global forces of dehumanization. It is ironic that while globalization links our lives to the wider world, it is also pushing us in the direction of isolated lives. The pursuit of material goods, whether amassing more or simply struggling to survive, has left many with no time and energy for the work of social change. We must resist the forces that isolate us. We need to counter the destructive global forces by establishing coalitions and networks in various places as well as at various levels. No "superman" can solve our problems. With his characteristic eloquence, Saul Alinsky reminds us that "solo is dodo."[60] Our history of global linkages has proven that we are not powerless and, in spite of the malleability of the forces of closure, something significant can happen.

The history of Amnesty International (AI) is encouraging and empowering. It started in 1961 when a British lawyer, Peter Benenson, learned of the arrest and seven-year imprisonment of two students in Portugal simply for raising their glasses in a toast to freedom. Indignant that this simple act could lead to a seven-year imprisonment, Benenson wondered how an oppressive regime might react to concerted global protests against acts of injustice. Benenson's idea attracted international support and within a few months the organization was formed. Fifteen years after its formation (1976), Amnesty International had 100,000 workers in seventy-two countries. Of the 13,000 political prisoners it investigated during this period, AI claimed that it played a significant role in the release of 8,500 prisoners.[61]

Amnesty International is one among many nongovernmental organizations that have made a significant difference in the lives of people. There are many grassroots communities around the world that have made a significant difference in their respective localities. We must not be dismayed by small beginnings, nor be intimidated to dream big as well as dream together. And our dreams must be woven and acted in a well-orchestrated manner. Good coordination is a critical aspect of our struggle for transformation.

I end this chapter with strategic response, which is typical of subaltern scholarship, for the pain of the victims of various forms of domination and exploitation is not appeased by any well-garbed intellectual exercise. Yes, the interlocking structure of the various forms of oppression is complex and insidious, which can lead us into a paralysis of analysis. But we can choose to struggle, and I say we must: We must walk our talks as we talk our walks.

Walking our talks is not meant to discount the significance of the talk. It is not to put in opposition the theoretical and the practical. Kurt Lewin's aphorism is very appropriate: "Nothing is so practical as a good theory."[62] What I am underscoring at this point is that theories must give way to living and acting. It is only in our acting that we come to the realization that, indeed, we have the power to live differently and make a difference. To arrive at this moment in our existence is already to experience a foretaste of a new humanity in the making.

## Notes

[1]Edna Bonacich, "Inequality in America: The Failure of the American System for the People of Color," in *Race, Class, and Gender: An Anthology*, ed. Margaret Andersen and Patricia Hill Collins (Belmont, Calif.: Wadsworth Publishing Company, 1992), 103.

[2]Mark Kline Taylor, *Remembering Esperanza: A Cultural-Political Theology for North American Praxis* (Maryknoll, N.Y.: Orbis Books, 1990), 80–82.

[3]Ibid., 82.

[4]See Elizabeth Spelman, *Inessential Woman: Problems of Exclusion in Feminist Thought* (Boston: Beacon Press, 1988), 116; Iris Marion Young, *Justice and the Politics of Difference* (Princeton, N.J.: Princeton University Press), 40.

[5]See George C. L. Cummings, "Black Theology and Latin American Liberation Theology: A Framework for Race and Class Analysis," in *New Visions for the Americas: Religious Engagement and Social Transformation*, ed. David Batstone (Minneapolis: Fortress Press, 1993), 220.

[6]Gustavo Gutiérrez, *A Theology of Liberation*, 15th Anniversary Edition with a new introduction by the author (Maryknoll, N.Y.: Orbis Books, 1988), xxii.

[7]Cornel West, "Black Theology of Liberation as Critique of Capitalist Civilization," in *Black Theology: A Documentary History, 1980–1992*, vol. 2, ed. James Cone and Gayraud Wilmore (Maryknoll, N.Y.: Orbis Books, 1993), 410–25; West, *Prophesy Deliverance: An Afro-American Revolutionary Christianity* (Philadelphia: Westminster Press, 1982); West, *Prophetic Fragments* (Grand Rapids, Mich.: William B. Eerdmans Publishing Company, 1988).

[8]See, for example, James Cone, "Preface," in *Minjung Theology: People as the Subjects of History*, ed. Commission on Theological Concerns of the Christian Conference of Asia (Maryknoll, N.Y.: Orbis Books, 1983), ix–xix.

[9]James H. Cone, *A Black Theology of Liberation*, Twentieth Anniversary Edition (Maryknoll, N.Y: Orbis Books, 1990), xvii.

[10]Sidonie Smith and Julia Watson, eds., *De/Colonizing the Subject: The Politics of Gender in Women's Autobiography* (Minneapolis:: University of Minnesota Press, 1992), xiv; Gayatri Chakravorty Spivak, "The Political Economy of Women as Seen by a Literary Critic," in *Coming to Terms: Feminism, Theory, Politics*, ed. Elizabeth Weed (New York: Routledge, 1989).

[11]Aida Hortado, *The Color of Privilege: Three Blasphemies on Race and Feminism* (Ann Arbor, Mich.: Univ. of Michigan Press, 1996), 18.

[12]It may be that the woman in question does not experience an independent identity, or that society does not attribute a separate identity to her.

[13]Janet L. Wolfe and Iris G. Fodor, "The Poverty of Privilege: Therapy with Women of the 'Upper' Classes," in *Classism and Feminist Therapy: Counting Costs*, ed. Marcia Hill and Esther D. Rothblum (New York: Haworth Press, 1996), 82.

[14]Bonnie J. Miller-McLemore, "What's a Feminist Mother to Do?" in *Setting the Table: Women in Theological Conversation*, ed. Rita Nakashima Brock, Claudia Camp, and Serene Jones (St. Louis: Chalice Press, 1995), 190, citing her own work, "Let the Children Come," *Second Opinion* 17/1 (1991): 12.

[15]Spelman, *Inessential Woman*, 94.

[16]Smith and Watson, "De/Colonization and the Politics of Discourse in Women's Autobiographical Practices," in *De/Colonizing the Subject*, xv.

[17]Eric Gamalinda, "Myth, Memory, Myopia: Or, I May Be Brown But I Hear America Singin'," in *Flippin': Filipinos on America* (New York: The American Writers' Workshop, 1996), 3.

[18]Spelman, *Inessential Woman*, 89.

[19]Nancy Chodorow, cited in Spelman, *Inessential Woman*, 95.

[20]Susan Brooks Thistlethwaite and Peter Crafts Hodgson, "The Church, Classism, and Ecclesial Community," in *Reconstructing Christian Theology*, ed. Rebecca Chopp and Mark Lewis Taylor (Minneapolis: Fortress Press, 1994), 312.

[21]Ibid., 312.

[22]Christine Smith, *Preaching as Weeping, Confession, and Resistance: Radical Responses to Radical Evil* (Louisville: Westminster/John Knox Press, 1992), 135.

[23]Ibid., 136.

[24]Anthony H. Richmond, *Global Apartheid: Refugees, Racism, and the New World Order* (Toronto, New York, and Oxford: Oxford University Press, 1994).

[25]Bonacich, "Inequality in America: The Failure of the American System for People of Color," in *Race, Class, and Gender*, 106–7.

[26]Robert Blauner, "Colonized and Immigrant Minorities," in *From Different Shores: Perspectives on Race and Ethnicity in America*, ed. Ronald Takaki (New York and Oxford, U.K.: Oxford Univ. Press, 1987), 159.

[27]Ronald Takaki, *Strangers from a Different Shore: A History of Asian Americans* (New York: Penguin Books, 1989), 25.

[28]Takaki, "Reflections on Racial Patterns in America," in *From Different Shores*, 28. Also see Stephen Steinberg, *The Ethnic Myth: Race, Ethnicity, and Class in America* (Boston: Beacon Press, 1989), specifically chapter 1. Steinberg writes that "it was out of economic necessity rather than a principled commitment to the idea of America as an asylum that the United States imposed no nationality restrictions on immigration, either before or after Independence" (11).

[29]Andrew Sung Park, *Racial Conflict and Healing: An Asian-American Theological Perspective* (Maryknoll, N.Y: Orbis Books, 1996), 35–37. See Ivan Light and Edna Bonacich, *Immigrant Entrepreneurs: Koreans in Los Angeles* (Berkeley, Calif.: Univ. of California Press, 1988), 17–18.

[30]Ruth Sidel, "Who Are the Poor?" in *Experiencing Race, Class, and Gender in the United States*, ed. Virginia Cyrus (Mountain View, Calif.: Mayfield Publishing Company, 1993), 126.

[31]Park, *Racial Conflict and Healing*, 38.

[32]Ada María Isasi-Diaz, *En La Lucha: A Hispanic Women's Liberation Theology* (Minneapolis: Fortress Press, 1993), 23.

[33]Stephanie M. Wildman and Margalynne Armstrong, "Concluding Thoughts on Noticing Privilege," in *Privilege Revealed: How Invisible Preference Undermines America*, ed. Stephanie Wildman (New York: New York University Press, 1996), 177.

[34]See Bonnie J. Miller-McLemore, "What's a Feminist Mother to Do?" in *Setting the Table*, 191.

[35]Sam Roberts, "Women's Work: What's New, What Isn't?" *The New York Times,* 27 April 1995, B-6.

[36]Cited in *Reading the Signs of the Times: Resources for Social and Cultural Analysis*, ed. T. Howland Sanks and John A. Coleman (Mahwah, N.J.: Paulist Press, 1993), 204.

[37]See Smith, *Preaching as Weeping, Confession, and Resistance*, 50.

[38]Takaki, *From Different Shores*, 164.

[39]Taylor, *Remembering Esperanza*, 132.

[40]See Lawrence Surenda, "Global Solidarity for the Future: Where Do We Go from Here in South-North Relations?" in *Spirituality of the Third World*, ed. K. C. Abraham and Bernadette Mbuy-Beya (Maryknoll, N.Y.: Orbis Books, 1994), 23.

[41]Rosemary Radford Ruether, *Sexism and God-Talk: Toward a Feminist Theology* (Boston: Beacon Press, 1983), 91.

[42]Alan S. Miller, *A Planet to Choose: Value Studies in Political Ecology* (New York and Philadelphia: Pilgrim Press, 1978), 79.

[43]Matthew Kaufman, *Christian Advocate* (September 14, 1898), 9, cited by Robert T. Handy, *A Christian America: Protestant Hopes and Political Realities* (New York: Oxford University Press, 1971), 126.

[44]Joseph Barndt, *Dismantling Racism: The Continuing Challenge to White America* (Minneapolis: Augsburg Fortress Press, 1991), 19.

[45]Ronald Takaki, *A Different Mirror: A History of Multicultural America* (Boston, New York, Toronto, and London: Little, Brown and Company, 1993), 415–16.

[46]Dolores Williams, *Sisters in the Wilderness: The Challenge of Womanist God-Talk* (Maryknoll, N.Y.: Orbis Books, 1993), 185.

[47]Grace Thorpe, "Our Homes Are Not Dumps: Creating Nuclear-Free Zones," in *Defending Mother Earth: Native American Perspectives on Environment Justice*, ed. Jace Weaver (Maryknoll, N.Y.: Orbis Books, 1996), 47–58.

[48]Leon White of the Commission for Racial Justice as cited by Charles Lee, "The Integrity of Justice: Evidence of Environmental Racism," *Sojourners* 19 (February–March 1990): 25.

[49]Aurora Tompar-Tiu and Juliana Sustento-Seneriches, *Depression and Other Mental Health Issues: The Filipino American Experience* (San Francisco: Jossey-Bass Publishers, 1995), 47.

[50]Catherine MacKinnon, *Sexual Harassment of Working Women: A Case of Sex Discrimination* (New Haven, Conn.: Yale University Press, 1979), 30; also see Pamela Cooper-White, *The Cry*

*of Tamar: Violence Against Women and the Church's Response* (Minneapolis: Fortress Press, 1995), 69.

[51]West, *Prophesy Deliverance* 47–65; Williams, *Sisters in the Wilderness,* 84–107.

[52]Takaki, *Strangers from a Different Shore,* 328.

[53]Marie Marshall Fortune, *Sexual Violence: The Unmentionable Sin; An Ethical and Pastoral Perspective* (New York: Pilgrim Press, 1983), 90, cited in Marvin Ellison, *Erotic Justice: A Liberating Ethic of Sexuality* (Louisville: Westminster John Knox Press, 1996), 47.

[54]Elizabeth Dodson Gray, *Patriarchy as a Conceptual Trap* (Wellesley, Mass.: Roundtable Press, 1982), 109.

[55]For Ruether's works on this issue, refer to *New Woman, New Earth* (New York: Seabury Press, 1975), 186.

[56]Charlotte Bunch, "Going Public with Our Vision," in *Experiencing Race, Class, and Gender in the United States,* 389.

[57]Hortado, *Color of Privilege,* 42.

[58]Ibid., 42; Patricia Zavella, "The Problematic Relationship of Feminism and Chicana Studies," *Women's Studies* 17:123–34.

[59]See Richmond, *Global Apartheid,* 227. The term "glocalization" is an attempt to link macroscopic and microscopic expressions.

[60]Cited in Larry Rasmussen, "Power Analysis: A Neglected Agenda in Christian Ethics," in *The Annual of the Society of Christian Ethics* (1991), 12.

[61]See Dennis Shoemaker, *The Global Connection: Local Action for World Justice* (New York: Friendship Press, Inc., 1977), 61.

[62]Kurt Lewin, cited by Donald Shriver, Jr., "The Taming of Mars: Can Humans of the Twenty-First Century Contain Their Propensity for Violence," in *Religion and the Powers of the Common Life,* ed. Max Stackhouse with Peter Paris (Harrisburg, Pa.: Trinity Press International, 2000), 144.

# CHAPTER 3

# A Theological Reading of the Interlocking Forms of Oppression

## Sin and Evil

I am aware that any mention of sin and evil conjures negative images and associations for some people. Nevertheless, I have opted to talk about sin and evil for two reasons. First, not to do so is to miss engaging in a topic that is still of vital importance to many and, thereby, to fail by default to seize the prospect of moving beyond the debilitating aspects of the traditional and mainstream interpretations of sin and evil. Second, I still believe that there are aspects of the tradition that can be reappropriated and revisioned. Peter Hodgson, appropriating George Wilhelm Friedrich Hegel, speaks of this revisioning as "sublation" (*Aufhebung*) or the process of "both annulling and preserving, of both passing-over and taking-up."[1]

### Sin and Evil: Dealing with the Terms

Some authors have made a distinction between sin and evil. Hodgson acknowledges this is a tenuous process, but finds it helpful to make the distinctions between the individual emphasis on sin and the systemic emphasis on evil. For Hodgson, evil is not a mere consequence of sin, for it has its own dynamic that reinforces and magnifies sin. In having its own dynamic, it precedes individual acts of sin as much as it is a consequence of individual acts of sin.[2]

Mary Potter Engel, reflecting from the context of sexual and domestic violence, considers the distinction between sin and evil crucial not only because it conveys distinct, though mutually reinforcing, dimensions, but also because the distinction is functionally or strategically critical.[3] Alongside

Latin American liberation theologies, she views evil as systemic in distinction from sin, which refers to discrete acts of individuals that reinforce structures of oppression (systemic evil).

Taking into consideration the varying contexts and audience, Engel argues that when one is speaking with perpetrators, sin needs to be stressed because it underscores personal responsibility. On the other hand, when one is speaking with the victims, the stress should fall on the systemic aspect (evil), so as not to perpetuate the feeling of self-blame among the victims. Yet, the other dimension should not be forgotten in dealing with both parties: for the perpetrators need to know that their actions are expressions of systemic evil that extends beyond their individual decisions, and the victims need to realize that they have a responsibility to resist and fight back. Though with varying emphasis in relation to varying contexts, the two concepts need to go together so that we may understand better the character of the human predicament.

Andrew Sung Park brings a different dimension to the discussion on sin and evil out of his background as an Asian American.[4] Unlike Engel and others who make a distinction between sin and evil, he makes a distinction between sin and *han* (sigh, deep anguish, suffering). Like the feminist and liberationist theologians, Park proposes an analysis of sin that does not trample the victims once again, but exposes their pain, taking seriously the well-being of all—the victims and the victimizers. While sin and *han* should not be separated, even as they are distinct, reflection from the experience and vantage point of victimization demands that we talk about the victim's *han*. It makes no sense to talk about sin from the experience of victimization when an individual or a community is a victim of the sinful acts of others. On the other hand, it is hermeneutically appropriate to speak of sin when we have to consider the actions of the perpetrators or when we want to hold the perpetrators accountable for their heinous acts. Because we are victims and victimizers at various levels and circumstances, what is critical is to speak of *han* to underscore victimization and sin when we speak of one's participation in acts that destroy individual and communal well-being.

Since I am using various theological resources that do not make the fine distinction between sin and evil, and I am also not consistent with my usage, I will continue using the two terms interchangeably. However, I am going to take into account the nuances conveyed by those who see the critical importance of the distinction between sin and evil or between sin and *han.* In cases when I use the term *sin* beyond discrete individual acts of wrongdoing, I will use the term *systemic sin* to underscore the structural dimension. When speaking of sin in relation to the victims of certain forms of oppression, I will cast my interpretation in ways that allow sin to be understood as victimization, but also in ways that will enable the victims to see their responsibility and calling to be active agents. I will also try to be sensitive to the mechanisms of survival that victims have evolved that may appear on the surface as acquiescence or participation. It is the temptation of the elites (including the so-called revolutionary vanguards) to readily condemn common people's mechanisms of survival as acquiescence, when mere survival in a brutalizing situation is already a triumph, as womanists and other Third World theologians have reminded us.[5]

## Setting the Framework and Focus

I am not searching for an "historical origin" of sin or for an etiological explanation of evil. Not only is such a search untenable, it is also based on a questionable hermeneutical framework. So far as our historical consciousness is concerned, we cannot establish a historical beginning before the "fall" when everything was perfect. The moment we think of human beings, we are already dealing with human beings as they exist. There is no beginning that is not beginning in the middle. The biblical creation myth posited a paradisical beginning before the fall, but I consider it a literary device depicting a people's awareness of their "falling out" from who they were and are meant to be and what they may become. Instead of advancing logical propositions to establish the whence of sin and evil, Hodgson suggests the telling of a story, just like the writers of the Genesis account did. "The story that we tell should not be understood as an historical account of origins or an etiological explanation of sin;" instead, Hodgson contends, "it has the character of disclosure, of insight into this mysterious transition that each of us makes individually and that the human species has made collectively."[6]

What is helpful as we chart direction, I believe, is for us to embrace the hermeneutical approach that considers the discourse on sin and evil as an attempt to understand our plight in relation to our pains and longings for a better tomorrow. Instead of taking account of sin and evil by finding their historical beginning before the "fall" when everything was all right, the soil of our present predicament and our awareness of our brokenness, I suggest, should be our starting point. It is this soil from which we should take account of sin and evil, and it is this soil from which we should interpret the biblical creation myth. An account of sin and evil, to be truly responsive to the plight of concrete human beings in their embodied social specificity, must starkly identify the expressions of brokenness. If we want to get a better sight of the devastating effects of sin and evil, we do not need to raise our eyes up high to the sky, but must lower our gaze here on earth. This is where the real drama of sin and evil is enacted daily; where the breaking of the web of life happens; where the victims continue to pile up. This is where I start; this is where we should start.

Shifting our hermeneutical eye to the earth or to the cosmos requires deconstruction of some of the theologies we have inherited. Instead of focusing on sin as primarily a rebellion against God, I agree with Marjorie

Hewitt Suchocki's position that sin is primarily the violation of creation, and thus a "rebellion against creation's well-being."[7] Sin is the violation or the breaking of the web of life that sustains us and makes us whole; it is the violation of right relation. It is from this perspective that we need to see the traditional notion of sin as a violation against God if it is to be of relevance today. Yes, sin is also a violation against God, but we discern this violation through our sinful constructions. It is a violation against God only if we begin to see the world, following Sallie McFague, as God's body. We sin against God because we sin against God's body. Sin is "living a lie" in relation to other members of God's body.[8]

Suchocki offers a pungent critique against an approach to sin as primarily a violation against God.[9] First, to speak of sin as rebellion against God tends to cast God in the role of a lawgiver who establishes boundaries for moral conduct as well as the judge in the event of a violation. As has been the case, divine moral codes often turn out to be cultural codes of society. When God is used to sanction these codes, it may be that the notion of God that is tied to such interpretations of social boundaries is part of the problem rather than a contributor to the solution. Second, sin as rebellion against God has been a ready ideological tool of those who want to maintain the established order, and it has been used to equate rebellion against the established order as rebellion against God. Third, the notion of sin as rebellion against God levels all distinctions between sins. Fourth, it makes the direct victims of sin invisible. What happens to God is what matters. Fifth, sin as primarily rebellion against God promotes the devaluation of creation and encourages its exploitation. Its hierarchical presupposition conveys the idea that sin can only be done against one who is over oneself or that which is above oneself, not against the world of nature. Sixth, it isolates as well as elevates the individual from the rest of creation; thus, it encourages the deification of the individual contrary to what it intends to overcome. Seventh, it makes human defiance against God the central problematic, which is remote from the experience of most people.

It is apparent from Suchocki's account that a critique of sin is also a critique of the doctrine of God. There is, indeed, a connection between the doctrine of God and the notion of sin. Suchocki articulated this connection in another essay in which she points out the close relation or the correlation between the doctrine of God, the notion of evil, and the social order. One's notion of evil reflects the doctrine of God one holds and vice versa. She contends: "So long as a particular interpretation of evil remains vibrantly cogent to a community, the social structure and the correlative doctrine of God will hold," but, on the other hand, when one's "interpretation of evil changes, both the social structure and the doctrine of God will creak and groan and then either be adapted or snap and be cast aside."[10] Sin as primarily a violation against God portrays a sovereign being who is above and aloof and as one who is construed as a lawgiver, an executioner, a guardian of the established order, and a being who must be continually appeased.

The notion of sin as primarily a violation against the sovereign God that Suchocki criticizes finds resonance in Michel Foucault's critique of political philosophy. Sin as primarily against a sovereign God corresponds to the notion of power revolving around the sovereign, which is personified by the monarch.[11] Under this political philosophy, denizens derive their subjecthood from the sovereign. Theories about rights and property revolve around the person of the monarch, and legitimate power belongs to the monarch alone. We may think that this notion belongs to the ancient world but, contends Foucault, we have not completely liberated ourselves from this sovereign-centered political philosophy. Even when questions are raised against the power of the sovereign and his rights and limitations, the Western legal system continues to revolve around the sovereign figure. "We need to cut off the King's head," says Foucault.[12] This obsession with the theory of power as sovereign conceals from our attention what Foucault calls the microphysics of power.

With insights from Foucault's critique of power, I would say that the notion of sin as primarily a violation against God also remains captive to a political philosophy that sees power through the person of the sovereign. Like the subjects of the sovereign power who have no subjecthood apart from the monarch, sinful acts against other individuals in society are crimes only because they are primarily against the sovereign God. I say this because in the notion of power as "sovereign," it is the sovereign who is the primary offended party, whether it be a crime directly against the sovereign or between the denizens of the empire. Since it is the honor of the sovereign that is being violated, the sovereign must be appeased, not the victims, for they are the sovereign's subjects. In a similar manner, the traditional notion of sin as primarily an offense against God (sovereign) has diverted our attention away from the embodied victims and has made us oblivious to the micro-physics of sin.

A similar ideological dynamic is present in cases of domestic violence. Rita Nakashima Brock's work, *Journeys by Heart: A Christology of Erotic Power*, is instructive here.[13] Like the sovereign monarch in political philosophy and the almighty Lord in Christendom theologies, we have the patriarchal head in the modern family. If the denizens of the sovereign power have no subjecthood apart from that of the monarch, likewise the children of the patriarchal household, explains Nakashima Brock, are "fused" with the parents and the parents are "unable to see their children as separate from themselves." With no selfhood and rights apart from the patriarchal head, it is the head's name and honor that must be protected at all cost. Whether the children experience violation from persons outside of the family or by members of the same family, the primary offended party is the patriarchal head, not the victimized children. The pain of the "extensions" (children) is not the center. Even if the patriarchal head is the one delivering the punishment to the erring children, it is the pain of the patriarchal head that is the primary focus, not the pain of the punished children. This scenario is summed up by the common formula parents often say to children when they punish: "This hurts me more than it hurts you."[14] Punishment to the offenders or restitution to the victims must satisfy the patriarchal head. This is a familial correlation of the almighty Godhead in theology.

What is true in familial relations and cases of domestic violence has resonance in the discourse regarding disability. In *A Healing Homiletic: Preaching and Disability*, Kathy Black calls our attention to the abuse that people with disabilities have experienced from the whims of an offended and executor God. Their suffering has been justified in various ways: a form of punishment, to test the faith, to educate humankind, or simply to prove God's power.[15] The punishment is not only rendered in the final parousia, but is hurled against the people of today who experience disabilities. A God who is understood as the epitome of power, strength, agility, and beauty is identified with the mindset and values of the powerful while punishing those who are considered weaklings, idiots, or failures. In the final analysis, the victims are further victimized.

Classical Christian theories of atonement are congruent with the sovereign power/patriarchal head/almighty God trajectory and the notion of sin as primarily a violation against God. All the classical atonement theories focus on what happened to God or to the pain of God and not on what happened to the beloved Son or to the people. It is God's pain that is the focus—God's woundedness; the pain of the victims is swallowed by God. Yes, it is God who renders the punishment, but it is also God who suffers terribly. Although the almighty God is the one who renders judgment, the interpretation has been that the sovereign God is no obdurate power wielder, but is also at the same time loving and self-sacrificing. Ultimately, it is God's pain that counts.

To continue this critical assessment, I would also say that sin as rebellion against God diverts our criticism from the order of things that produces victimization. It sidetracks us from our concrete experience of sin and evil toward an abstract Being, thus resulting in our bizarre and abstract notion of forgiveness. With an abstract notion of sin committed against an abstract Being, it is no wonder that pious Christians continue to commit crimes and still shout—"hallelujah, praise the Lord!"—having been assured that they are cleansed by the blood of the Lamb, without making any concrete amends to the victims (nature and human beings) of their concrete sins. As sin is not committed in the abstract, so healing and forgiveness must be concrete in relation to creation's well-being.

While well-intentioned, it appears that the focus of some theologians on the suffering God serves to divert attention from the suffering of creation to God's suffering itself. In my work, *Toward a Theology of Struggle*, I raised the possibility of the obfuscation of historical suffering by its quick absorption into God's very own eternal suffering, especially in the form of the trinitarian character of God.[16]

The classical notion continues to obfuscate sin and does a disservice to those who suffer the most by leveling the distinction between sins. If sin is primarily a violation against God, then it does not matter what type of sin: they are all equal in the sight of God.[17] Criticizing the prevalent Protestant consciousness of sin, Dorothee Sölle contends that it is "innocuous and distresses no one in its indiscriminate universality, for it identifies sin, not theoretically but *de facto*, with a universal human fate comparable perhaps to a smallpox, against which we are protected by vaccination."[18]

Ted Peters supports the idea of making distinctions between sins. Peters said that he would prefer for people to gossip against him rather than murder him on his way home from his office. "At the mundane level," he argues, "there are degrees in the kind and amount of evil that is produced."[19] Not surprisingly he opted not to be murdered. But because he operated within the framework of the classical notion of sin as primarily a violation against God, he was only able to take account of the distinction between sins with much theological arm-twisting and shifting gears from the God-level to the mundane level. This cumbersome maneuver only suggests, in my view, that Suchocki's relational approach and McFague's notion of the world as the body of God offer a much better approach to the matter.

In resonance with Suchocki's points, I consider it a crucial corrective to the traditionally prevalent approach to discern sin in our acts of violence against creation's well-being and in our social constructions. When the specific experience of brokenness is the theological locus for interpreting evil, we cannot remain content with a generalized theological account of sin and evil. Our varied positions in the interlocking structure of forms of oppression (classism, racism, sexism, naturism) put us in different positions of vulnerabilities and privileges. One could argue, and with theological sense, that both the master and the slave are alienated from their true humanity. But this is a vacuous universalistic statement, for the socio-political face of the alienation of the slave and that of the master are not the same. There is, in fact, a conspicuous contradiction. Most often, this generalized account muffles the experience of the marginalized. It also helps to conceal the operative ideological undergirding. Although universal categories, argues Thomas Ogletree,

> enjoy formal clarity and precision, they always carry with them
> unstated and even unacknowledged meanings and assumptions
> of a more concrete sort. The accompanying meanings and
> assumptions tend, moreover, to affect decisively the specific
> applications of the principles themselves. When moral principles
> are applied without critical awareness of the concrete meanings

associated with them, they are apt in their universalistic grandeur
to serve as ideological cover for what is actually going on.[20]

A context-bound hermeneutic takes seriously the varied experiences
of groups with regard to the various forms of oppression, and these varied
experiences warrant a differentiated articulation of sin and evil.
Indiscriminate universality does not happen when one views sin from the
earth; nor when one views it from the prism of the violation of creation's
well-being; nor when it is viewed as a social construction. Feminist, black,
and ecologist theologians have done work in the direction of a context-
bound hermeneutics of sin, and their insights offer breakthroughs in our
notions of sin and evil.

Feminist theologians, for example, have pointed out that the notion of
sin as pride and hunger for power does not clearly articulate the condition
of those who have been subjugated and have lost their sense of self-worth.
Disastrously, the definition of sin as hunger for power works to perpetuate
the situation of the disempowered, for it is an outward warning and judgment
against those who are seeking empowerment. More fittingly, sin as laziness
or failure to resist is the prevalent sin of oppressed people.[21] Their sin, to
use Erich Fromm's book title, is "escape from freedom," a point I elaborated
elsewhere.[22]

In response to the feminist interpretations of sin, several theologians
modified their theological positions to incorporate feminist analysis, but
rebounded by reasserting pride as the "primal" sin and swallowing sloth in
it, as James Nash does. One can interpret sloth under the rubric of pride,
but this interpretation does not take into account what it means for those
who have lost their sense of self-worth, or those whose dignity has been
trampled upon.[23] No oppressed community or group, of course, can be
totally innocent. But a crucial difference is present when we probe deeper:
What does the sin of pride or to be supercilious mean for a colonized
person who has learned to despise his or her race? What does the sin of
pride mean for a person of color who has internalized racism such that, if it
were possible, he or she would like to be born in another life as a white
person? What does the sin of pride mean for many gays and lesbians who
are still hiding in their closets and who have not gained the courage to
speak out?

More in line with feminist articulation is one offered by Ismael Garcia,
a Hispanic theologian and ethicist. For the power wielders, Garcia argues,
"sin usually takes the form of human pride" and all its varied expressions.
The poor, on the other hand, often manifest sin in forms opposite that of
the power wielders. Instead of self-pride, they tend to engage in self-
deprecation or self-hatred. "In their sin, the oppressed," continues Garcia,
"seek security in the present order, no matter how fragile and unjust, and

avoid and refuse to endure the risks and pains that come from being obedient to God's call for justice."[24]

Black theologians have also reminded us that in the context of racism, sin is quite distinct for blacks and whites. What, for whites, is the yardstick of who they are—whiteness—and by which others are judged, is also whites' lurid sin, while the capitulation of blacks to the normative whiteness—desiring to be white—is also the blacks' "fall."[25]

Sin would also get a contextual interpretation when viewed from an ecological standpoint. One way to look at sin from this angle is to interpret it as "living a lie" and as a refusal of human beings to live within the "scheme of things."[26] Nash speaks of the ecological sin of human egoism, arrogance, turning inward, rebellion against God, and grasping more than our due without regard to the integrity of the ecosystem. But, what does the sin of ecological rebellion mean to a poor peasant in Brazil cutting trees for firewood and to a U.S. logging company that has to ship the wood to the U.S. for the construction of Mr. Nash's house? What does rebellion against God mean for many indigenous peoples who have been evicted from their traditional lands in order to give way to the construction of nuclear power plants to support the industries?

I believe the shift in the interpretation of sin in the direction of the creation's well-being is an important move. Reconciliation requires not only that we are reconciled with God, but also that we are reconciled with the rest of creation. To know God is to do justice and to love mercy. The message of 1 John 4:20 is very direct: "Those who say, 'I love God,' and hate their brothers or sisters, are liars; for those who do not love a brother or sister whom they have seen, cannot love God whom they have not seen." There is no other way of knowing God that bypasses the neighbor in need, but always in and through the neighbor. To push further, the neighbor is not simply my bridge to God but God has become the neighbor. Gutiérrez puts it well: "It is not enough to say that love of God is inseparable from the love of one's neighbor. It must be added that love for God is unavoidably expressed *through* love of one's neighbor. Moreover, God is loved in the neighbor."[27]

It is lip service to love God in abstraction, as it is always lip service to love humanity in abstraction. What we can say of loving God in abstraction is also true of loving anybody in abstraction. In *The Brothers Karamazov*, Dostoyevsky's doctor said: "I love humanity, but I wonder at myself. The more I love humanity in general, the less I love man in particular."[28] Encounter with individual lives and living communities is necessary to move beyond abstraction, lip service, and chilly apathy.

This shift of focus to creation's well-being is not a "spillover" from the love we have of God, though our love for God certainly overflows in love for the neighbor (including the cosmic neighbor).[29] Rather, I interpret the love of neighbor as indivisibly a dimension of the love of God. It is not that the love for God is one and the love for the neighbor is another, but they are one in two dimensions. My shift to the priority of creation's well-being is not simply for practical consideration in distinction from the ontological, but is itself an ontological assertion.

## Sin: Not an Inherent Flaw in Human Beings

In a constructive theology course I taught at United Theological Seminary of the Twin Cities in the fall of 1995, I encountered some students who expressed a strong resentment about the category of sin and evil. I learned from that encounter that one of the reasons why some do not want to employ the term *sin* is its association with a "tragic flaw" in human nature. It means, for these students, an outright declaration that human beings are inherently bad. For them, it is only making people feel bad and helpless; it means that people cannot get out of their rotten condition. Based on this construal, these students raised the question about our ability to participate in the transformation of our lives and society. This concern is very valid, and I am taking this seriously. But this concern is based on a theological presupposition that I do not share, and I also do not think that it is the view that the mainstream Christian tradition and major theologians have endorsed.

While there is a difference in the way I would approach the topic of sin from theologians who are approaching it by focusing on the ontological existentials, there is an agreement that sin is not a tragic ontological flaw. Edward Farley, for example, speaks of the "tragic structure" of human existence or "tragic vulnerability," but the tragic is not an ontological defect.[30] The tragic is constitutive of human being as such: It refers to the inextricable interdependence of the conditions of well-being with conditions of limitations, frustration, challenge, and suffering. This tragic structure pervades in all three spheres of human reality that Farley speaks about (individual, interhuman, and social).[31]

Other theologians take a different account of the ontological structure, but the notion of the tragic that Farley speaks about is present. We have this notion in Hodgson when he refers to the structures of human being as fragile, fallible, and characterized by instability, which is inherent in the synthesis of finitude and freedom (finite freedom or embodied freedom). What Hodgson calls structures of freedom—(1) agency, (2) community, (3) society, and (4) transpersonal—are subject to distinctive or tragic vulnerabilities.[32]

In Paul Tillich's work, this notion of the tragic is explained through his account of the polarities of human existence that constitute (1) individuation and participation, (2) dynamics and form, and (3) freedom and destiny.[33] The polar character of these ontological elements makes human beings vulnerable to the threat of nonbeing. With the impact of finitude, these polarities create a tension as the various elements draw away from one another in opposite directions, instead of complementing one another or maintaining a balanced relation. Under the first element, human being faces the threat of loneliness on one hand and the threat of collectivization on the other. Under the second element, finitude transforms the polarity of dynamics and form into a tension between being and becoming, stability and change, rest and movement. And, under the third element, finitude transforms the polarity of freedom and destiny into a tension as human being is threatened by the possible loss of freedom implied in one's destiny and the equal threat of the loss of destiny implied in one's freedom. This polarity of human existence, under the impact of finitude, constitutes the tragic structure. It is tragic in the sense that the seat of human limitation is also the seat of creativity and possibility.

The Kierkegaardian and Niebuhrian account of the tragic follows what David Kelsey calls the "dynamics of self-choosing."[34] This dynamic of self-choosing occurs within the confines of an ontological structure that is open to various possibilities, depending on the decisions being made by the subject. As a being capable of transcendence, human being sees open possibilities as well as vulnerabilities. Transcendence enables human beings to see possibilities for realization, but it also enables human beings to be aware of their contingencies brought about by temporality and embodiment. Caught up in the tension between one's possibilities and the awareness that one may cease to be, human being experiences anxiety or dread. Anxiety is not just a simple fear. Anxiety is concomitant of one's finitude and freedom; it is an internal threat (internal precondition), not external (temptation); it proceeds out of living at the juncture between freedom and necessity. For Søren Kierkegaard, anxiety is the "dizziness of freedom," and it occurs when "freedom...gazes down into its own possibility, grasping at finiteness to sustain itself."[35] Anxious about one's own finiteness, human being, according to Reinhold Niebuhr, "seeks to transmute his finiteness into infinity, his weakness into strength, his dependence into independence."[36] Threatened by deep-seated anxiety and insecurity, human being makes every effort to secure all windows of vulnerability, even at the expense of others.

Freedom, in its dizziness, finally succumbs to false securities as human beings refuse to accept their finiteness. Anxiety, the dizziness of freedom, brings forth the sin of pride as human beings refuse to accept finiteness. This sin of pride, for Niebuhr, has various expressions: pride of power, pride of knowledge, pride of virtue, and spiritual pride.[37]

On the other hand, human beings' abdication of freedom or surrender into the demands of finitude leads to what Niebuhr calls the sin of sensuality.[38] In the sin of sensuality we have a being who has failed to exercise transcendence, freedom, and responsibility—a being who has failed to become a subject of his or her destiny. It is characterized by flight, despair, sloth, and submission. Fatalism, a social sickness common among subjugated peoples, is a form of this sin of sensuality.

Because human being is basically a being-in-the-world or is primordially related to others, sin always means the destruction of others. It means then that there is no disruption in the ontological and transcendental region that does not destroy the intersubjective life; there is no corruption of the individual that does not express itself in behavior toward others; there is no corruption that does not alienate others. Estrangement does not only result in self-destruction but also destruction of others. To use Walter Rauschenbusch's words: "Sin is not a private transaction between the sinner and God."[39] There is no idolatry that does not do violence to other selves; there is no self-securing act that is not done at the expense of others; no concupiscence without victims; no hubris without others being put down, no separation from the Ground of Being without being separated from the neighbor; no flight without being a flight from other beings; no flight without being an escape from obligation and responsibility.

In this cursory account of the ontological structure of human being, there is a common understanding among the scholars I have cited that sin is not the result of a tragic flaw in the structure of human being as such. The tragic structure serves as the precondition, but not the cause of sin. There is nothing inherently bad in finite freedom, but it establishes the conditions for temptation. Even as the ontological structure must be dealt with in utmost seriousness in taking account of sin, as Farley argues, the theologians whom I have considered do not establish a causal link between the ontological structure and sin.[40] Tillich speaks of the coinciding of creation and fall and of the identical character of "actualized creation" and "estranged existence," but this does not suggest that human beings are inherently bad.[41] Even Niebuhr, who takes the paradoxical position that sin is inevitable, still clings to the idea that sin is not necessary, that is, a nonessential part of human nature even if it always, in fact, happens.[42] There is certainly that pervasive character of sin (preconditioned by human ontological structure), which tells us that we cannot completely eradicate it. But in all the theological positions that I explored, human agency is part of the dynamics. It also shows that the ontological account of the human is open to the interpretation of the socially constructed dimension of sin and evil.

## Sin and Evil as Social Construction

In distinction from the ontological accounts that focus on the underlying structures that provide the internal preconditions to sin, my focus is on the "social preconditions" of sin and evil. I think this focus coincides, in a sense, with the "external preconditions" of ontological approaches, but it is also different because I look at social preconditions as constructions. Rather than spend more space in taking account of the underlying deep structures that constitute preconditions for sin, which many theologians have already done so well, I see the need to underscore our social constructions, especially constructions that are hurtful. These sinful constructions are embedded in our ideologies, cultural rules, and practices. This focus on the social construction of sin is, I believe, consistent with my hermeneutic framework.

### Social Institutions and Their Functions in Society

While one may speak of the antecedence of individuals in the sense that individuals create society and institutions, there has never been a point in time when human beings have not been shaped by society and social institutions. As much as we think about a point in time when there was this neutral historical ground, and as much as we think that there was this self-originating and self-conscious free-choosing individual prior to the social, this is not the case. By our historicity, we are born into the social world; by our solidarity, we share in it. We did not choose our own parents, nor did we have a choice about the kind of society we wanted to be born into. Even what we consider the private domain and the most intimate is structured by society. We are born with an existing framework of social interactions and expectations.

No interaction in society is possible without some shared understanding of meaning, of expected roles and behavior, of some stable social structures or patterns that govern the interactions. In the process of people's interaction certain ways of relating are structured, which in turn make interaction possible. Sociologists call these patterns institutions. An institution "provides everyone with a stable social order with a minimum of emotional and intellectual agonizing each day about what should be done."[43] Institutions emerge out of social interaction, and, in return, give stability, order, coherence, legitimacy, and shape to social interactions. They stabilize behavior or stabilize society; solidify the interactions so that they do not become haphazard; raise reciprocity to the level of obligation; order meaning; mediate the relations of individuals to each other into a meaningful and coherent whole; and regulate relations among individuals in connection to basic and secondary needs.[44] These patterns are perpetuated over time, bridging several generations. Society and its social institutions, while creations of human beings, outlast the lives of individuals. Institutions acquire a status or life of their own; they are bigger than the sum of all individuals; and they transcend individuals in space and time. This point is very crucial in understanding how we become inheritors of previous acts and how our collective acts influence and shape the coming generations.

As the inherited ways of seeing, thinking, and behaving get perpetuated over time, they become part of society's common stock of knowledge. And, "the common stock of knowledge which dictates people's understanding of 'how things are' is assumed to be all there is to know."[45] Peter Berger and Thomas Luckmann help advance this point aptly: "What is taken for granted as knowledge in the society comes to be coextensive with the knowable, or at any rate provides the framework within which anything not yet known will come to be known in the future."[46]

All the various nuances that I enumerated about institution–orders behavior and interaction, integrates activities, creates a sense of obligation, solidifies and shapes interaction, mediates relations, stabilizes interaction, orders meaning and roles, establishes patterns of behavior, and finally bridges previous generations and the generations yet to be born–point to the crucial role that institution plays in shaping the lives of people. As every relation, activity, and interaction is mediated by institutions, it is clear that the influence of institutions permeates every point in the life and action of individuals. And this is where potential danger lies.

### When Institutions Get Corrupted: Institutional Evil

When institutions get corrupted they become instruments of human evils and vehicles for transmitting these evils into the next generation. This leads Erich Fromm to say that society and its institutions are the great corrupters of individuals.[47] It is at this juncture that I embark on an analysis of institutional evil.

In order to clarify institutional evil, Gregory Baum placed it against the background of the common notion of sin–the individual sin. For Baum, the illustration that best conveys the idea of a private understanding of sin is the confession.[48] A confessional understanding of sin implies that sin, for it to be confessed, has to be conscious and deliberate. This, for Baum, does not take an accurate account of sin. At worst, it fails to take into consideration the work of sin that most of us have suffered in the most odious form imaginable. This has to do with what he calls social sin; it is a notion of sin that enables us to understand the collective evil in which we are involved. Baum notes that social sin is not simply an evil act of a person that affects large segments of the population. While not negating that this is one aspect of social sin, he notes that by its being egregiously blatant or overtly intentional, it remains very close to personal sin. Social sin proper is when the subject who is corrupted and is responsible for the perpetuation of corruption is the collectivity. It is at this collective level that structures, systems, and institutions become instruments of human evil. It is here that sin enters into the realm of social sin, or to a stage in which we can speak of sinful social structures.

Baum clarifies the dynamics of social sin at four levels. First level: Social sin is made up of unjust and dehumanizing trends that are built into various societal institutions. The destructive trends corrupt the individuals and dehumanize them. Second level: Social sin refers to cultural and religious symbols that legitimize and reinforce unjust social institutions. Third level: Social sin refers to false consciousness that institutions have created and perpetuated. Fourth level: Social sin refers to collective decisions, generated by distorted consciousness, which exacerbate the injustices in society as well as intensify the power of the dehumanizing trends.

Through the above-mentioned alchemy, distortion interweaves with another distortion to the point where collective decision results in collective distortion that magnifies evil to an unprecedented proportion. Soon the institution becomes so corrupt that it poisons the whole social atmosphere. It contaminates the air that people breathe and it bequeaths the same atmosphere to the generations that are yet to be born. What were once willful acts of individuals have now permeated the institutions and have acquired the status of normalcy. Once considered normal or the way things are, these acts escape close scrutiny. We have reached the apex of our analysis of human sin: collective corruption, or what I specifically refer to as evil or social sin. Systemic sin transcends the lives of individuals and ensnares the collective life.

I think it is in the notion of social sin that the early church theologians (Augustine in particular) and the Protestant Reformers' emphasis on the doctrine of "original sin" acquires intelligibility. Genetically, we do not inherit the sin of our parents, but we inherit it by virtue of being born in a society that is marred by sin; we inherit it because we live in a society whose institutions have been corrupted and have perpetuated the corruption. We do not start from a "neutral" and "sanitized" ground. Our values and choices are shaped by the unjust structures in which we happen to be born. We start with a will already in bondage as we struggle to be free. We are already inheritors of sin via society and the institutional media, and we perpetuate this sin to the next generations. Original sin, to use Farley's language, points to the "always-already-thereness" of sin.[49]

Paul Ricoeur offers some insights on how we may think of the always-already-thereness of sin in his interpretation of the Genesis account of the fall. Ricoeur refers to the serpent as a part of ourselves that we do not recognize: The serpent-seducer is the seduction of ourselves by ourselves projected into the seductive object—the serpent. But, continues Ricoeur, the serpent is also outside in a more radical fashion. It symbolizes the always-already-thereness of sin, even before we become conscious of its presence. All of us find evil already there. Like language, tools, and institutions, there is this "anteriority of evil to itself."[50]

## Sin and Evil: Beyond Good Intentions

In this account of sin and evil I am convinced of the need to put in tension the human agency that leads to acts of sin and the reality of the antecedence, or the anteriority, so we might respond adequately as human agents in our sinful situations. The always-already-thereness of sin tells us that no one is born from a "neutral" and "sanitized, sin-free ground." Yet, on the other hand, it is the human subject who creates these sinful structures. Human beings are not mere products of society and institutions; they are also subjects in the sense that their behavior alters and reformulates the social dynamics. Though not totally free from the bondage of sin, agency belongs to the human subject. Thus, accountability and responsibility for sinful acts belongs to human beings.

There is more, however, to the antecedence of sin or evil that forces us to look beyond individual agency. Having acquired a life of its own, systemic evil operates beyond the good intentions of individuals and beyond individual personal goodness. "I do not have to be greedy; the system does it for me," one of my students said. Aida Hurtado puts this point well:

> Significantly, it does not matter how good you are, as a person, if the political structures provide privilege to you individually based on the group oppression of others; in fact, individuals belonging to dominant groups can be infinitely good because they never are required to be personally bad. That is the irony of structural privilege: the more you have, the less you have to fight for it. Conversely, it does not matter how "good" you are as a subordinate; your actions are almost entirely independent of your individual character, and social judgments about you are based on your group membership.[51]

It is even the case that many of the worst crimes in history have been committed by people with good intentions. We are not bereft of good intentions. Many have been oppressed and killed because of good intentions. The early global colonizers did not lack good intentions; rather, they were full of good intentions. The new global conquerors are not lacking in good intentions either. As the familiar saying goes, "The road to hell is paved with good intentions." An African story is instructive here.

> The rainy season that year had been the strongest ever, and the river had broken its banks. There were floods everywhere, and the animals were all running up into the hills. The floods came so fast that many drowned except the lucky monkeys who used their proverbial agility to climb into the treetops. They looked down on the surface of the water where the fish were swimming and gracefully jumping out of the water as if they were the only ones enjoying the devastating flood.
>
> One of the monkeys saw the fish and shouted to his companion:
>
> "Look down, my friend, look at those poor creatures. They are going to drown. Do you see how they struggle in the water?"
>
> "Yes," said the other monkey. "What a pity! Probably they were late in escaping to the hills because they seem to have no legs. How can we save them?"

"I think we must do something. Let's go close to the edge of the flood were the water is not deep enough to cover us, and we can help them to get out."

So the monkeys did just that. They started catching the fish, but not without difficulty. One by one, they brought them out of the water and put them carefully on the dry land. After a short time there was a pile of fish lying on the grass motionless. One of the monkeys said, "Do you see? They were tired, but now they are just sleeping and resting. Had it not been for us, my friend, all these poor people without legs would have drowned."

The other monkey said, "They were trying to escape from us because they could not understand our good intentions. But when they wake up they will be grateful because we have brought them salvation."[52]

## Social Conversion or Transformation

The systemic character of evils that plague our society calls for a kind of responsibility that operates beyond individual goodness and good intentions. It calls for a more nuanced interpretation of the manifestations of sin in our society so that we may respond adequately to the crises and help ameliorate dehumanizing situations. Systemic evil demands not only individual confession and conversion but also the transformation of our collective ways of thinking, being, and acting. As the interlocking forms of oppression are systemic and structural in nature, so, too, must transformation happen at the structural-societal level.

What must happen is social conversion or social transformation. To speak of social conversion does not mean the neglect of the personal; rather social conversion embraces the personal and social and the various avenues that make us who we are and what we have become. I say this for the reason that the social is personal, as the personal is social through and through. To put it differently, the social is an outward and wider expression of the personal, as the personal is an expression of the social life. Bernard Lonergan offers a helpful comment on the matter of conversion that embraces both the personal and the social:

> Conversion is existential, intensely personal, utterly intimate. But it is not so private as to be solitary. It can happen to many, and they can form a community to sustain one another in their self-transformation and to help one another in working out the implications and fulfilling the promise of their new life. Finally, what can become communal, can become historical.[53]

In keeping with the indivisible intertwining of the personal and the social, for me it is not an issue of changing the personal first and the social follows, or changing the social structures first and personal conversion will come as a result. The first one suffers from an "idealist illusion" while the second suffers from a "materialist illusion."[54] I agree with Mark O'Keefe Brown that the two opposing extreme positions need to be rejected.[55]

Since we are indivisibly personal and social through and through, the conversion happens simultaneously. I affirm with those who say that there is no societal conversion without changed individuals, but changed individuals are not isolated monads. Even what we call personal conversion is not the same as privatistic and exclusive, but a social reality. As social individuals, if I may use the term, our experience of personal conversion cannot be isolated from the wider transforming energy that sustains us and opens our prophetic consciousness. No one can go on with the task of social transformation without having a deep experience of spiritual nourishment from within. Without this deep personal experience, even the most socially committed individual is going to experience compassion fatigue and spiritual drought. Liberation theologians all over the world are well aware of this. In short, the personal and the social mutually nourish and support each other.

From this basic understanding, I do not only reject the extreme idealist and materialist positions, I also reject the prioritizing of one over the other. I cite the 1971 statement of the Roman Catholic Bishops' Synod to substantiate my point:

> Action on behalf of justice and participation in the transformation of the world fully appear to us as a constitutive dimension of the preaching of the Gospel, or, in other words, of the Church's mission for the redemption of the human race and its liberation from every oppressive situation.[56]

Participation in the "transformation of the world" is "constitutive" of the "[c]hurch's mission for the redemption of the human race." The term "constitutive," in my view, suggests that actions for justice and social transformation are at the heart of redemption. There is no redemption that does not involve justice and social transformation. They are not peripherals to redemption, but at its very core; they are not secondary to personal conversion.

It can be argued that at some points in our own individual and temporal social journeys one must be given priority. To this I concede, for there are moments in our lives when we experience the imbalance or that our needs tilt in favor of one. Wherever we are on our faith journeys, we need to address both personal and social transformation. For those of us who are committed to social transformation, our commitment and acts of social transformation are only authentic when they are nourished by the wellspring of our deep personal transformation. Uprooted from this deep spiritual experience, we can only expect spiritual drought, compassion fatigue, and eventually bitterness and cynicism.

It is only when our faith is anchored in a deep experience of conversion that we can continue to believe, along with Julia Esquivel, in the certainty of spring. Esquivel's poem, "Certainty," speaks of this deep faith in the certainty of the spring of life amidst a "thousand years of death."

> "They can cut all the flowers
> But Spring will always return."
> Guatemala you will bloom.
> Every drop of blood,
> every tear,
> every sob extinguished by bullets,
> every cry of honor,
> every shred of skin
> torn away in hatred
> by the anti-humans—
> will bloom.
> The sweat that broke out
> of our anguish
> fleeing from the police
> and the sigh concealed
> in the most secret of our fears—
> will bloom.
> We have lived a thousand years of death
> in a homeland
> that will be altogether
> "An eternal Spring." [57]

We live amidst a "thousand years of death." The forces of death have continued to dominate our individual and collective lives. And there are no clear signs that the reign of the forces of death will end soon. It can even be argued that the death-giving forces are gaining more strength and sophistication. But even as the darkness has not lifted, we see signs of a new humanity everywhere. These signs are discernible in those human beings who have maintained an abiding faith in the certainty of the "eternal Spring."

## Notes

[1] Peter Hodgson, *Revisioning the Church: Ecclesial Freedom in the New Paradigm* (Minneapolis: Fortress Press, 1988), 17.

[2] Peter Hodgson, *Winds of the Spirit: A Constructive Christian Theology* (Louisville: Westminster John Knox Press, 1994), 222.

[3] Mary Potter Engel, "Evil, Sin, and the Violation of the Vulnerable," in *Lift Every Voice: Constructing Christian Theologies from the Underside*, ed. Susan Brooks Thistlethwaite and Mary Potter Engel (San Francisco: Harper and Row, Publishers, 1990), 152–64.

[4]Andrew Sung Park, *The Wounded Heart of God: The Asian Concept of Han and the Christian Doctrine of Sin* (Nashville: Abingdon Press, 1993); also his *Racial Conflict and Healing: An Asian-American Theological Perspective* (Maryknoll, N.Y.: Orbis Books, 1996).

[5]See Dolores Williams, *Sisters in the Wilderness: The Challenge of Womanist God-Talk* (Maryknoll, N.Y.: Orbis Books, 1993).

[6]Hodgson, *Winds of the Spirit*, 212.

[7]Marjorie Hewitt Suchocki, *The Fall to Violence: Original Sin in Relational Theology* (New York: Continuum Publishing Company, 1995), 16.

[8]Sallie McFague, *The Body of God: An Ecological Theology* (Minneapolis: Fortress Press, 1993), 99–129.

[9]Suchocki, *Fall to Violence*, 17–18.

[10]Marjorie Hewitt Suchocki, "God, Sexism, and Transformation," in *Reconstructing Christian Theology*, ed. Rebecca S. Chopp and Mark Lewis Taylor (Minneapolis: Fortress Press, 1994), 26.

[11]See Michel Foucault, in *Power/Knowledge: Selected Interviews and Other Writings, 1972–1977*, ed. Colin Gordon (New York: Pantheon Books, 1980), 92–108, 109–33.

[12]Ibid., 121.

[13]Rita Nakashima Brock, *Journeys by Heart: A Christology of Erotic Power* (New York: Crossroad, 1988).

[14]Ibid., 55.

[15]Kathy Black, *A Healing Homiletic: Preaching and Disability* (Nashville: Abingdon Press, 1996), 19–42.

[16]Eleazar S. Fernandez, *Toward a Theology of Struggle* (Maryknoll, N.Y.: Orbis Books, 1994), 40.

[17]Suchocki, *Fall to Violence*, 18.

[18]Dorothee Sölle, *Political Theology*, trans. John Shelley (Philadelphia: Fortress Press, 1974), 89; also see Park, *Wounded Heart of God*, 69–85.

[19]Ted Peters, *Sin: Radical Evil in Soul and Society* (Grand Rapids, Mich.: Wm. B. Eerdmans, 1994), 11.

[20]Thomas Ogletree, *Hospitality to the Stranger: Dimensions of Moral Understanding* (Philadelphia: Fortress Press, 1985), 98.

[21]See Valerie Saiving, "The Human Situation: A Feminine View," *The Journal of Religion* (April 1960); Judith Plaskow, *Sex, Sin, and Grace: Women's Experience and the Theologies of Reinhold Niebuhr and Paul Tillich* (Washington: University Press of America, 1980); Susan Thistlethwaite, *Sex, Race, and God: Christian Feminism in Black and White* (New York: Crossroad, 1991), 77–91.

[22]Fernandez, *Toward a Theology of Struggle*, 47, citing Erich Fromm, *Escape from Freedom* (New York: Holt, Rinehart and Winston, 1941).

[23]James Nash, *Loving Nature: Ecological Integrity and Christian Responsibility* (Nashville: Abingdon Press, 1991), 118.

[24]Ismael Garcia, *Dignidad: Ethics Through Hispanic Eyes* (Nashville: Abingdon Press, 1997), 139.

[25]James Cone, *A Black Theology of Liberation* (Maryknoll, N.Y.: Orbis Books, 1990), 108.

[26]McFague, *The Body of God*, 112–29; also her essay, "Human Beings, Embodiment, and Our Home the Earth," in *Reconstructing Christian Theology*, 141–69.

[27]Gustavo Gutiérrez, *A Theology of Liberation*, 15th Anniversary Edition (Maryknoll, N.Y.: Orbis Books, 1988), 115.

[28]Fyodor Dostoyevsky, *The Brothers Karamazov*, trans. Constance Garnett (New York: Modern Library, 1950), 64.

[29]Paul Knitter, *One Earth, Many Religions: Multifaith Dialogue and Global Responsibility* (Maryknoll, N.Y.: Orbis Books, 1995), 165.

[30]Edward Farley, *Good and Evil: Interpreting a Human Condition* (Minneapolis: Fortress Press, 1990).

[31]Ibid., 27–75.

[32]Hodgson, *Winds of the Spirit*, 199–210.

[33]Paul Tillich, *Systematic Theology*, vol. 1 (Chicago: Univ. of Chicago Press, 1951), 174–204.

[34]David Kelsey, "Human Being," in *Christian Theology: An Introduction to Its Traditions and Tasks*, revised and enlarged ed., ed. Peter C. Hodgson and Robert Williams (Philadelphia: Fortress Press, 1985), 187–88.

[35]Søren Kierkegaard, *The Concept of Dread*, trans.Walter Lowrie (Princeton, N.J.: Princeton Univ. Press, 1944), 55.

[36]Reinhold Niebuhr, *The Nature and Destiny of Man*, vol. 1 (New York: Charles Scribner's Sons, 1964), 251.

[37]Ibid., 186–203.

[38]Ibid., 228–40.

[39]Walter Rauschenbusch, *A Theology for the Social Gospel* (Louisville: Westminster John Knox Press, 1997), 48.

[40]Farley, *Good and Evil*, xxi.

[41]Paul Tillich, *Systematic Theology*, vol. 2 (Chicago: Univ. of Chicago Press, 1957), 44.

[42]Niebuhr, *Nature and Destiny of Man*, vol. 1, 242.

[43]Patrick Kerans, *Sinful Social Structures* (Paramus, N.J.: Paulist Press, 1974), 75.

[44]See Wolfhart Pannenberg, *Anthropology in Theological Perspective*, trans. Matthew J. O'Connell (Philadelphia: Westminster Press, 1985), 397–484.

[45]Kerans, *Sinful Social Structures*, 75.

[46]Peter Berger and Thomas Luckmann, *The Social Construction of Reality: A Treatise in the Sociology of Knowledge* (New York: Doubleday and Company, 1966), 62.

[47]J. Stanley Glen, *Erich Fromm: A Protestant Critique* (Philadelphia: Westminster Press, 1966), 137–155.

[48]Gregory Baum, *Religion and Alienation: A Theological Reading of Sociology* (New York: Paulist Press, 1975), 198.

[49]See Farley, *Good and Evil*.

[50]Paul Ricoeur, *The Symbolism of Evil*, trans. Emerson Buchanan (Boston: Beacon Press, 1969), 257–59.

[51]Aida Hurtado, *The Color of Privilege: Three Blasphemies on Race and Feminism* (Ann Arbor, Mich.: Univ. of Michigan Press, 1996), 34–35.

[52]Joseph Healey and Donald Sybertz, *Towards an African Narrative Theology* (Maryknoll, N.Y.: Orbis Books, 1997), 136.

[53]Bernard Lonergan, *Method in Theology* (New York: Herder and Herder, 1972), 130.

[54]Jürgen Moltmann, *The Crucified God*, trans. R. A. Wilson and John Bowden (London: SCM Press, 1974), 23.

[55]Mark O'Keefe, *What Are They Saying About Social Sin?* (New York and Mahwah, N.J.: Paulist Press, 1990), 93.

[56]"Justice in the World," #6, *Gremillion*, 514. Cited in O'Keefe, Ibid., 95.

[57]Julia Esquivel, *The Certainty of Spring: Poems by a Guatemalan in Exile*, trans. Anne Woehrle (Washington: Ecumenical Program on Central America, 1993).

# CHAPTER 4

# *Humanity in the Crucible of Classism*

## Reimagining the Human in
## Response to Classism

Classism, a form of systemic evil, has been so deeply embedded in our institutional life that it has acquired the status of the always-already-there. Yet this form of evil, as I argued earlier, is a creation of history and not eternal; thus, it is open to alteration by us as historical agents. This chapter is an expression of this conviction. There would be no reason for me to write this chapter if classism was not subject to alteration. The first part of this chapter is a critique of the evil of classism and its undergirding anthropology. The second part is devoted to my search for an alternative theological anthropology in response to the violence of classism. Even as I am focusing on classism, I am aware that it is best understood only in relation to other forms of oppression.

The heart of classism is commonly defined in political and economic terms, but it also takes on other dimensions such as social status, attitude, and lifestyle. Classism is a societal institution that creates and perpetuates economic exploitation, political domination, social stratification, and differential treatment. It has to do with unearned privileges of certain groups, alienation of laborers from the fruits of their labor, unequal access to resources and accumulation of the wealth by the few, marginalization, elitist lifestyle, powerlessness, colonization, cynicism and fatalism, and other class injuries. Classism, as José Comblin rightly pointed out, is a "civilization of privilege."[1]

As I noted earlier, citing Susan Brooks Thistlethwaite and Peter Hodgson, classism is a system of prejudice that belongs in a category by itself. While ethnic, gender, and sexual differences are good in themselves because of the diversities that they represent, class is not. Thistlethwaite and Hodgson argue that "class carries with it *necessarily* its ideological legitimation in the form of classism—the belief that social stratification or class division is justified on the basis of inherent human inequality, or the will of God, or accommodation to the fallen condition, or productive efficiency, or some other reason."[2]

## Society's Denial and Evasion of Classism

Classism is with us, yet people have a way of evading or denying it. One way of evading classism is to view it as a form of "social differentiation," comparable to social roles and division of labor, but with no suggestion of hierarchical ordering and "social inequality."[3] Since there is no society without social differentiation, classism, under the facade of social differentiation, is taken as natural.

The stories of those who have "made it" in any society have also been used to deny the existence of classism. If there are those who have "made it," then why do others fail? There is nothing wrong with the system, it is argued, because others have "made it." Instead, the fault lies with the individual person. The overused line, "You've come a long way, baby," serves a similar purpose. This line, explains Paula S. Rothenberg, often

> accompanied by photographs of models representing women who clearly travel the "fast lane," creates an impression that some find hard to shake. Magazine covers displaying female and Black and Asian male astronauts, female jockeys, and Black business executives would have us believe that women and people of color have been fully integrated into society.[4]

In the United States, where the myth of classlessness has been propagated, there is a general avoidance of class-laden vocabulary that exposes class boundaries. It seems that class is not a domain of public discourse, and any talk about issues that deal with class is un-American. There are, nevertheless, a few exceptions: people talk about the "middle class" and the "affluent." But they are acceptable only because they hide or mute class differences. "References to the middle class by politicians for example," argues Gregory Mantsios, "are designed to encompass and attract the broadest possible constituency. Not only do references to the middle class gloss over differences, but also these references avoid any suggestion of conflict or exploitation."[5]

Barbara Ehrenreich pursues a similar point taken by Mantsios with regard to the general avoidance of class-laden vocabularies.[6] Ehrenreich critiques the term "affluent." She claims:

If the problem had been described as wealth, one would have to specify *whose* wealth. Wealth is property, it belongs to someone. Affluence was seen as a general condition, attached to no particular persons or groups. It hung over the entire landscape like a bright, numbing haze, a kind of smog with no known source or cure. Since it had no proprietors and perpetrators, affluence could be attacked without seeming to question the priorities of a business-dominated economy. It was a politically innocuous target–and a comfortably snobbish one.[7]

Another way of evading classism and its causal connection to the poverty of the many is the relegation of poverty to humankind's infancy stage. This is what Ehrenreich calls "infantilizing the poor."[8] The infant-poor do not constitute a class, though they constitute a distinct infantile culture–the "culture of poverty." This culture of poverty is a psychopathology characterized by two related traits: (1) "present-time orientation" and (2) "insufficiently developed 'deferred gratification pattern.'"[9] Such an ideology identifies the poor as half children and half psychopaths who are not able to think ahead and who do not have the self-discipline to control their impulses of the moment for long-term gain. Thus, there is nothing wrong with the classist system; we are simply dealing with a contingent of people who have remained infants.

Karen Bloomquist suggests four other ways in which people, especially those marginalized by the socioeconomic system, tend to justify their situation or compensate for it: (1) blaming poverty on the situation in which one does not have full control; (2) lowering personal aspirations so that they are in line with one's actual achievements; (3) inflating or counterfeiting one's achievements for the purpose of convincing oneself and others that one has not really fallen short; (4) contrasting one's relative "success" with those who have visibly failed so as to feel superior to them.[10]

Common to these forms of evasion or justification is the failure to see the systemic character of classism. Whether the justifications come from the dominant class or from the poor, both sets of justifications avoid and deny classism. Those in the lower socio-political class often do not see that their very own situation is a product of classism because they continue to aspire to climb to the top of the social scale.

## The Ideology, Dynamics, and Theology of Classism

Classism operates on certain dynamics supported by some forms of ideology and theology. It is undergirded by a religious worldview, a space-devouring and material-possessing anthropology, notions of sin that are based on class morality and values, and by an ideology that blames the victims. The effects of classism are devastating: It alienates human beings from the products of their labors, from the act of production, from fellow human beings, from the self, and from the world of nature. (More on the alienation from nature will appear in chapter 7.)

### Classism and the Total Market: The Market's Religious Metaphysics

The linkage between the poverty of the many and the wealth of the few suggests that an analysis of classism has to be done within the wider context that makes this causal connection possible. Of course classism is not a new phenomenon, but in the modern world I name this context as the capitalist total market. The modern capitalist market is the wider context that generates and nourishes a classist worldview, lifestyle, and organization of power differentials; it provides the overall context in which individuals are given values in relation to things. Classism, in its modern complex expression, cannot be adequately understood apart from the capitalist total market.

Capitalism, it is argued, comes from the Latin term *caput* (head), which means that "the cause of the wealth of nations is inventive intellect, the creativity of human intelligence seeking to decipher the wealth hidden in creation by the Creator himself."[11] A defense of the capitalist free market, Michael Novak contends, is "first, a defense of efficiency, productivity, inventiveness and prosperity." Moreover, he continues, "it is also a defense of the free-conscience—free not only in the realm of the spirit, and not only in politics, but also in the economic decisions of everyday life."[12]

The market is the medium through which exchange relations happen in a capitalist system, in which some gain and others lose; some win and others are defeated; some are rewarded and others are punished. Immanuel Wallerstein identifies the market as the "principal arena of economic struggle."[13] It is also here that the product of human labor becomes alienated from the laborers and becomes a capital that stands against its producer. In turn labor becomes a commodity subservient to the alienated labor (capital), just like any other commodity.

At the surface level it seems that the total market is devoid of any religiosity. On the contrary, it has religious and theological undergirding, though shallow. M. Douglas Meeks argues that "even though modern people tend to think of and live before God in ways shaped by the demands and accumulation of wealth ostensibly through the market logic and rules, the economy nevertheless continues to require certain narrow views of God for its justification."[14] Without this religious backing, the coercion of the market would be blatant. Even at the level of semantics, as Meeks points out, there are obvious correlations: Both fields regularly employ such words as trust, fidelity, bond, confidence, fiduciary, debt, redemption, saving, security, and futures.[15]

The total market operates, according to Franz Hinkelammert, on an "entrepreneurial metaphysics," a "metaphysics of commodities, money, marketing, and capital."[16] Entrepreneurial metaphysics promotes certain values and morality. For its devotees, this metaphysics has the aura of religion. Devotees of this metaphysics speak of "commodities, money, marketing, and capital as the great object of their devotion; a pseudo-divine world towers over human beings, and dictates their laws to them."[17] Values and rules of the market appear as paths of virtue. The primary virtues are obedience and humility. One must bow down to the laws of the market. If there are virtues, there are also sins against the market; sins that need repentance, amends, and compensation.

The "invisible hand" of the market takes the function of a god. Under the guidance of this "invisible hand," the welfare of the whole society is promoted even as each one seeks his or her own self-interest. "By pursuing his own interest," Adam Smith argues, "he frequently promotes that of society more effectually than when he really intends to promote it."[18] The appeal to the "invisible hand," however, hides the fact that economy is not independent from politics (power); it mystifies the question of politics and the market.[19]

Since the objects of devotion in the total market are human creations and, more specifically, alienated and reified products of human labor, they are metamorphosed into idols. What could be more alienating than a product of alienation becoming a god—an object of devotion, a fetish? Misunderstanding the story of the alienation of the fruits of one's labor and attributing independent life and qualities to the objects/products of human labor leads to "fetishism of commodities." It is "the subjugation of the human being and human life to a product of human labor, with the consequent destruction of the human being per se through the relationship that is established with an idol."[20]

### God, Social Order, and Classism

Classism (evil), social order, and certain conceptions of God go together, to reiterate a point I mentioned in the previous chapter. The ideology of classism supports a particular notion of God as a legitimator of the social order. If the invisible hand has made the exchange of goods and services possible in the market, the social class formation, which is an outcome of market exchange, is consequently an act of the invisible hand. There is nothing morally wrong with the class system: It is natural; it is part of the divine scheme of things; it is a divine institution. To go against classism is to go against the divine market architect—God.

The marginalized have also bought into this way of thinking and have become avid defenders of the classist system. Not only do they believe it is a divine institution, they also dream of climbing up the class ladder. The dream of the poor can only be to move away from their negative economic condition, and the way to do that, they believe, is to climb up the class ladder. To think as if there is no up, from their point of view, is to be enslaved to their present plight. So the class ladder functions as a divine promise for them, without an awareness that their present position on the social ladder is the making of the class system itself.

The poor most often do not see their situation as a product of classism. Instead, they are likely, as Karen Bloomquist expresses,

> to cling to a hierarchical, authoritarian, fixed social order, which ironically has been the source of their victimization. They do so because of the precariousness of life in an age when the dream is being betrayed all around them. They cling to a privatized religion removed from their worldly struggles because in their private realm they can be themselves, the real self or "soul" can live and the wounds be forgotten. They adopt the upwardly mobile values and religious orientation of those above them because of their tenacious belief that in the end the dream will "save" them. In other words, their religious expressions have been colonized or become captive to the dynamics of domination from which they seek salvation.[21]

## Classism and Related Forms of Alienation

Classism breeds radical alienation; it produces class injuries of various sorts. The three forms of alienation identified by Karl Marx—alienation of the workers from the fruits of their labors, alienation from the act of production itself, and alienation from fellow human beings—continue to shed light on our present experience of alienation, but there are other dimensions that need to be explored.[22]

### Alienation from the Fruits of One's Labor

It is perceptive of Marx to note that "the more value [the worker] creates the more worthless he becomes; the more refined his product the more crude and misshapen the worker; the more civilized the product the more barbarous the worker."[23] Several years separated Marx and Michael Moore, author of *Downsize This!*, but Moore, in his satirical style, pursues Marx's point to its odious consequences. In the American Dream, says Moore, "If you work hard, and your company prospers, you, too, shall prosper." But not anymore. "If you work hard, and the company prospers— you lose your job!" This is a reversal of the American Dream. Many of the top companies that downsized their employees registered high profit earnings and hefty increases of their CEOs' salaries, who earned as much as 212 times the salary of their average workers.[24]

The new economic liberation and globalization thrust has brought untold new wealth to some. Instead of millionaires, we now brag of mega-billionaires. But it has also created and promoted asymmetries both globally and locally as well as pessimism and fatalism for those who are pushed to the sidelines. While most of those who fall by the wayside are still concentrated in the so-called developing countries, citizens of the affluent North have not been spared.

Economic hardships, job prospects in other places, media enticement of a comfortable life, and political conflicts all conspire to push people from the Third World to seek employment outside of their localities or to immigrate to affluent countries when possible. The numbers of internal and international refugees are swelling. In 1995, twenty-six million people were displaced in their own countries, while twenty-three million refugees had fled across borders.[25] Economies of many developing countries have stayed afloat because of remittances from overseas contract workers and domestic helpers to their home countries, and from immigrants to their original homelands.

When the products of human labor are alienated from the laborer, these products acquire a life that now enslaves the creator–the laborer. Labor creates value, but in the process, labor (as alienated labor), which is the creator of value, becomes a commodity serving the product of its alienated activity–capital. The product of alienation further alienates the laborer because it is already in the hands of people whose interests are diametrically opposed to those of the producers. Capital, which is nothing other than a surplus-value of one's labor, has now become a value that kills the value-creating power. Dead matter, a product of human labor, dominates living people. This situation is the story of the "metamorphosis of value." As Bertell Ollman writes, "The metamorphosis of value is a tale about man, his productive activity and products, and what happens to them all in capitalist society."[26]

In the metamorphosis of value or in its merry-go-round journey, the products of labor are ossified into independent forms and they now appear in the form of capital, commodity, landed property, profit, interest, rent, wages, and money. Then they are given independent life and the creator of value is subordinated. What could be more degrading than the creator of capital (labor) turning out to be at the mercy of capital. Instead, with the inverted situation, capital becomes the creator and labor is subservient to capital, though palliative remarks are often made in praise of labor. The product of labor now assumes a separate existence, assuming a power independent of and even against the producer.[27]

Money, as a crystallization of exchange value in an easily exchangeable form, is the mediator between a person and what he or she wants. Everyone in the market system relates to the other in the form of money. Like the biblical passage in which one cannot go to the Father without passing through the incarnate Son, so, too, one cannot have access to what one desires without money. Cast in this role, people risk their lives and bear loneliness and separation from loved ones in search of it. People from the Third World flock to where they can get more money while leaving their immediate families behind.

Alienated human beings ultimately appropriate the properties of money. Marx's critique is very powerful:

> The properties of money are my own (the possessor's) properties and faculties. What I *am* and *can do is,* therefore, not at all determined by my individuality. I *am* ugly, but I can buy the *most beautiful* woman for myself. Consequently, I am not *ugly,* for the effect of *ugliness,* its power to repel, is annulled by money...Money is the highest good, and so its possessor is good...I am *stupid,* but since money is the *real mind* of all things, how should its possessor be stupid?[28]

### Alienation from the Acts of Production

The Industrial Revolution has been a mixed blessing. It revolutionized production, but alienated the workers from the acts of production in the process. Common workers have become cogs in the industrial machine, performing jobs that do not require much creativity or freedom. They are expected to produce more and work like machines. Industrial capitalism has trapped them into stations on a conveyor belt and turned them into simple appendages of the machine.

In the era in which labor is a commodity being sold and bought, many workers do not identify with their work as a life's project. There is a separation between a life's project and the job. The job is simply to survive or to earn enough to do something else. This is especially the case with those workers who have less control of their jobs. For most of these workers, there is a clear demarcation between working days and nonworking days. A strong aversion to any mention of work or its association may be present. Where there is less congruence between the job and daily life, the day off is always a welcome respite. Most workers who lack control of their labor look forward to early retirement.

Deep is the alienation when the worker finds it impossible to be at home in his or her place of work. Work, for the worker, is not in any sense a fulfillment of her or his being; the laborer works because she or he wants to survive. As the alienation of labor proceeds, the laborer loses his or her personhood altogether and he or she becomes like the things he or she makes, a commodity.

### Alienation from Fellow Human Beings

Classism sets human beings against one another. The interest of one group stands in diametrical opposition to that of another. When this exists, communal life is broken. Individual lives reflect this breakdown of communal bonding. Healthy subjectivity, which only happens in relationships among equals, remains frustrated in a society that continues to devalue the worth of another.

The various social units of society bear the alienation of classism. Classism exacerbates ethnic antagonism, especially as various ethnic communities compete for jobs and other benefits. Ethnic antagonism works to the benefit of capitalism and classism, for the antagonism of ethnic groups makes them vulnerable to the control of the market forces and power wielders.

What happens at the domestic level finds expression at the global level and vice versa. When millions of people move from one country to another to look for jobs as migrants or as immigrants, these hordes of newcomers threaten the inhabitants of that country and heighten anti-immigrant sentiments. The effects of immigration, guest workers, and waves of refugees on hitherto relatively homogeneous societies can induce reactionary forms of nationalism that threaten democratic values.[29] In the U.S. and European countries, refugees and immigrants have become targets of attacks.

Familial relations are not exempt. Parents, brothers, and sisters turn against each other in the pursuit of wealth and class status. Even the good intentions of poor parents, like the sacrifices they make to help children elevate their social status, can turn into alienation. What happens when the children let the parents down? What happens to the relationship between brothers and sisters when parents sell their only parcel of land to pay for the college tuition fee of the eldest son or daughter (usually the son, which is the case in many Asian countries) with the hope that the eldest son or daughter will help the rest of the siblings, but that son or daughter ends up getting married before finishing college? Those who have sacrificed feel betrayed. And, "if children do achieve upward mobility, they seem to pull rank," notes Bloomquist. Then "they acquire different values and life styles, move away psychologically if not geographically, and often develop a disdain for their parents' reality. As a result, parents feel betrayed in an even deeper sense."[30] What Bloomquist is saying is not only true in the United States but in other countries as well.

Relationships between spouses or lovers suffer the brunt of a classist society. "When labor is geared to exchange value and the universal need for money," says Dorothee Sölle, "our human relationships are not immune to laws of exchange production." Intimate relations, Sölle continues, are not immune from the incursion of the rules of exchange:

> It is an illusion to think that people who work from nine to five for exchange value, treating their own work and their relationships to co-workers and products according to the rules of commodity exchange, can then return home and relate to others and to themselves as unalienated human beings capable of fulfilling their suppressed needs.[31]

Prostitution and the mail-order bride business, especially between Third World and First World countries, are glaring examples of relationships defined by the rules of market exchange. Men from more affluent countries flock to the Third World not only for sexual pleasure, but also to find brides. Many Third World women have found their way to Japan, North America, and Europe through the mail-order bride business. The brides are usually much younger than their husbands. By means of the mail-order bride business, poor women of the Third World, often with the help of their parents, have acquired what may be their only means to elevate their own economic status and that of the rest of the family.

But one may also ask why more men from affluent countries are seeking brides from poorer countries? For the price of one, the relatively affluent male gets a wife and a *maid.* Even in such intimate matters as finding a wife, the market idea of "buy one get one free" is operative. There is also the common perception among European American men that Asian women and many other Third World women are more passive than white women. Thus, the men can exercise more control. Hence, we can only say, as many of the mail-order brides have expressed, that the reasons have little to do with love but are shaped by the dynamics of socio-political economy.[32]

## Classism and Elitism

Classism breeds elitism. Those who occupy the top of the social scale—people with wealth and prestige, high educational level, money, political and military power—form the elite group of any country. Not only do they control the economic and political direction of the country, they also create an elitist or highbrow culture that disdains the so-called lowbrow culture of the common people. This is seen not only in the social clubs in which they circulate, but also in the kinds of social entertainment they choose. Those who have so-called refined musical and artistic tastes attend expensive opera performances, while the lower class remains confined to inexpensive neighborhood theaters.

Elitism in the Third World arises from a distinctive configuration of factors. While it has roots in the earlier pre-colonial times, its present expression includes a mixture of several factors: colonial bureaucracy, economic disparity, urban-rural disparity, and civilian and military rule.[33] Elites of the Third World tend to ally themselves with the elites of wealthy nations, which furthers the core-periphery relation not only domestically but globally.

The lower class people are not mere bystanders in the perpetuation of elitism. They help legitimize it and dream of becoming elites someday, even if their dreams have often become nightmares. They grab whatever opportunities come in order to experience a taste of elitism. By becoming adjuncts of the elite group or an authoritarian power, they get a taste of the elite's privilege. With connections to the elite power holder, they readily make use of whatever power they derive from the connections for their personal gain. When they elevate their social status, they also tend to develop contempt for their former class status. This is what we call in a Filipino language: "mata pobre," one who looks (*mata*) down on the poor (*pobre*). In my native culture a common saying is appropriate: "A fly who happens to rest on the back of a carabao (water buffalo), thinks and acts like a carabao."

The church is no exception with regard to the ugly presence of classism and elitism. If Martin Luther King, Jr., could speak of Sunday as the most racially segregated day of the week, Sunday is also the most segregated day of the week because of classism and elitism. Where and with whom people sit during worship services indicates the presence of classism. No amount of sermonizing would encourage the lower class members to assume leadership because of the prevailing classism and elitism in the churches. Liberal churches of the mainline denominations are no better than the evangelicals when it comes to classism and elitism.

## Classism, Consumerism, and Identity

Don Oldenburg's article in the *Washington Post* conveys the idea of a day-to-day life in the U.S. in which holidays have become shopping days. If one is to observe every major holiday, one cannot miss the shopping days as well. The major holiday that leads us to the spirit of U.S. consumerism is the day after Thanksgiving. "Many Americans," says Oldenburg, "think of today [Friday] as an unofficial day off. Now there's a campaign afoot to establish the Friday after Thanksgiving as an annual holiday."[34] Friday is the beginning of the "countdown" of the holiday shopping binge until Christmas. The panic on the faces of people is what literally greets a person if he or she goes to the mall during this season. Former United States President Dwight Eisenhower, faced with the market backwash that threatened U.S. industries, expressed it in crystal clear terms: "It is the duty of every American to consume."[35]

This is also the case in many Third World countries. While one often hears the lament that people are in economic crisis, malls are always crowded and many more are being constructed. Of course, there are other reasons why malls in the Third World are crowded: They serve as air-conditioned hang-outs. A similar phenomenon is happening in the U.S. as teenagers dubbed "mall rats" use malls as hang-outs.[36] From the First World to the Third World, from the North to the South, globalization is creating a "global culture" typified, writes Robert Schreiter, "by American cola drinks, athletic and casual clothing, and American movie and television entertainment."[37] In short, it is the culture of consumption.

Classism breeds consumerism of various sorts. If status, identity, and self-esteem are derived by what and how much one consumes, then consumerism is part and parcel of a class society. Possession and consumption define one's subjectivity and identity. The "endless acts of consumption provoked by the *danse macabre* of capitalism," says Peter McLaren, "organizes subjectivity in specific ways around the general maxim: I purchase, therefore I am."[38] In his trenchant critique, McLaren speaks of the hybrid and splayed identity of the postmodern self as being patterned after the cathedral of capitalism and the shopping mall. The "shopping mall self (the self as the rhetorical effect of image value)," as McLaren calls it, "has become the quintessential model of panic identity in the contemporary United States."[39]

Possession and consumption define who one is or how one is perceived and given value by others. What is possessed and consumed is not simply the use value of something but the exchange value. That which is consumed is not simply the thing that is purchased but, more specifically, the image value. Commodities are more than material objects; they are also social signifiers. Image enhancement, not use value, defines what is of value. The exchange happens not between use values but between image values. Image value supersedes use value and exchange value is the object of fixation. Everyone is driven to consume and acquire the goods that elevate one's status in society. Designer footwear and workclothes have become the homeboys' and homegirls' obsessions of the hip-hop nation. Even poor people in the Third World know the expensive brand names of shoes, watches, and clothing. They would try to get them at the expense of their meals just to get the status derived from buying an expensive brand name. Outward trappings provide the sense of identity that is desperately needed in a class-based society.

When the consumer attains a certain level of taste, sophistication, and, of course, financial means, he or she seeks compatible commodities of high social signification, pushing him or her deeper into the consumer trap. But, just as consumers seek compatible commodities, or, just as commodities seek compatibilities, consumers seek subject compatibility or compatible social relations. This means that people who own similar commodities (social signifiers) are more likely to limit their interaction to other people who own similar commodities. Thus, commodities (social signifiers) dictate the horizons of relations and interaction.[40]

Consumerism not only involves the consumption of an image value that an individual desperately needs to elevate his or her status, it is also an expression of a deep psychological alienation. Greater conspicuous consumption provides greater psychological compensation for the rote meaninglessness of the job. The solution to boredom in a consumeristic society, especially when the communal bond is weak, is to consume. This statement sounds simplistic, but it says a lot, and it is true to the experience of common people. If one is bored, one may engage in the act of consumption by watching (consuming) a movie and munching (consuming) something while watching. Or, one of the major ways in which people address boredom is to "shop around" (consume).

The more one buys and consumes, the deeper one falls into bondage to the job in order to pay the bills. Eventually, a second job is needed. But the second job leaves less time for the family, with whom to enjoy life. Just as one has something to pay for the monthly mortgage for the cabin by the lake and a boat to enjoy on weekends, one has to work during weekends to pay for the bills. It is an irony that many people live everyday.

Consumeristic globalization has created an idol—an idol that sucks the blood of people around the world, though unevenly and differently. True to its name, consumerism consumes and globalization gobbles the consumers and the gobblers. John B. Cobb, Jr., offers a critique of the religious metaphysics of this global market. Economism is the name of this religion and its god is endless economic growth. The priests are the economists; evangelists are the advertisers; and the laity are the consumers. The shopping mall is the cathedral; virtue is competitive spirit; and sin is inefficiency. "Shop 'til you drop" is the only way to salvation.[41]

### Classism, Self-Sacrifice, Obedience, and Conformity

The unquestioned aim of climbing the ladder of social stratification creates and nourishes a culture of self-sacrifice, obedience, and conformity. When I was growing up, I heard my parents' admonition to sacrifice, not to complain or rock the boat, and to conform to social expectations. Critical thinking was never encouraged. It was considered a hindrance to success. If one was to be successful, conformity to the set of expectations was the recipe.

What was true of my growing-up years in the Philippine context resonates with Bloomquist's observation about the way working class parents in the U.S. train their children. Because of the parents' desire that their children move upward, they are taught to conform and avoid critical questioning. Self-direction is not encouraged. This is based on the assumption of parents that conformity to external authority is a necessary requirement for their children to move upward. In this context, "sin becomes operationally equivalent to class values." The sinner asks the question: "How have I failed to measure up to the codes, ideology, and god of the American dream?"[42] or to the dream of climbing the social ladder.

The training at home gets played out in the wider society (or vice versa). With the "Oriental despot" often circulated as an example of authoritarian leadership, I thought for a time that the U.S. corporate structure was an expression of democratic management. Far from the truth, hierarchy, conformity, and playing by the rules are the trademarks of corporate life. The one who hires has the sole power to fire. The corporate elites have no problem playing by the rules they created, since they are the beneficiaries. Yet, as Thomas Naylor and company point out,

> [T]here is a price to be paid for this access to the benefit stream of large corporations: corporate loyalty and unremitting conformity. A good corporate citizen is one who is always agreeable and abides

by the rules. Dissent is not perceived as a virtue in the corporate world.[43]

## Classism, Inferiority, Contempt, Resentment, and Fear of Falling

Classism causes injuries of various sorts, which Richard Sennett and Jonathan Cobb call "hidden injuries."[44] They are not exactly hidden, but they are less visible than the economic dimension commonly associated with classism. These injuries are experienced differently depending on one's position on the social ladder.

The sense of inferiority is an injury that lower class people experience in a classist society. It is devastating and traumatic for a person, especially at a growing age, to experience discrimination because of her or his class position in the community. In an overtly classist society, the social demarcation is so sharp that those in the lower class can only see themselves as lowly as the earthworms. The feeling of inferiority can be so deep that it continues to haunt the person even after he or she has climbed the economic ladder.

Inferiority may be coupled with self-contempt when, in striving to move up the social ladder, one fails again and again. Self-contempt or self-accusation may include blaming oneself for the failure by being weak, stupid, lazy, or in lacking good character. Sennett and Cobb have noted this self-accusation in the words of a garbage man: "Look, I know it's nobody's fault but mine that I got stuck here where I am, I mean…if I wasn't such a dumb shit." And, the "lower" one defines oneself in society, "the more it seems his fault."[45] Even for a person who says he or she was deprived of opportunities during his or her growing years, class is still considered a personal responsibility.

Complicating this feeling of inferiority, self-contempt, and the desire to be like those at the top of the social ladder is the dimension of resentment. Sennett and Cobb document a few expressions of this resentment among working class people in the U.S. toward the middle and upper class. Working class people have the idea that those who are in the managerial positions are just banking on their academic credentials and constructed privilege, which do not really mean much in terms of the hard stuff of day-to-day production. There is anger in many working class people at those who can "order you around," but this gets complicated when those who "order you around" are also perceived to "have the right to tell you what to do."[46]

If the lower-class people deal with other injuries, the middle- and the upper-class people fear the prospect of falling. The fall can be devastating to those who have lived above their secure means, which is getting more common as loans and credit cards become easily available. It means the loss of their house, cabin, boat, and other expensive properties. Not only that, it means the diminishment of one's self-worth, which is measured by one's class position. The rising tide of bankruptcies filed in recent years is an indication that many have fallen from the economic ladder.

Upper-class women who have acquired their class status through marriage to wealthy men are more vulnerable in the event of divorce. But, even if a woman remains the wife of a wealthy CEO, her upper class position is not only derivative, but is always subordinate to that of her husband. Often, the division of labor among upper class husbands and wives is even more rigid than in other social classes, with the husband in full control of the financial resources and carefully monitoring all the money doled out to the wife.[47]

While falling is always associated with falling down, Ehrenreich highlights a different dimension of falling that is experienced by the middle class in the U.S. Except for the most securely wealthy, the middle class is also afraid of the downward slide, but there is another dimension: It is "a fear of inner weakness, of growing soft, of failing to strive, of losing discipline and will…Whether the middle class looks down toward the realm of less, or up toward the realm of more, there is fear, always, of falling."[48]

### Classism, Powerlessness, and Fatalism

Classism breeds powerlessness and fatalism among those whose dreams have always been betrayed. In my years of work in the parish and in community organizing, it was disheartening to observe the painfully slow growth of people's empowerment. People on the lower rung of society would rather have the wealthy and educated make decisions for them. They often express their willingness to volunteer their labor and time, but relegate the planning and decisions to the so-called educated and the wealthy. The powerlessness of many has reached the level of fatalism.

Fatalism is the death of hope and the subversion of the future. Fatalism or resignation, a disease common among those who have been subjugated for so long, is a form of not facing the future—the open future. The future, by its being a future, is open for transformative action. However, people in submerged conditions do not see this future as a possibility for something new and better. Domesticated, they feel the way many Israelites did in the biblical account: They would rather remain in Egyptian captivity than journey into the wilderness where new possibilities and risks await. Refusal to face the open future is for them a form of refuge, because everything that is associated with the open future—freedom, decision, and responsibility—is already relegated to somebody else, to those who dominate them.

I think this helps to explain why, in spite of the years that the Filipino people were plundered under the Marcos' dictatorial regime, many have remained loyal even long after the collapse of his reign. This helps to explain why the poor people in the rural churches where I worked would be content to have others think and decide for them, that is, the pastor and the more educated and monied church council members. I can recall one occasion when I heard someone say, "Whatever is agreed upon, I will follow," to which I retorted quickly, "What if we will agree to sell your carabao or water buffalo?" (There was laughter). By fleeing from the open future that calls them to be active freedom-seeking agents, they escape from freedom and fall into the hands of an authoritarian power.

If the major sin of the "successfuls" is pride in their ability to forge their destiny, this is not so with the underdogs. After so many years of working overly hard or buying lottery tickets without success or good luck, they have grown fatalistic. Their religious upbringing compounds this fatalism. As an old hymn goes:

> The rich man in his castle,
> The poor man at his gate,
> God made them high or lowly,
> And ordered their estate.[49]

This sense of powerlessness, fatalism, and cynicism may find other expressions, like "bad-ass" behavior and violence. The term "bad-ass" combines two words, "bad" and "ass." The "bad" indicates deviance from wider social values, and "ass" connotes a combination of toughness and meanness."[50] In East Los Angeles, "bad-ass" is shown in the way one walks, often called the "barrio stroll." It is characterized, says Peters, by "a slow, rhythmic walk with flamboyant arm movement, chesty posture, and head up toward the heavens." Even as the "bad-ass" posture shows pride, it is more of an expression of powerlessness; it is a form of compensating for one's powerlessness in a society that has pushed the powerless to the margin.

## The Human Face Reimagined

A fundamental distortion is happening at the very core of our conception of who we are, which can be observed in the way we relate to ourselves, one another, the material goods at hand, and the ecosystem. This fundamental distortion has found expression in the systemic evil of classism.

### Dismantling Class Privilege: A Theological Task

A commentary about the 2000 presidential election in the United States hits the target about class privilege. Using the metaphor of a baseball game, the writer says George W. Bush believed he just made a home run. But the reality is that Bush was born on the third base. He did not start in the batter's box. This perspective is central to the nature of class privilege. Those who are in the privileged position often think that they deserve all that they have and expect more privileges as if they were rights.

Classism is supported by an anthropology that rests on the basis of class privilege, which is the outcome of a long process of various forms of alienated relationship. The human being in a classist society stands on the backs of others. From an explicitly theological viewpoint, the subject in a class society is constructed on the basis of human sin. The classist self is constructed out of the debris of human sin and profound alienation.

Seeing our social reality from the experience of the poor helps us to discern that the presence of the marginalized is a nagging reminder that there is something deeply wrong with the system. When we see reality from the experience of the poor, we are prevented from equating the present reality with the final *telos* of history, and we are prevented from making an idol of the successes of the modern society. The cry of the poor obliges the whole of society to search, to innovate, to create something new, to break down barriers; it is an ongoing ferment of destabilization and invention.

Overcoming the reigning classist anthropology is not going to be easy, both at the theoretical and practical level. Since the classist anthropology has its theological undergirding, the task of theological deconstruction is a necessity. We must deconstruct the notion that class stratification is a divine arrangement. It is not a divine arrangement, nor ordained by God, and it does not serve the purposes of God under the condition of human alienation. Instead, class stratification is a violation of God's intention for the whole of creation. It is not an instance of right relationship because it violates greater well-being. It is a human construct backed by theological ideas in order to perpetuate a system of privilege to a few and the marginalization of many. It is founded on the false assumption of human worth, which elevates one class over the other. It alienates both the elite and those who are relegated to the lower rung of the social order, though the brunt of its disastrous effects falls primarily on the marginalized.

Our Hebraic-Christian prophetic tradition is clear in its denunciation of systems of stratification and marginalization. Likewise, it is replete with images and metaphors of an alternative social arrangement, such as the *basileia* vision, the communal vision that springs from the Holy Communion, the radical ministry of Jesus of Nazareth, and the egalitarian practices of the early Christian communities. These visions of an alternative social arrangement must find expression in social movements of our times if something tangible is to happen.

### Restoring the Fruits of Labor: Meeting the Needs of the Poor

Classism is constructed on the transfer of the fruits of the labor of the many into the hands of the few elites. Once in the hands of the few, these alienated fruits of labor become instruments of deeper alienation of the laborers. While it is true that class injuries are experienced by both the elites and the lower class, the brunt of human suffering is experienced by the lower class. Hence, the restoration of the fruits of the laborers is, for me, a barometer of restored right relationship. Securing the basic survival needs of the underclass takes precedence over the class injuries of the upper class.

Liberation from want is a fundamental necessity in the restoration of one's humanity. No one can be fully human in a situation in which one's basic needs are not met. Liberation from want is a basic human right. This is the right to survival, more elementary than what many people in the northern hemisphere define as "privileges," which are available for those who can afford to pay for them. It is a right that is often neglected in common discourse about human rights violations because it is identified as a right belonging to a certain class of people. But, as Robert McAfee Brown argues, "as long as children are growing up in a society where their parents cannot get jobs, so that children grow up undernourished, as long as people cannot get decent housing or education and health care for their children, human rights are being violated."[51]

Basic needs for human existence have always been violated in a classist society. They remain violated in a classist society because the economic priority is getting more profits for the upper class rather than the well-being of the whole community. It is appalling that as the salaries of top executives are rising, the living wage of common workers has remained at the bottom. These living wages do not qualify as "livable" wages. Rather, they are "death" wages, wages that do not sustain life.

Restoration of the alienated fruits of one's labor is a fundamental necessity. The restoration of the fruits of one's labor does not only satisfy basic biological needs, it also enhances the societal and psychological well-being of a person. As long as workers are alienated from the fruits of their labor, their humanity is being violated. Restoration of the fruits of one's labor is an urgent task that must be pursued with determination, for those who are presently reaping the fruits will not willingly surrender their privilege.

## Empowering the Underprivileged

Along with the goal of restoring the fruits of the laborers is the goal of empowering the underprivileged. The structural character of classism means that meeting the needs of the poor is not a simple matter of giving them something to eat or offering them jobs. Countering classism demands the empowerment of those who have been relegated to the lower rung of the social ladder. Empowerment requires that they decolonize themselves from the classist worldview, organize and mobilize themselves, demand active participation in the decision-making process, and exercise greater control over the fruits of their labor.

A people empowered is a people who has realized that its situation is not eternal, nor is it the will of God; instead, it is alterable. Empowered people are those who have overcome fatalism and cynicism and are being sustained by the power of hope. Recognizing that their plight is alterable and the future is open, they have resolved to transform their given situation. Rather than submit to the forces of death and closure, they have become active moral agents.

The work of people's empowerment is a calling of the people of God. It is an expression of the Spirit at work. The Spirit working in us empowers us to work for the empowerment of others even in the midst of various threats. I would extend the apostle Paul's enumeration of the fruits of the Spirit to include empowerment. Spirit as life-giving power works for people's empowerment and bears fruit in empowered people.

## Reshaping Our Socioeconomic Life

The emergence of a new human being liberated from the thrall of classism cannot happen in a piecemeal fashion. It requires a major rethinking of anthropology in relation to our socioeconomic system. I cannot imagine a new anthropology within the current socioeconomic system. Thus, I am suggesting that we re-conceive theological anthropology along with our socioeconomic system.

### *Reorienting Ourselves: Growth or Well-being*

Rethinking who we are (being) is a precondition for putting in perspective the purposes of production and possession. This is not an easy task, for who we think we are is always shaped by production and possession. More often than we think, production and possession strongly shape our self- and collective understanding. Production and possession not only respond to our desires, they also create desires that make us believe they are part of the very nature of who we are. What would liberate us, I believe, from the clutches of production and possession is not their complete renunciation—after all, we cannot live without them—but putting them within the broader perspective of our quest for well-being. When Jesus spoke about seeking first the kingdom, in response to the anxious disciples, Jesus wanted to reorient his disciples toward a greater value, that which promotes life (Lk. 12:31). And when we seek life, other things will find their place.

Well-being is the category I use for saying that life is more than producing and having. There is more to life that warrants our serious attention. One can buy things, but one cannot buy joy, as we can see in the lives of the rich and famous. One can buy a spouse or partner, but not necessarily genuine love and affection. One can use possessions to instill fear and demand obedience, but not generate respect. Joy, love, affection, and respect are indicators of human well-being. Well-being is more important than producing or possessing, and should define the role of production and possession.

On the contrary, growth (production, accumulation, and consumption), with its undergirding anthropology, has been the defining norm of our lives and society. There is this pervasive understanding that higher economic growth is good, and higher growth than ever before is better. But there can be growth without well-being, and there can be growth without integration. Cancer is uncontrolled growth of certain cells; it is growth that is not fully integrated into the overall system; it is growth that does not promote well-being; it is growth that can result in death. Our economic growth is a cancerous growth. It has not "trickled down" to those at the bottom of the social scale. It has not led to a quality life even to those who are at the top of the social ladder. Economic growth has increased production, accumulation, and consumption, but, paradoxically, it has not led to overall well-being.

### Homo Economicus as Person-in-Community

Well-being is only well-being in relation to others. This is what being a *homo economicus* is. In their joint work, *For the Common Good,* Herman Daly and John Cobb, Jr., call for a way of understanding *homo economicus* as person-in-community.[52] Theirs is an understanding of the human as being fundamentally related to the community even while individuality is maintained. The fundamental significance of this model as distinct from the classical, according to Daly and Cobb, "is the recognition that the well-being of a community as a whole is constitutive of each person's welfare."[53] Patterns of relationship and how those patterns are affected by the market are as important as the possession of commodities. *Homo economicus* as person-in-community is a fundamentally different anthropology than that which undergirds Adam Smith's classic book, *Wealth of Nations,* and the capitalist societies informed by Smith's economics, in which societal well-being is assumed to happen as individuals seek their own interests. Societal well-being is not, as our common experience testifies, a natural outcome of separate individuals seeking their own interests mediated by the market; rather, it is grounded in the understanding that one's humanity is intrinsically bound to the wider community.

Classism undermines the notion that human beings only find their well-being in relation to others. It is an infringement of mutual relation; it is an expression of a fundamental breach of covenanted relationship. When classism is present in the church, it is an infraction of an ecclesial community. Employing a broader term, it runs at variance with, and is in opposition to, God's *basileia* (the reign of God).

### Economics for Community: Economy of Care

The *homo economicus* as person-in-community calls for an economic order beyond what is called "chrematistics" economics. According to Cobb and Daly, chrematistics economics refers to the branch of political economy that deals with the manipulation of property and wealth in order to maximize short-term monetary value for the owners. What happens on

Wall Street is an excellent example of chrematistics economics. Economic success is measured, not in terms of well-being or the system's effectiveness to deliver care, but in terms of increased production and consumption. When it deals with increased production and consumption, it only refers to GNP, not to the protein intake of individuals and families.

An alternative to chrematistics economics is economics in line with its Greek root *oikonomia*, or "economics for community." *Oikonomia* is different from chrematistics. Daly and Cobb offer three features of economics as *oikonomia*: (1) it takes seriously the long-term interest rather than the short-term gains; (2) business transactions take into consideration the costs and benefits to the whole community, not only the benefits of the transacting parties; (3) instead of prioritizing abstract value and its stimulus for unlimited accumulation, *oikonomia* focuses on concrete value in relation to specific needs that can find objective satisfaction.[54]

What Cobb and Daly refer to as economics for community (*oikonomia*) resonates with what Bod Goudzwaard and Harry de Lange call the economy of care. To speak of an economy of care is to speak of a community of care or of a caring community. An economy of care happens only when we see human beings as persons-in-community. Economy is geared toward the care of the community, both human and other beings. Success, as an economic criterion, is based on what builds and supports the community as a whole.

If well-being is the defining norm for both production and consumption, then care is a fundamental economic category. Economics is not simply a matter of production, but one of care: care for the overall well-being of both human beings and the rest of creation. Care is a basic element in the oldest definition of the Greek word *oikonomia* or economy. Our conception of economics must recover this dimension.

What is this economy of care and how does it view human beings in relation to economic forces? An economy of care is a precare economy. In principle, it places income and consumption in service to care needs. It does not consider the care needs of the people only after production, income, and profits have been secured, but puts care at the forefront of economic decision-making.

In contrast, the dominant economic model operative today is postcare economics. In postcare economics, Goudzwaard and de Lange contend, "we engage in the highest possible consumption and production and only afterwards attempt to mitigate the mounting care needs, often with extremely expensive forms of compensation."[55] In this economic model we find the subordination of human and ecological well-being to production and consumption.

## Critique of Works Righteousness: Rethinking the Value of Labor

In a society that values worth by works and achievements, it goes against the grain to tell people that they may not deserve all of what they are enjoying now. Or that they have not earned all of what they enjoy by their own efforts. It is an irony that the descendants of the religious groups who accused the ancient church of works righteousness and argued in favor of justification by grace through faith are no less captive to works righteousness than those they criticized. In a capitalist global market every person is justified according to works, regardless of faith convictions.

The work that justifies is not, however, plain work or labor, but one that passes the criterion of success as defined by our capitalist and classist society. In a classist society a person is justified by the kinds of works that elevate his or her social and economic status. Common laborers may work from morning until evening (or from evening until morning), but the kinds of work they engage do not fit the criterion of success. The works that they do, though essential for the life of society, are not given their appropriate monetary and societal value. The value of one's work in a classist society is a function of class stratification.

Work is intrinsic to who we are, and we cannot divorce ourselves from our work. We are creatures of work, and our works reveal much of who we are. More than something that we do in order to provide for our basic needs, work is a way we express ourselves, our creativity, talents, ideas, and dreams. In work we seek self-fulfillment. Work is intrinsic to our identity. Work, according to Meeks, "has to do with livelihood, with inclusion in the community, and with a sense of personal dignity and well-being...Work is a way of belonging to, sharing in, and contributing to the life of the community."[56] To deny a person work is to diminish his or her humanity.

Our work defines us. It is an avenue to fulfillment. Yet, it is also the source of pain for many people. Many of them are forced to work in order to survive, but do not find self-fulfillment or meaning in their work. Going to work is something that many people do not look forward to. If they had a choice, they would be somewhere other than their workplace. People often say, "Thank God it's Friday," but not, "Thank God it's Monday." Larry Dossey is more blunt: "There must be a reason more heart attacks occur between 8:00 and 9:00 a.m. on Monday mornings than at any other time during the week. There is; it is returning to work that one hates."[57]

Work, in a market society, is reduced to a commodity and given value according to the criteria set by chrematistics economics. The market has skewed the conception of work by devaluing those forms of work that cannot be easily transacted in the market and assigned a monetary equivalent. Goudzwaard and de Lange call these devalued forms of work "transductive labor."[58] Works that are classified under transductive labor are not geared toward producing goods for the market, but are oriented toward care of the community, social relations, and the ecosystem. Such forms of work may include housekeeping, taking care of children, volunteering in some civic organizations, providing food and care for the hungry and the needy, community organizing, and caring for the environment.

Because these forms of work are not easily quantifiable, they are not considered in factoring economic gains. But transductive labor is essential to any society. Without it chrematistics economics would collapse and society would be in chaos. The forms of work or services classified as transductive labor have, in many ways, provided the much-needed "safety nets" for the victims of corporate greed. In a sense, churches and other civic organizations subsidize business corporations through the social care (transductive labor) they provide, allowing corporations to continue their profit-making ventures. Who says there is no free lunch in America? Who says that only Jane Doe, not the business corporation, is the welfare mother? How about the corporate "welfare mother" who gets government subsidies, bailouts, and transductive safety nets provided by civic organizations?[59] And yet it is ironic that as civic and religious organizations are expected to do more, government financial support has been tremendously reduced, of course under pressure from corporate lobbyists acting in concert with neo-conservative politicians.

The distinction between productive and transductive labor sheds light on the economic paradox: increasing wealth while decreasing care. As chrematistics economics produces more wealth, it continues to trample transductive labor and siphon the alienated fruits of labor from the laboring masses. Our view of work will not change significantly unless we stop thinking of it as a simple commodity that can be totally transacted and assigned worth according to the price set by the global market.

### Human Being and the Economy of Time

Under the rubric of chrematistics economics, time is valued in relation to the wealth it generates. Time is money and waste of time is waste of money. Time is an adjunct of production. Its value is determined in relation to productive forces. The value of an upper level manager's time is worth more than the time of a common employee or laborer. One can waste a low paid employee or laborer's time but not the boss's time. The CEO's time is well guarded by their secretaries from obstructions by those whose time is deemed less important, though CEOs seem to have time for people of their own class. Since it is assumed that the time of an ordinary employee has less monetary value, and it is also assumed that she or he has more time to spare, scheduling always revolves around the time of the executive officer. The value of one's time is indicative of the worth of a person. This matter lies at the heart of anthropology. When time is tied to production, the efficient use of time must always be observed to speed up production and profit. Driven by quantifiable output, process is often sacrificed. As the democratic process is time consuming, corporations dispense with it.

Democratic process, an essential part of our humanity and participation in the productive life of society, is violated. Social relations, which are constitutive of our well-being, are often neglected.

Also, with time evaluated in terms of money, time spent with people who do not generate money is considered a waste of time. The person who thinks that time is money tends to view social encounters as a way to expand his or her financial portfolio. Time, once made an adjunct of production and profit, has painful repercussions in relationships with people. There is little time to give on social interactions that do not translate into financial reward and, more specifically, less time to commit with those who cannot boost one's economic standing. If any encounter between the wealthy class and the lower class happens, it happens at the level of labor-capital transactions.

If we say that time is an adjunct of production in chrematistics economics, then time is also an adjunct of consumption. What is production for if not to support consumption? Greater production requires greater consumption, and greater consumption means more time is spent acquiring the goods that are produced. But the market creates so many desires that people become confused between basic needs and wants. So consumption increases and expands, requiring more time for production and the satisfaction of consumptive desires. The cycle is endless and vicious.

What kind of solutions do we hear from management specialists? Use time efficiently and buy gadgets that promise fast performance so that we can "save" some time–time for the family and time for each other. But what is the result? Do we have more time with each other because we now have computers and supersonic communication networks? Not at all. The volume of work increases and more time is used in front of machines.

Greater consumption means more time spent away from building healthy relations with people. The more time is allotted in acquiring goods for consumption, the less time is available for close personal and communal relations. As society continues to elevate its material prosperity, it pays a high price: increasing loneliness and isolation among citizens. People in materially rich countries, in spite of their time-saving tips and devices, live more harried and lonely lives.

There is a fundamental need to reorient our concept of time in relation to the forces of production and consumption. Time, in consonance with the concept of economy proposed here, is not simply an adjunct of production and consumption. The value of time must be placed within the wider perspective of an economy oriented toward promoting greater well-being and an economy of care.

### Living Abundantly and the Economy of Enough

The abstraction of use value that we find in chrematistics economics leads to endless consumerism. As value is abstracted, so, too, is satisfaction abstracted and pushed to infinity. Image value, which is an example of exchange value, does not set any limit. Enhancing one's image in a class society through the consumption of luxury goods is an endless process. Use value reaches satisfaction, but not when value is abstracted. Abstraction of use value does not offer any criterion or limit to consumption.

This abstraction of value and its concomitant effect in infinite dissatisfaction corresponds, according to Meeks, to a God who is viewed as infinite. "Classical theology," he says, "depicted the infinity of God as the boundary of human finiteness...This empty infinity in God is the reverse side of the sense of insatiability in the human being."[60] Divine infinity corresponds to human insatiability. The common saying that the "sky is the limit" is simply another way of saying "God is the limit." God and sky are correlative terms because the infinite God can only find an abode in the infinite sky.

When use value is abstracted in favor of exchange value, more specifically image value, a sense of abundance is never experienced even in the midst of plenty. In the realm of economics understood as chrematistics, in which insatiability works in tandem with the sense of scarcity, the experience of abundance is always beyond reach. Insatiability is like a gaping mouth that devours whatever is fed to it without any satisfaction. "'Enough' is always just over the horizon, and like the horizon it recedes as we approach it," says Paul Wachtel.[61]

It is by reorienting ourselves and taking steps in the direction of the economy of care that we will experience liberation from our decreasing sense of abundance. A sense of abundance can only be experienced when one has a sense of enough, "for abundance," de Lange and Goudzwaard contend, "is the awareness of having more than enough."[62]

### *Homo Economicus as Imago Dei: Our Economic Commission*

God, says Douglas Meeks, is an economist.[63] When we say God is an economist, we mean it in its deeper sense as *oikonomia*, in which God takes care of the whole household, making sure that the needs of all are met and that justice reigns while sustaining the ecosystem's well-being. God is not, as many Christians have been led to think, outside the pale of economy. God is not outside the pale of economy, and economy is not outside the pale of God. This is not to conflate theology and economics, but to say that our theological understanding of being created in the image of God has economic implications.

As God is an economist, we, too, are economists and must live up to this noble calling. To be created in the image of God is to be a *homo economicus*, for God is an economist. God's economic acts call forth economic acts on the part of human beings. Meeks rightly states that "being human is an economic commission to join God the economist in distributing righteousness so that the world may live."[64] Being human, continues Meeks, means "to be sent as God's economist to live and work for God's will for the creation."[65]

A fundamental reorientation must happen in terms of the way we understand who we are (anthropology) and the way we view the economy. This reorientation considers the well-being of all as the criterion of economic success: Care is of paramount economic consideration, production is made subservient to that which builds up communal life, consumption is linked to use value, and the future of those who are yet to be born is protected. *Homo economicus* must join with God the economist in dismantling classism and in building a society in which the economy is directed toward care and greater well-being. Classism, poverty in the midst of affluence, powerlessness and fatalism, commoditization of labor, fetishism of commodities, destruction of familial relations, and devastation of the ecosystem are hallmarks of an economy gone awry.

### The Promise of a Humanity Liberated from Classism

We may not in this earthly life of ours live in a society without classism, but a humanity experiencing liberation from classism is already in the making. It is happening in individuals who struggle to live the promise of the new humanity in the present. We see this new humanity emerging among those who resist the culture of consumerism and who refuse to define their identities according to the logic of consumption and the image value of things. It is birthing among individuals who have realized that they do not have to hoard material goods in order to find joy and meaning in life.

The authors of *Affluenza: The All-Consuming Epidemic* tell a story of a woman named Evy McDonald. "My goal," she recalls, "was to be the youngest female hospital administrator in the country." Her promotion was fast. With each promotion she lavished herself with material goods. She bought a new house and an expensive car. Then disaster struck. Evy was diagnosed with a fatal disease. Suddenly, the feisty, cheerful, and determined woman was confronted with questions about the meaning of her own life. "Who did I want to be when I die?" Evy asked herself. "And what I discovered was that I didn't want to have the most things. What I wanted my life to be about was understanding love, understanding service, and feeling whole and complete."[66]

Likewise, the new humanity is present in the life of a person who has continued to affirm his or her dignity as a child of God even in the midst of poverty. We can discern this new humanity in Bacoral, a boy who lives in Acre, Brazil, and suffers from Hansen's disease (leprosy). During a meeting of evangelization group instructors, Bacoral offered his commentary on the gospel story of Our Lady's visit to Saint Elizabeth.

I'm amazed. One poor woman visiting another simple woman, and they talked about salvation and the fate of the world! That happens here too. The gospel happens today. Here in this very meeting. But many people aren't simple and that's why they don't discover the great tasks waiting them. You get people who go around saying, "I'm a friend of so-and-so," the doctor, the mayor, the senator, the landowner, or millionaire. They hang their greatness on the wrong hook. It's rubbish. What makes us valuable is that we're children of God! That's what I think.[67]

The new humanity is coming into being among people's organizations and alternative communities around the world that struggle to dismantle classism and practice an economy that promotes greater well-being. Various alternative communities and critical social movements around the world embody the presence of this new humanity in the way they dwell and in their social activism. They embody the presence of a new humanity because critical social movements, in the words of R. B. J. Walker,

> challenge the reduction of economic life to processes of material accumulation. They push beyond existing horizons of what it means to know and to be in the world. They explore and invent, interpret and act. What is at stake is not the possibility of storming the palaces of culture but of developing ways of being together, ways of creating and relating, of expressing and speaking, that are empowering.[68]

I know that it is an enormous challenge to live differently in a world defined by classism, but the challenge remains nonetheless. It is our calling to live differently from the classist system. Our ability to dismantle classism and to live a life counter to the classist lifestyle will be enhanced only as we learn to support each other. We need to support one another in unlearning class-laden attitudes and changing values and lifestyles at the personal level. Moreover, we need to bond together in reimagining and constructing a mode of relationship that is mutually liberating.

### Notes

[1]José Comblin, *Retrieving the Human: A Christian Anthropology* (Maryknoll, N.Y.: Orbis Books, 1990), 151.

[2]Susan Brooks Thistlethwaite and Peter Hodgson, "The Church, Classism, and Ecclesial Community," in *Reconstructing Christian Theology*, ed. Rebecca Chopp and Mark Lewis Taylor (Minneapolis: Fortress Press, 1994), 312.

[3]Harold R. Kerbo, *Social Stratification and Inequality* (New York: McGraw-Hill, 1983), 10–24.

[4]Paula S. Rothenberg, ed. *Racism and Sexism: An Integrated Study* (New York: St. Martin's Press, 1988), 50.

[5]Gregory Mantsios, "Class in America: Myths and Realities," in Rothenberg, *Racism and Sexism*, 57.

[6]Barbara Ehrenreich, *Fear of Falling: The Inner Life of the Middle Class* (New York: HarperCollins Publishers, 1989), 30.

[7]Ibid.

[8]Ibid., 48.

[9]Ibid., 50.

[10]Karen Bloomquist, *The Dream Betrayed: Religious Challenge of the Working Class* (Minneapolis: Fortress Press, 1990), 21.

[11]A response to the Catholic Bishop of the United States pastoral letter (1984) on the modern capitalist economy. Cited in Timothy J. Gorringe, *Capital and the Kingdom: Theological Ethics and Economic Order* (Maryknoll, N.Y.: Orbis Books, 1994), 160.

[12]Michael Novak, *The Spirit of Democratic Capitalism* (New York: American Enterprise Institute/Simon and Schuster, 1982), 113.

[13]Immanuel Wallerstein, *The Capitalist World Economy* (Cambridge: Cambridge University Press, 1979), 285.

[14]M. Douglas Meeks, *God the Economist: The Doctrine of God and Political Economy* (Minneapolis: Fortress Press, 1989), xi.

[15]Ibid., 29.

[16]Franz Hinkelammert, "The Economic Roots of Idolatry: Entrepreneurial Metaphysics," in *The Idols of Death and the God of Life: A Theology*, ed. Pablo Richard, et al. (Maryknoll, N.Y.: Orbis Books, 1983), 165.

[17]Ibid., 166.

[18]Adam Smith, *An Inquiry into the Nature and Causes of the Wealth of Nations*, ed. Edwin Cannan (New York: Random House, 1937), 423.

[19]Gorringe, *Capital and the Kingdom*, 37.

[20]Hinkelammert, "Economic Roots of Idolatry," 191.

[21]Bloomquist, *Dream Betrayed*, 48.

[22]Gorringe, *Capital and the Kingdom*, 80–81.

[23]Karl Marx, *Early Writings*, translated and edited by T. Bottomore (New York, Toronto, and London: McGraw-Hill Book Company, 1964), 123.

[24]Michael Moore, *Downsize This! Random Threats from an Unarmed American* (New York: Crown Publishers, Inc., 1996), 10–11.

[25]Zillah Eisenstein, *Hatreds: Racialized and Sexualized Conflicts in the 21st Century* (New York and London: Routledge, 1996), 94.

[26]Bertell Ollman, *Alienation: Marx's Conception of Man in Capitalist Society* (Cambridge: Cambridge University Press, 1976), 198.

[27]Erich Fromm, *Marx's Concept of Man* (New York: Frederick Ungar Publishing, 1961), 47.

[28]Ibid., 165–66.

[29]Anthony H. Richmond, *Global Apartheid: Refugees, Racism, and the New World Order* (Toronto, New York, and Oxford: Oxford University Press, 1994), 41.

[30]Bloomquist, *Dream Betrayed*, 39.

[31]Dorothee Sölle with Shirley Cloyes, *To Work and To Love: A Theology of Creation* (Philadelphia: Fortress Press, 1984), 116.

[32]See Luz Rimban, "Filipino Brides in Japan," *Filipinas* (April 1998), 30.

[33]Elizabeth Morgan with Van Weigel and Eric DeBaufre, *Global Poverty and Personal Responsibility: Integrity Through Commitment* (New York and Mahwah, N.J.: Paulist Press, 1989), 109.

[34]Don Oldenburg, "'Buy Nothing Day' Counters 'Shop Till You Drop' Message," in *The Washington Post*, 29 Nov. 1996, 1A.

[35]Eisenhower, cited in Bob Goudzwaard and Harry de Lange, *Beyond Poverty and Affluence: Toward an Economy of Care* (Geneva: WCC Publications; Grand Rapids, Mich.: Wm. B. Eerdmans, 1995), 93.

[36]Thomas H. Naylor and William H. Willimon, *Downsizing the U.S.A.* (Grand Rapids, Mich.: William B. Eerdmans Publishing Company, 1997), 59.

[37]Robert Schreiter, "Contextualization from a World Perspective," in *ATS Theological Education* Volume 30, Supplement 1 (Autumn 1993), 82; Schreiter, *The New Catholicity: Theology*

*Between the Global and the Local*, Faith and Culture Series (Maryknoll, N.Y.: Orbis Books, 1997).

[38]Peter McLaren, *Revolutionary Multiculturalism: Pedagogies of Dissent for the New Millennium* (Boulder, Colo.: Westview Press, 1997), 197.

[39]Ibid., 198.

[40]Ibid., 120.

[41]John B. Cobb, Jr., "Economism or Planetism: The Coming Choice," *Earth Ethics 3* (Fall 1991), cited in Sallie McFague, *Super, Natural Christians: How We Should Love Nature* (Minneapolis: Fortress Press, 1997), 13.

[42]Bloomquist, *Dream Betrayed*, 83.

[43]Thomas Naylor, William Willimon, and Rolf Österberg, *The Search for Meaning in the Workplace* (Nashville: Abingdon Press, 1996), 117.

[44]Richard Sennett and Jonathan Cobb, *The Hidden Injuries of Class* (New York: Vintage Books, 1972).

[45]Ibid., 96.

[46]Ibid., 97; also, see Ehrenreich, *Fear of Falling*, 132–43.

[47]Janet L. Wolfe and Iris G. Fodor, "The Poverty of Privilege: Therapy with Women of the 'Upper' Class," in *Classism and Feminist Therapy: Counting Costs*, ed. Marcia Hill and Esther Rothblum (New York and London: Haworth Press, 1996), 81–83.

[48]Ehrenreich, *Fear of Falling*, 15.

[49]Cited in Bloomquist, *Dream Betrayed*, 49.

[50]Ted Peters, *Sin: Radical Evil in Soul and Society* (Grand Rapids, Mich.: Wm B. Eerdmans, 1994), 99–101.

[51]Robert McAfee Brown, preface, in Gustavo Gutiérrez, *The Power of the Poor in History: Selected Writings* (Maryknoll, N.Y.: Orbis Books, 1983), xiv–xv.

[52]John Cobb, Jr., and Herman Daly, *For the Common Good: Redirecting the Economy Toward Community, the Environment, and a Sustainable Future* (Boston: Beacon Press, 1989), 161.

[53]Ibid., 164.

[54]Ibid., 139.

[55]Goudzwaard and de Lange, *Beyond Poverty and Affluence*, 63.

[56]Meeks, *God the Economist*, 151.

[57]Larry Dossey, address to Mystics and Scientists Conference, Winchester, England, April 3, 1993. Cited in Thomas Naylor, William Willimon, and Rolf Österberg, *The Search for Meaning in the Workplace*, 58.

[58]Goudzwaard and de Lange, *Beyond Poverty and Affluence*, 57.

[59]See Michael Moore, *Downsize This!*

[60]Meeks, *God the Economist*, 168.

[61]Paul Wachtel, *Poverty of Affluence: A Psychological Portrait of the American Way of Life* (Philadelphia: New Society Publishers, 1989), 17.

[62]Goudzwaard and de Lange, *Beyond Poverty and Affluence*, 161.

[63]Meeks, *God the Economist*.

[64]Ibid., 90.

[65]Ibid.

[66]John de Graaf, David Wann, and Thomas Naylor, *Affluenza: The All-Consuming Epidemic* (San Francisco: Berrett-Koehler Publishers, Inc., 2001), 172–173.

[67]Carlos Mesters, *Defenseless Flower: A New Reading of the Bible* (Maryknoll, N.Y.: Orbis Books, 1989), 78–79.

[68]R. B. J. Walker, *One World, Many Worlds: Struggles for a Just World Peace* (London: Zed Books; Boulder, Colo.: Lynne Rienner, 1988), 151.

# CHAPTER 5

# Reimagining the Human in Response to Sexism

## Toward an Integrated Man and Woman

We are not only afflicted by classism but also by sexism. Just like the viruses of classism and racism, this form of evil is resistant, entrenched, and pervasive. It is not simply an enemy out there, which we can easily isolate, but it is in us and around us. Because sexism is pervasive, complex, and enduring we need to stand together and employ multiple means in our struggle against it. Theology is one arena in which this struggle has to be waged, because sexism has an entrenched theological undergirding.

As in other forms of oppression, sexism shapes and is shaped by other forms of oppression. I agree with Mark Kline Taylor that a singular focus on sexism would be inadequate to explore its complexity, "a complexity that includes a multifarious intersecting with other modes of oppression. To think of sexism fully is to think also of heterosexism, racism, and classism."[1] Nevertheless, these forms of oppression have distinct matrixes.

Several authors have dealt more extensively with sexism and its multifarious ramifications, and it is not my intention to give a full rehearsal of the burgeoning literature on this complex topic. Whatever cursory account of sexism I am going to give, it is for the purpose of providing some basic materials that may lead to a theological reimagining of anthropology in response to sexism. Feminist theologians have already done extensive work in this direction, so what I seek to do is to navigate among the various positions and put forward an interpretation that is coherent and consistent with the overall direction of this project.

I am aware that my reconstruction of anthropology in light of sexism is one among many interpretations. There are competing positions because there are different construals of what it means to be human. Rather than placing blame for this cacophony of interpretations on the doorstep of feminism, we should welcome it as an expression of the richness of feminist reflections. Feminist reflections remind us that there is no single model of what it means to be human that can exhaust every dimension. This work seeks to contribute to the large and complex project of anthropological reconstruction.

## Sexism: A Systemic Problem

Sexism, like classism, disfigures the human face, but this time the brunt falls on one sex–female. Sexism is the systemic oppression and exploitation of more than half of the world's population–women. Through its systemic or structural character, sexism assures and secures male domination by elevating men and subordinating women. It is an ideology and a cluster of practices that justify male privilege and support the continuing oppression of women on the basis of gender difference.

The manifestations of sexism can be blatant or overt as in the case of murder, rape, and various forms of domestic violence. It is wrong to assume that these overt forms of violence happen only among poor or dysfunctional families. Statistics challenging this assumption are overwhelming. In South Africa, one out of every six adult women experiences routine assaults from her male partner. Sixty percent of persons murdered in Papua, New Guinea, in 1981 were women. In France, 95 percent of the victims of violence are women, and most of these acts of violence are perpetrated by their husbands.[2]

Sexism may also take a more covert form, as feminists have articulated well. It may appear without an identifiable single perpetrator in the sexual division of labor, the wage system, female-dominated child care, male-dominated breadwinner roles, and in men's control of women's bodies. It may also appear in commonly accepted practices, rules, customs, and cultural stereotypes that relegate women to a lower rank in the hierarchy. Any attempt on my part to articulate some of its manifestations is limited, while feminists have articulated it extensively and well.

Sexism is undergirded by the dominant patriarchal worldview of our time. In her work *Heart of Flesh: A Feminist Spirituality for Women and Men*, Joan Chittister identities four interlocking principles of the patriarchal worldview: dualism, hierarchy, domination, and essential inequality.[3] It is a worldview or a way of thinking and perceiving that is hierarchical and dualistic–mind over body, reason over passion–with women identified on the lower side of the dualism. As mind rules over body and reason over passion, so man rules over woman (domination). Men exercising power over women is thus derived from the nature of things. Hence, to change this arrangement, the argument goes, is to violate the nature of things or "the way things are" (essential inequality). This patriarchal worldview is buttressed by pseudo-science, justifying the putative biological inferiority of women. Based on this putative biological reality, it is the unquestioned duty of men to rule over women. Women are assigned roles governed by this putative biological hierarchization and bifurcation. As M. Shawn Copeland puts it:

> Sexism is expressed in artificial, arbitrary biological limitation of the plasticity and perfectibility of women; in restriction of the quality and character of women's participation in social cooperations by way of generalised assignment of biologically patterned roles and tasks; in culturally generated taxonomy that bifurcates along physiological lines; and in structured disregard for women's capacity for liberty.[4]

Society is patriarchal, argues Allan Johnson, to the extent that it is "male-dominated," "male-identified," and "male-centered."[5] Patriarchy is present where males dominate positions of authority and women are relegated to positions that are often devalued, however essential they may be for the survival of a society. Of course there are women who have reached the upper level of patriarchal society, but they are always measured against men of the same position. This male dominance promotes a power differential in favor of men and promotes the idea that men are superior to women.

A society is also patriarchal to the degree that it is male-identified. In a male-identified society, the core cultural ideals of what is good and desirable are identified with maleness and masculinity. We can identify a few, such as: competitiveness, control, toughness, decisiveness, rationality, autonomy, and the ability to conceal emotions in tough situations. On the other hand, qualities that are stereotypically identified with women are shunned: emotional expressiveness, dependence, vulnerability, care and compassion, intuitive and nonlinear ways of thinking. Because patriarchy is male-identified, women identify with the role assigned to them by society, and any violation of these socially assigned roles is fraught with painful consequences. When a woman achieves success under the patriarchal system and assumes a powerful position, she is often viewed as having been "desexualized." Her socially ascribed female identity recedes under the veil of male-identified power. For men, the effect of their assumption of a powerful office is the opposite: they become more truly what being a man is. A common perception pervades that "[p]ower looks sexy on men but not on women."[6]

Moreover, a society is patriarchal to the extent that it is male-centered. In a patriarchal society, activities that revolve around men are the focus of attention. Major events revolve around the activities of men. The things that are commonly done by women do not get much attention. But when men do things that women normally do, they get the attention and credit. Men do not usually notice their being at the center, yet this is precisely what it means to be privileged.

There is no one expression of patriarchy and there is no one expression of sexism (just as there is no one expression of colonialism, feminism, or nationalism). People's experience of sexism is shaped by their physical and social location and the interweaving of other forms of oppression. Sexism interweaves with other forms of oppression and its expression is shaped to the extent that it influences and is influenced by other forms of oppression.

Sexism interweaves with classism, relegating women in general to the bottom of the economic totem pole. But women have different positions on the social ladder of any society, which impacts the way they experience sexism. Upper-class women do not have to force themselves to seek employment even in the face of sexual discrimination, which lower-class women have to undergo in order to survive. Although some women are at the top of the economic-social scale, this does not erase their victimization by sexism.

Sexism is compounded by racism, which is to say that women of color experience sexism differently than white women. A woman of color does not experience sexism as a woman—like any white woman—and then experience racism like any woman of color; she experiences sexism as a woman-of-color. Asian women's experience of sexism, for example, is always interwoven with their experience of racism. They are stereotyped as docile and submissive (the "perfect wife") and as the exotic sexpot who will cater to the sexual desire of any man.

It is not only women who experience sexism in different ways. Men's participation in the perpetuation of sexism is also affected by the interweaving of class and race. The dynamics of class undermine the male privilege of those men who are economically at the bottom of the social ladder, impacting their ability to engage in sexual discrimination against upper-class women. Racism undermines black males' gender privilege, especially in relation to white women, not only because of their skin color but also because of the challenges they face in assuming the patriarchal position of being the male provider. Nevertheless, the fact that not all men are better off than all women does not erase the reality of male privilege. The privilege is available to all men, though not to the same degree.

Sexism is a global phenomenon, and this global dimension tells us of the global commonalities as well as the differences in the ways sexism is encountered and experienced. Sexism is not only a Western problem; it is pervasive throughout the world. It is not only a problem of the white society, argues Chung Hyun Kyung, a feminist theologian from Korea, much less a white women's issue.[7] Women all over the world have been victimized by patriarchal capitalism or, in the words of Zillah Eisenstein, the "phallocratic market."[8] Sexism cuts across borders and is inscribed in the bodies of women who are forced to undergo genital mutilation, imprisoned and banished for questioning the role of women in the Islamic world, tortured and raped (such as in Bosnia-Herzegovina), and killed for not wearing the veil.[9]

On the other hand, the global dimension of sexism reminds us, and Western feminists in particular, to be cautious about making quick judgments regarding what may be deemed sexist practices in other countries. While there are commonalities, women's experience of sexism is influenced by such factors as colonialism, racism, nationalism, and global capitalism, to name a few. Western feminists ought to be cautious not only because of the complicity of Western feminism with Western imperialism, but because of the increasing momentum of globalism, which makes white hegemonic culture easily exportable to other countries.

## The Internalization of Sexism by Its Primary Victims

The systemic character of sexism can be discerned in its power to colonize its victims. This colonization reaches its zenith in the male identification of women. Like the poor and oppressed who identify with their masters, and people of color who become whites inside (like the Oreo cookie), women in a male-dominated society become male-identified. As victims of sexism, women also learn to internalize the sexist worldview and identity. Christine Smith is very lucid on this:

> Women in a male-dominated world become more male-identified
> than female-identified. There are severe repercussions for women
> who step outside male identification. The violence women witness
> and experience is a powerful silencing and compromising agent.
> Many women live under the illusion that male identification and
> female submission will render them safe from the most blatant
> violences of male domination.[10]

This does not mean, of course, that women's male identification is total, but it is thorough, and women know how serious the consequences are when they deviate from the patriarchal norm. Male identification can even be interpreted as a mode of survival. Delores Williams, a womanist theologian, sees in the survival strategy of black women not a complete acquiescence to the system of domination, but a critical way of living in a violent situation.[11]

Nancy Gabalac and Mary Ballou expose a process that finally leads to the colonization or patriarchalization of women's identity and consciousness.[12] This long process includes humiliation, inculcation, retribution, conversion, and finally, conscription. Women's experience of humiliation includes being constantly exposed to negative images and stereotypes of women in the media. After constant bombardment by negative images and subjection to the humiliation process, women become ready for the inculcation of "correct" gender behavior. When the ascribed gender behavior is violated, retribution is applied. Humiliation, inculcation, and retribution finally lead to conversion, a stage in the colonization process in which women learn to believe that who they are under the patriarchal society is natural and what they are obligated to do must be right. And, what can we expect from converted women if not also to convert or conscript other women? Conscription can be interpreted as the betrayal of women by women. The cycle of humiliation, inculcation, retribution, conversion, and conscription continues unless decolonization, which is a long process, takes place.

### Sexism and the Male's Pain

It is not only women who suffer from sexism but also men. Sexism exacts a high price from men, but it is the price paid for being the main beneficiary of system. If I cannot grant whites the claim that they suffer so much from racism that it balances the pain that people of color suffer, I also say that the price men pay for their active perpetuation of sexism does not balance out the price that women pay. There is a need to underscore this point especially in light of a growing literature which claims that men suffer as much as women in a sexist society.

Herb Golberg, a male-liberation proponent, argues that men are the major sufferers under a patriarchal and sexist society.[13] Men, indeed, suffer under a patriarchal society, but to assert that they are the major victims is to go overboard. It is this kind of claim that erases the unequal power relations that happen in a patriarchal and sexist society. To level the suffering that men and women undergo in a sexist society, much more to assert that men are the major victims, is tantamount to a denial of men's oppression of women and a perpetuation of the sexist rule. It is a refusal to acknowledge one's privilege and responsibility for the perpetuation of sexism.

If it is accepted that men suffer as much as women in a sexist society, then it is logical to assert, as Warren Farrel does, that men deserve as much sympathy as women.[14] This assertion is like saying: "Don't blame me, I am hurt as much as you are." "Men's misery *does* deserve sympathy," says Johnson, "but not if it means we ignore where it comes from and what men get in exchange for it."[15] This must be clear before we can speak about men's pain.

Indeed, men pay a high price in a patriarchal-male-dominated society. Patriarchal society diminishes male's being. Men pay a high price for being "manly." Being a "real man" in a patriarchal-sexist society means masking one's feelings to prevent any show of "femaleness." "Real men," unlike women, must not show their emotions, must not cry, and must deal with painful events without wincing. They suppress their feelings until their bodies betray them. Mark Gerzon states:

> Our bodies often speak more eloquently than our words. When the twentieth century began, men could expect to live nearly as long as women. A woman's life expectancy was 48 years, a man's 46. But by the mid-1970s, according to the U.S. Department of Health, Education and Welfare, the average woman could expect to live 76.5 years, while the life expectancy of the average man was only 68.7 years.[16]

Males in a patriarchal-sexist society avoid any close association with femininity or vulnerability. Traits associated with "real manliness" are encouraged such as competition, assertiveness, independence, decisiveness, and rationality. Trained to hide their feelings and compete with others, men are more reluctant to share their inner emotions than women. It is not unlikely, therefore, that men develop fewer intimate and lasting friendships than women do. And, with the specter of heterosexism, men, as I have observed in the U.S., are all the more curtailed in close friendships with other men.[17] What is quite common in a country like the Philippines, where men put their arms around each other's shoulders while standing or walking, is likely to be interpreted in the U.S. as a sign of homosexual behavior. As a result of men's social upbringing, there is some truth in Chittister's comment that men do not have friends, they have buddies.[18]

Sexism takes its toll among the perpetrators, the males. They are betrayed by their own power and privilege. Like other forms of evil, sexism turns back on the evildoers. Sexism makes men out of touch with their emotions, their deepest feelings, and fearful of establishing mutuality and interdependence. It does not only cut them off from their feelings, it denies them the blessings of being together. They are alienated from who they are and from who they can become.

### Theological Critique: Theological Canopy of Sexism

Like classism and racism, sexism is undergirded by deeply held theological beliefs. This tells us that theology, much as it is a discourse about God, is at the same time a discourse about ourselves in relation to what we call God. And, as a discourse about ourselves in relation to God, it cannot escape ideological distortions. Theology has undergirded various forms of evil, and this is certainly true with sexism. Since theology has played an active role in the legitimation and perpetuation of sexism, the theological deconstruction of sexism and reconstruction of an alternative theological position is an important part of our struggle against sexism.

Feminist theologians have produced significant works that expose the theological underpinnings of patriarchy and sexism. Though sexism cannot be solely attributed to Christianity, Christian theology has played an important role in supporting and perpetuating sexism. Feminist theologians have pointed out that the Bible, even while prophetic in many respects, has supported and nourished sexism. Instead of simply "mining" the Bible for gems of its liberating content, which early feminists had done, many feminists are now questioning the Bible itself. "Merely pointing to the portions of scripture whose content supports justice and liberation is not adequate," argues Sharon Ringe, "for these interpreters recognize that at the very heart of scripture itself women are on alien and even hostile ground."[19]

The creation account in Genesis is often cited to prescribe the proper place of women in the overall scheme of things and particularly in relation to men. The role played by Eve in the story of the fall has from generation to generation been used to legitimize the subordinate status of women and to bar them from the ordained ministry. In 1 Timothy 2:11–14 we have the apostle Paul using the Genesis creation account to buttress his position in support of the subordinate status of women: "Let woman learn in silence with full submission. I permit no woman to teach or to have authority over a man; she is to keep silent. For Adam was formed first, then Eve; and Adam was not deceived, but the woman was deceived and became a transgressor." The same argument is still being used. In recent years I heard a preacher quoting the apostle Paul in support of the subordinate status of women. He said: "Don't ask me why this is so. I can only say that this is what the Bible says."

The teachings of the church fathers perpetuated the subordinate status of women. Not only was Adam formed first, but it was also Eve who was tempted first. Tertullian could say this of Eve: "*You* are the Devil's gateway. *You* are the unsealer of that forbidden tree. *You* are the first deserter of the divine law."[20] Eve's sin deepened and justified her subordinate status in relation to Adam.

No one can speak of the formative theology of the church without taking account of the thoughts of Augustine of Hippo (354–430). Feminist interpreters of Augustine have pointed to his view of women as a classical representation of patriarchal anthropology. Rosemary Radford Ruether makes the point that although Augustine grants woman's redeemability and participation in the image of God, "it is so overbalanced by her bodily representation of inferior, sin-prone self that he regards her as possessing the image of God only secondarily. The male alone possesses the image of God normatively."[21]

Though with some modifications, Thomas Aquinas continued the Augustinian view that subordinated women to men, especially in his adoption of the Aristotelian notion of women as "misbegotten males" (deficient). Linda Maloney, critiquing Aristotle, points out that the notion of "misbegotten male" in Aristotle is a consequence of his whole system. Her interpretation runs:

> Since it was a fundamental principle for him that, of the two factors or components in every being, 'form' is superior to 'matter,' sexual reproduction was considered beneficial, because it demanded that the one who gives the 'form' (the male) be separate from the one who supplies the 'matter' (the female). Thus the 'lower' is not mingled with the 'higher' in the same individual.[22]

What about the Protestant reformers? They claimed major reforms in the life of the church, but did not make a major shift in their view of women. Martin Luther brought slight modification by acknowledging women's original equality with men, but again he continued the pattern of subordinating women by saying that women lost their original equality with men through the fall. Luther's commentary on Genesis 2:18 illustrates my point:

> Hence it follows that if the woman had not been deceived by the serpent and had not sinned, she would have been the equal of Adam in all respects. For the punishment, that she is now subjected to the man, was imposed on her after sin and because of sin, just as the other hardships and dangers: travail, pain, and countless other vexations.[23]

The Genevan reformer, John Calvin, did not use the argument of the fall to put women in a subordinate position, but again he found a way to justify the inferior status of women through the rhetoric of God-given order. For Calvin, women are not subordinate because of essential inferiority before or after the fall, but due to the fact that God appointed or ordained them to different "social offices."[24] It follows from this position that what society considers "woman's place" is ordained by God for the good of all, and to go against this appointment is to go against God.

Recent theological pronouncements continue to perpetuate the subordinate status of women, but in more subtle ways. It is generally accepted that because women are created in the image of God, they stand equal in relation to men. But subtle theological arguments against full equality are also advanced. Cardinal Simonis, for example, makes a fine distinction between man as the image of God in relation to God's transcendence and woman as the image of God in relation to God's immanence. This argument perpetuates men's elevated status over that of women because immanence is considered subordinate to transcendence.[25] Also, even as women are considered equal by virtue of their being created in the image of God, male church judicatories continue to subordinate women by arguing that women are called to a distinct office.

Christology is often used by the patriarchal church to marginalize women, especially on the issue of women's ordination. In the Roman Catholic Church, for example, arguments against ordination have revolved, according to Ruether, around "christology," "maleness," and "priesthood." If Christ is viewed as the bridegroom (male) and the church as the bride, then Christ's representatives (the priests) can only be males; women cannot represent Christ. Christ has his physical semblance in the male priest. What is the primary physical semblance that warrants the notion that only male priests can represent Christ? It is the "possession of male genitalia," says Ruether. Possession of male genitalia is "the essential prerequisite for representing Christ, who is the disclosure of the male God."[26]

I am aware that my treatment of the theological arsenal of patriarchal and sexist theologies is not exhaustive. What I have done, in a very general way, is to cite examples of how Christian theology has deliberately and subtly undergirded the marginalization and oppression of women.

## Reinterpreting Sin and Evil in Light of Sexism

Sexism is a deadly sin that has infested our society. But to call it sin or evil is not enough; the classical notion of sin must be reinterpreted as part of our struggle to dismantle sexism. Feminist theologians have come up with interpretations of sin that are more in keeping with women's experience of sexism and more in keeping with their vision of a redeemed humanity. In listening to women talk about their experience of sexism, men have also been challenged to reinterpret sin in relation to their active role in the perpetuation of sexism. So, rather than limiting my account of sin to women's experience, I will also highlight some dimensions of how men might view sin, with particular focus on their active participation in the perpetuation of sexism.

Sexism, like other forms of oppression, is a form of idolatry. If racism is "epidermal fetishism," so sexism is "genital fetishism." Here, the male genitalia functions as a symbol of all that our society associates with the myth of "maleness." Sexism is the worship of the male genitalia as an idol; for it is an expression of human folly elevated to a level that demands devotion. Idolatry is present here because sexism demands daily sacrificial offerings: It feeds on the blood of its victims.

As an expression of idolatry, sexism is predicated or grounded on the male's contempt for weakness (read: femininity) and the drive for control. Threatened by the sight of weakness or any association with weakness and lack of control, men in a patriarchal culture are not trained to handle their fears in any way except by closing all possible windows of vulnerability through investment in various mechanisms of control. As they continue to organize their lives around control, they become more tied to the fear of not being in control. When we dig into the inner lives of men who look physically "macho" and men who assume powerful social positions, we may find men who are deeply insecure and terribly afraid that they might be construed by others as "wimps." I am not saying that all men who look physically macho are deeply insecure. What I want to say is that male insecurity may hide behind the facade of macho physicality.

Dependence, intimate relationships, and other human traits associated with weakness (femininity) must be shunned by men in a patriarchal and sexist society. Dependence and intimate relationships are perceived to make one more vulnerable to others; thus, the "self-made man" becomes the ideal, rather than an oxymoron. Instead of establishing connections, intimate relations, and mutual openness, the male figure learns to disconnect and to be always on the lookout for others who might take advantage of his weakness. The patriarchal-sexist society is grounded, according to Johnson, in a "Great Lie" that

> the answer to life's need is disconnection and control rather than connection, sharing, and cooperation. The Great Lie separates men from what they need most by encouraging them to be autonomous and disconnected when in fact human existence is fundamentally relational.[27]

We are back again to the very basic notion of sin as "living a lie." Men in a patriarchal and sexist society "live a lie" in relation to their innermost selves and others. It is a "Great Lie" to live as if one were a "self-made man." The "self-made man" is a theology of death because it celebrates disconnection.

Having interpreted the evil of sexism primarily, but not exclusively, from the experience of the main beneficiaries of sexism, I would like to devote the rest of this section to feminists' attempts to interpret sin and evil from the perspective of the main victims of sexism—women. Several feminist theologians have laid the groundwork in this direction, and what I would like to do is to highlight the main points.

Smith presents an overview of the trend in feminist interpretations of sin and evil.[28] She identifies four points: (1) feminists are generally critical of the individualistic-privatistic understanding of sin that has dominated traditional theology; (2) a shift from the dominant interpretation of sin as pride, disobedience, idolatry, and alienation to notions of sin and evil that are congruent with women's experience, e.g., betrayal of trusted relationships, brokenheartedness, the violation of right relation, and systemic injustice and oppression; (3) a focus on naming and defining the systemic reality of sin and evil; and (4) a call for theologians to identify their social location and to take seriously the specific contexts that give shape to concrete expressions of sin and evil.

Valerie Saiving is one of the early feminists who attempted to interpret sin in the direction Smith identifies. Critical of the dominant notion of sin as disobedience and pride, Saiving thought sin is better described as:

triviality, distractibility, and diffuseness; lack of an organizing center or focus; dependence on others for one's own self-definition; tolerance at the expense of standards of excellence, inability to respect the boundaries of privacy; sentimentality, gossipy sociability, and mistrust of reason—in short, underdevelopment or negation of the self.[29]

This notion of sin is, of course, shaped by Saiving's Western middle-class upbringing, but hers is a pioneering and trailblazing work in the development of feminist interpretations of sin and evil. Rather than leveling all sin as rooted in pride, arrogance, and self-assertion, the primary expression of sin that women experience (not necessarily denying other expressions) is self-negation, servility, and self-loss. In a context in which women have been conditioned to deny themselves, sin is not self-assertion but continuing self-denial in favor of the needs of others at the expense of women's self-actualization.

Judith Plaskow, though she disagrees with Saiving's assumption that the differences between men and women rest primarily on biological grounds, concurs with Saiving that the dominant interpretation of sin and evil does not take seriously the experience of women. Plaskow critiqued the works of some major theologians to show that the dominant interpretation of sin has been oblivious to the experience of women.[30]

One feminist theologian who has taken on the challenge of constructing sin and evil from women's specific experience and location, especially those who are victim-survivors of domestic and sexual violence, is Mary Potter Engel.[31] Engel explores four dimensions of sin: (1) distortion of feeling; (2) betrayal of trust; (3) lack of care; (4) lack of consent to vulnerability.

Sin as distortion of feeling comes when women, instead of being angry at the abuse that they suffer, suppress their anger and engage in self-blaming. Women who are victims of domestic abuse often blame themselves for the situation. Instead of confronting their perpetrators, they turn their anger inward and blame themselves.

Betrayal of trust is another significant dimension of sin interpreted in the context of domestic abuse. Sin, in the context of domestic violence, involves the betrayal of trusted relationship. The primary expression of sin in this context is not prideful arrogance and self-love, but betrayal of trust. Instead of focusing on sin as disobedience, which results in a focus on the actions of abused women in relation to their abusers, we should aim our attention on the breach of trust committed by the perpetrator. For a woman to disobey an abuser is not sinful. Rather, "sinful disobedience" is a way toward liberation and healing.

Lack of care is another dimension that Engel wants us to interpret as sin. While men in a patriarchal society are socialized to inflate the boundaries of the self and annex others, women are socialized to deflate themselves, to become diffused, and to lose themselves in relationship. Calling women's struggle for self-actualization "prideful arrogance" is absurd, and functions as a means to perpetuate male domination. Self-love, for victims, is not sin. In fact, they have not loved themselves. A battered woman's experience of sin is lack of care and self-love.

Lastly, sin involves a lack of consent to vulnerability. Men in our society have been socialized to ignore mutual dependence and vulnerability. As I said in the previous section, their usual response to vulnerability or any sign of weakness is control and putting on the facade of manliness. In this context many men (and women) learn contempt for weakness. However, while women learn contempt for weakness as men do, there is a difference. Men generally respond to weakness by control and domination; whereas women tend to respond, like other oppressed people, by escaping into false dependence. Thus, they fall deeper into the hands of the oppressor-abuser.

Other dimensions to sin appear only as we theologize from specific locations and specific experiences of people, as feminist theological interpretations on sin and evil have made us aware. These other dimensions await exposure as theologians continue to listen closely to the pains of people.

### Grace and Liberation through Acts of "Sinful Disobedience"

Our brief account of sin and evil illustrates that many of the interpretations of sin that we have learned to accept have supported further victimization rather than promoting salvation. These interpretations are expressions of a patriarchal culture that continue to subvert the unfolding of women's humanity, and, concomitantly, the male's humanity. It follows that part of the journey toward liberation and healing is, in fact, "sinning clearly and boldly" (*pecca fortiter*), or committing the sins defined as such by the patriarchal and sexist society.[32] We need to say, to paraphrase the Lord's Prayer, "O God, lead us into committing the sins dreaded by the Fathers." Disobedience is the proper and prophetic stance in response to situations of exploitative and violent relation. Disobedience to the abusive god incarnated in abusive persons is obedience to the God of life.

The abusive person demands not only obedience but trust. In spite of repeated assaults, violence, and exploitation, oppressors unabashedly demand trust from their victims. When trusted relations are violated, the salvation of the victims does not lie in becoming more trusting of their perpetrators. In fact, the effect of the betrayal of trust is distrust. Victims must distrust if they are to survive. The antidote to the lack of trust that victims have learned throughout the history of abuse is not to increase trust, but to acknowledge the victims' damaged capacity to trust before talking about moving toward a necessary life-affirming trust.

If sinful disobedience is a path to liberation in the context in which obedience means the perpetuation of abuse, then sinful self-assertion is an expression of liberation and a way toward healing in the setting in which the victims have learned self-deflation, self-hatred, and self-blame. If victims have been trained to love others, but not themselves, self-love is not a sin to be overcome, but a requirement for liberation and healing.

Anger, which arises from the realization that one has been wronged, is not sin, as patriarchal society has made us believe. Beverly Harrison's influential essay "The Power of Anger in the Work of Love" reminds us that anger is a "feeling-signal that all is not well in our relation to other persons or groups or to the world around us."[33] What we should worry about is not anger, but when the victims have become numbed to their repeated experience of abuse. What is sinful is when the victims harden their hearts and fail to express outrage. Anger in the face of oppression is not the opposite of love, but love's expression. As Harrison notes: "Christians have come very close to killing love precisely because we have understood anger to be a deadly sin."[34] The sin of anger needs to be committed by all people who have experienced exploitation and abuse.

It follows from our account of sin that understanding the way we think about sin is necessary in our struggle against it. I concur with Engel's affirmation: "I believe that the capacity of human beings to do good and to repair the effects of evil by transforming them into good is co-original with this sinfulness."[35]

## Deconstructing "Human Nature" and Transgressing Genderized Identities

Sexism is founded on a Great Lie, on a distorted notion of who we are; it is undergirded by a patriarchal construction of reality that is accepted as human nature; and it is reflected in our construals of sin and evil. It is enlightening as well as disheartening to find out that many acts we have labeled as sinful might well be the sins we need to commit, and the ideals we have aspired to may be the supreme expressions of patriarchal and sexist society.

Our identity in a patriarchal and sexist society is a domain that is thoroughly genderized along patriarchal and sexist categories. Yet, through our long history of socialization, this identity has acquired the status of being "natural"–human nature. Finding out who we are and who we can become (identity) requires the deconstruction of the so-called human nature and the transgression of our gendered identities. But if we are to deconstruct human nature as a requisite for transgressing and finding our identities, we also need to explore a framework by which to approach human nature.

The discourse on human nature has been a terrain of discursive skirmishes and theoretical explorations. Feminists are in the thick of discursive contestation and are proposing various frameworks. I am of the opinion that both biology and socio-cultural factors ought to be part of a feminist redefinition of "human nature." Biology affects women's (and men's) destinies, but, as Katherine Zappone puts it, *"it does not...affect the course of our lives by taking choices from us.* Instead, it's by the way in which those biological differences interact with other cultural, social and historical realities that human choice is restricted (or enhanced)."[36] Biology is not destiny; rather, "biology plus cultural construction and exploitation is destiny."[37]

What Zappone has articulated finds resonance in Audre Lorde's succinct point regarding difference. For Lorde, the problem is not our differences, but how we interpret (misname) and misuse those differences in the "service of separation and confusion."[38] Our biological make-up is given and surely has to be dealt with, but our interpretations of it make an enormous difference in how we experience our bodies. Our biological differences need not lead to sexism, but because of our patriarchal interpretive lenses our differences have been treated in sexist terms. In this regard, within the context of sexism, gender–not woman–is the primary category. It is through a faulty gender construction that women have suffered; it is on this construction-interpretation that we need to focus.

This shows that transgression of our genderized identities in a patriarchal-sexist society is a must, if men and women are to develop their full potentials as human beings. If racism creates and promotes "racialized identities," sexism creates and promotes "genderized identities." More particularly, our identities have been genderized according to patriarchal categories. As long as patriarchal ideology remains intact, we will continue to have distorted identities. We need to transgress the patriarchalization of our gender identities in order for men and women to develop identities established not on the hierarchization of sex, but according to egalitarian and holistic categories.

### Theology of Vulnerability and Connections: Beyond the "Self-Made Man"

Feminist theology, contrary to the perception of some, is not simply a theology done by and for women, but a theology articulated from the perspective of women's experience for the well-being of all. This certainly includes men. The healing of men requires the liberation and healing of women, and the healing of women requires the liberation of men.

As I pointed out earlier, the idea of a "self-made man" is a Great Lie, a lie from which men and those who have bought into this way of thinking need to be liberated. No one is a "self-made man"; every person comes into this world through relationship. When one claims and behaves otherwise, one breaks the web of relationship, which is tantamount to breaking the web of life. The consequences of denying our fundamental relatedness are deep, causing a rupture in our very being. And this rupture in our being always finds expressions in our day-to-day relationships with people, animals, and the natural environment. Hence, the liberation and healing of the "self-made man" requires an articulation of a theological anthropology of connections.

We are made for each other, and we cannot find our humanity apart from each other, even as other human beings have dehumanized us. The world around us, experienced through particular people and relationships, is not a barrier to be avoided. It is only because of it and through it, not in spite of it, that full human life is realized. From the Genesis account to the book of Revelation, either by way of looking backward to an Edenic place or imagining the "not yet" (the new heaven and new earth), we find a picture of the human who finds fulfillment only in the community of beings.

Finding God and realizing our humanity are experiences that are always mediated through our relationships with people and the natural world. It is not in being a "self-made man," free from personal attachments, that makes me truly human, but my deep connections. This is a challenge to all of us, but most especially to men who are socialized to the idea of the "self-made man." Connections, intimacy, and openness are not to be dreaded; they are not marks of weakness, which our sexist society makes us believe, but sources and marks of strength. Connections may hurt us, but we cannot be sustained and nourished without them. Intimacy requires openness and self-disclosure. This openness makes us vulnerable, but intimacy can only thrive on vulnerability. Intimacy, says Chittister,

> is a coming out of hiding that makes me vulnerable for the rest of my life…However it comes, there is nothing like it to help me take the measure of myself, to grow to full stature, to find mystery in the commonplace, and to retire forever from my attempts to be God.[39]

The most liberating way to respond to our vulnerability is not through obsessive denial, nor by closing all possible windows of vulnerability, but by accepting that vulnerability is part of our humanness. Human vulnerability is not the problem: The problem is the denial of our vulnerability and its attendant expression in the control over others, and in losing oneself to the control of others. As we recognize our vulnerability, we know that we must come together and support one another. It bonds us to each other to establish a league of life. Vulnerability, when taken as part of who we are, can turn the potential for narcissism into an avenue for service to the community. It can become a doorway for caring.

## Theological Anthropology of Embodiment

Women's experience of sexism in a patriarchal society has given birth to an intense reflection on the body. Among theologians, it has given birth to a theology of embodiment. Susan Wendell identifies some of the concerns that triggered feminists to theorize on the body subject.[40] One central concern of feminist thinking on the subject of body, Wendell notes, is women's struggle against men's control of women's bodies. Charlotte Bunch concurs with Wendell's observation: "The physical territory of this political struggle over what constitutes women's human rights is women's bodies."[41]

Men control women's bodies in many aspects, such as sexuality, reproduction, health care, cosmetics, pornography, the work place, etc. Patriarchal ideology basically sees women as sexual objects, fit to serve men's sexual needs and to bear and raise children for society. Beyond reproduction, men's control over women extends to the domain of pornography. Radical feminists note that pornography not only portrays women as sexual objects for men's gratification, it also eroticizes the pain and humiliation of women. Pornography, as Kathleen Barry puts it, is the "ideology of cultural sadism."[42] Furthermore, men's control of women's bodies extends to the work place. Women's bodies are exposed to pollution and industrial hazards. Women are not only imprisoned in homes, but also in offices, sweatshops, and factories.

Another concern Wendell identifies that has triggered women's reclamation of the body is the issue about men and women's alienation from their bodies and the ways this alienation contributes to women's oppression. Men who are alienated from their bodies and from their feelings project their alienation onto the female body. Wendell also notes that other feminists, instead of focusing on the body alienation, have focused on overcoming women's socio-cultural alienation from their bodies. Because patriarchal ideology has appropriated the authority to describe women's bodily experiences and has devalued women's bodies, a major feminist concern has been the reclamation and re-description of experiences unique to women.

These concerns–men's control of women's bodies, men and women's alienation from their bodies and the ways this alienation contributes to the oppression of women, and the valuing and re-description of experiences unique to women–have not only prompted a feminist discourse on the body and given birth to the theology of embodiment, but have also given shape to the task of re-description or theoretical reconstruction of the body.

Given these concerns, reconstruction must involve the articulation of women's rights as human rights and, more specifically, of the rights of women in relation to their bodies. In light of the alienation of men and women from their bodies, healing and liberation must involve the reuniting of men and women to their alienated bodily experiences and selves. And, in the context where women's bodies have been devalued and the interpretation of their experience has been controlled by men, reconstruction must involve the celebration of women's bodies and the re-articulation of women's experience from the perspective of women, not of men.

On the other hand, we must recognize that the move toward embodiment is ambivalent. Wendell points out that her experience of disability has led her to adopt a form of "bodily disembodiment," which has given her a sense of freedom from an ailing body. This notion of "bodily disembodiment," along lines of feminist interpretation, can be interpreted as a form of survival. As Wendell argues, "bodily disembodiment" is not a retreat to Cartesian dualism, but a response that is itself shaped by the experience of the body. One thing is clear, writes Wendell:

> We cannot speak only of reducing our alienation from our bodies, becoming more aware of them, and celebrating their strengths and pleasures; we must also talk about how to live with the suffering body, with that which cannot be noticed without pain, and that which cannot be celebrated without ambivalence.[43]

As much as we think of the body as a social construct that is shaped by discursive practices, the body is something literally physical. Biology is not destiny, but this does not erase the reality of the limits that the body imposes. Social constructionism that forgets biology does not help those who struggle daily in physical pain, and those who are fighting for work benefits because of certain physical ailments. This is not to discount the constructed nature of what we call biological givens, but to give a warning and, perhaps, a corrective.[44] Feminists themselves have expressed the danger of idealizing the body, and erasing the reality of lived bodies as social constructionism is emphasized. Susan Bordo makes this point: "The deconstructionist erasure of the body is not effected, as in the Cartesian version, by a trip to 'nowhere,' but in resistance to the recognition that one is always *somewhere*, and limited."[45]

Theological anthropology constructed from the experience and perspective of women enables us to see the body as an avenue for God's grace. We are what we are because of our bodies. We do not simply possess our bodies; we are our bodies. We must celebrate the pleasure that the body brings, and work for the liberation of women's bodies from negative images. The tyranny of the Barbie-type body, slimness and styling according to the dominant male gaze, needs to be dismantled and overcome. Theological reconstruction must take into account the denigrated women's bodies and the denigrated woman's image.

## Image of Women, Image of God

The notion of the image of God is still considered by feminist theologians as very important to the anthropological reconstruction of the devalued and denigrated woman's image. But this is not and cannot be a simple "me too" theological claim, for the notion of the image of God in a patriarchal and sexist society is itself problematic. Yes, women must reclaim their being created in the image of God, but there are questions that cannot be bypassed: What images of God do we embrace in the context of a patriarchal and sexist society? Whose image is God's image in a patriarchal society? These questions must be asked first, if women are not to be continually colonized by male images of God.

That women–not just men–are created in God's image is a crucial discursive claim in the context in which men have appropriated the image of God solely for themselves. Mary McClintock Fulkerson points out that this is not a simple "me too" claim, which simply absorbs women into the patriarchal domain, but an anti-hegemonic-destabilizing-multi-pronged move, in which poststructuralism is very insightful.[46] The claim that women are created in the image of God is not a simple assertion that women, like men, are created in the image of God; this assertion destabilizes the male claim. Men cannot be the image of God because men's image is constructed on the pernicious system of significations that denigrates women and elevates men. By no means does this make a claim, contends Fulkerson, that "woman is the real image of God; it is not even to say that both are." Rather, she continues, "in this particular set of discursive arrangements, in this context of male dominance, what the reigning discursive system means by *man* is not the *imago Dei*."[47] This destabilizing move must be executed if we are to speak about women being created in God's image.

In the chapter on classism and the economy, Meeks pointed out that our view of God as infinite has functioned, most often without our awareness, as an expression of market production and consumption pushed to the infinite. What Meeks has articulated for the economy resonates with feminists' critique of God in relation to patriarchy and sexism. The attributes we give to God–omnipotence, transcendence, impassibility, self-containment–are the same as the attributes of the real man–"self-made man"–in a patriarchal society.

The doctrine of God, more specifically the notion of the image of God, sheds light on our image of the self. This is because God is not only a subject of reflection and ultimate religious devotion, but also a symbolic superstructure. Our notion of God expresses who we are, our pains, and our longings. More particularly, the image of God expresses what the self idolizes or deifies; thus, our image of God is an image of our own genesis.

Catherine Keller, in her famous work *From a Broken Web: Separation, Sexism, and the Self,* gives an excellent account of the connection between the self and our images of God.[48] In a context dominated by the patriarchal superstructure, Keller points out that the image of God is a supreme expression of the male's self-desire. Patriarchal selfhood projects a God who is self-sufficient, self-originating, and needs no one for self-fulfillment (aseity). Divine aseity or self-sufficiency also links with impassionability, for God can only be self-sufficient if God is impassionable. If God were affected emotionally, God would not be the pure active cause or the Unmoved Mover. Likewise, divine impassionability is only possible if God is immutable; thus, we have the notion of divine immutability. But how can we talk of a loving and compassionate God that the tradition speaks about? The church fathers responded to this question with the idea that God loves but without passion; God is compassionate without passion. St. Augustine's lines from the *Confessions* speak of this kind of love: "You love, but with no storm of passion; you are jealous, but with no anxious fear; you repent, but do not grieve."[49]

Not only the church fathers', but our own images of God continue to reflect the patriarchal ego. It is difficult for us to imagine that God could embody expressions associated with the feminine. To those who think God needs others for self-fulfillment, Sören Kierkegaard could only hurl the epithet "stupid."[50] It is "stupidity" for one to think that God is dependent on others for God's self-fulfillment; it is the absurdity of all absurdity to even imagine that God could be otherwise. "It would otherwise be a highly embarrassing thing to be a creator," says Kierkegaard, "if the result was that the creator came to depend upon the creature. On the contrary, God may require everything of every human being, everything and for nothing."[51] In a patriarchal culture this God can only take the pronoun "He." Keller can only say that the patriarchal God is the "absolute instance of the traditional sin," a God who is more "curved upon himself" than merely a separative supersubject. "Embarrassed by feeling, could this deity be other than a magnified He?" Keller asks rhetorically.[52]

Our task of interpreting the image of God can only progress if it goes hand in hand with the struggle to dismantle patriarchy and sexism. The task of articulating an image of God that is liberating for women is the other side of women's struggle to define their self-identities.[53] Positive self-imaging of women is, in turn, the other side of seeking a liberating image of God. This process does not involve a mere mining of the scriptures and traditions to find a previously unnoticed image of God. Instead, the quest for a positive image involves relentless mirroring, exposing of distortions, and following the clues to where women's pain leads us.

### Can a Male Savior Save Women? Can a Male Savior Save Men?

If the image of God is not unambiguous, does not Jesus the Christ, as the full incarnation of God, provide us the clearest picture of the positive image we are seeking? Just as the image of God can epitomize the patriarchal male self-image, so can the man Jesus of Nazareth and the cacophony of interpretations surrounding him. Nevertheless, a Christian theological account of anthropology cannot bypass christology, for Jesus occupies a central place in Christian theology.

Feminists' struggle to interpret Jesus in ways liberating to women is articulated in the question: "Can a male savior save women?" Some have definitely said "no," and are calling themselves post-Christian feminists. On the other hand, many are trying to construct a christology that moves away from patriarchy and sexism. How successful this move is, is a matter of serious controversy. I would like to focus on the interpretations of those who are working to reinterpret christology.

Elizabeth Johnson puts forth the position of those who are convinced that christology can be salvaged from its patriarchal milieu: "The image of Christ does not lie in sexual similarity to the human man Jesus, but in coherence with the narrative shape of his compassionate, liberating life in the world, through the power of the Spirit."[54] I agree in general with this statement, but not without raising hermeneutics of suspicion. While it is easy to say that Christ's image does not lie in Jesus' maleness, it is much more difficult to disentangle our association of Christ with maleness. Therefore, I always entertain doubts about attempts to cleanse Jesus of his patriarchal upbringing.

My argument against racism can be applied here. If I can say that there is nothing inherently wrong in having a white skin, I can also say, like many feminists, that there is nothing inherently wrong in Jesus' maleness. So what if Jesus is a male? After all, we may argue, though he was a male he embodied a compassionate and liberating life. However, we cannot simply say "so what" of Jesus' maleness, even if his life was counter to patriarchal ideology and sexist practices. We cannot say "so what" of Jesus' maleness, for being a male in a male-dominated society is already a privilege. If in the case of white racism I made the point that even those whites who are fighting courageously against racism benefit from being white, why can we not say that Jesus benefited from being a male in a patriarchal society? We may say that Jesus was not sexist, but he did not have to suffer from sexism like women of his time simply by virtue of being a male. Why is it that in the so-called divine scheme of things God's decisive incarnation was in the man Jesus—and not a woman? Would we not raise the suspicion that this in itself is an expression of a patriarchal bias projected onto the divine mystery?

In spite of, or because of, the serious questions I raise about Jesus in a patriarchal society, the Jesus of the Christian scriptures remains a powerful image of what it means to live differently and to live humanly. Jesus shows us what it means to live in a liberating way and to live with integrity in the midst of the brutal reality that defines our world. Nevertheless, because it is hard to dislodge Christness from maleness in a patriarchal society, I believe there is a need to expand our image of Christness. If Allen Warrior, from an American Indian perspective, could say that no amount of excellent biblical scholarship can change the exodus-conquest-elect narrative, I also say that no amount of good argument about the nonidentification of Christness with Jesus' maleness would suffice to dislodge identification.[55] Symbols, representations, and narratives have a pervasive, encompassing, controlling, and enduring power that a scrupulous argument or a scholarly treatise does not have.

For the above reason I see the necessity of enlarging our symbols, representations, and narratives of Christ. It is not my intention to diminish the significance of Jesus of Nazareth, but to put him in a proper perspective in relation to Christ. The Christ (divine logos) was "truly" and "fully" embodied in Jesus of Nazareth, but the "fullness" of Christ is more than what can be contained in one historical person. Jesus as the Christ is "totally divine" (*totus Dei*) but not the "totality" of the divine (*totum Dei*).[56]

Rita Nakashima Brock articulates a notion of Christ that is not limited to the historical Jesus of Nazareth, pointing instead to the ongoing possibility of a Christa/community in which we can participate as did Jesus. Brock makes the point that "Jesus participates centrally in this Christa/Community, but he neither brings erotic power into being nor controls it. He is brought into being through it and participates in the co-creation of it."[57] The Christa/community is much larger than Jesus, and Jesus, though a central figure, is nourished by the Christa/community. To illustrate the relationship of Jesus with the Christa/community, Brock uses the metaphor of the "whitecap on a wave." This is how she describes it:

> Jesus is like the whitecap on a wave. The whitecap is momentarily set off from the swell that is pushing it up, making us notice it. But the visibility of the whitecap, which draws our attention, rests on the enormous pushing power of the sea—of its power to push with life-giving labor, to buoy up all lives, and to unite diverse shores with its restless energy. The sea becomes monstrous and chaotically destructive when we try to control it, and its life-giving power is denied. Jesus' power lies with the great swells of the ocean without which the white foam is not brought to visibility. To understand the fullness of erotic power we must look to the ocean which is the whole and compassionate being, including ourselves.[58]

Peter Hodgson and Mark K. Taylor offer a similar emphasis by arguing for a Christ gestalt or a christic shape that is much larger than can be contained in the life of Jesus of Nazareth, though with distinctive nuances. For Hodgson, the person of Jesus continues to play a central role in mediating the gestalt of God in history, which is the gestalt of love in freedom, but Jesus' personal identity did not exhaust the shape, which is intrinsically communal.[59]

Taylor, likewise, proposes an understanding of Christ that accentuates the intersubjective and the communal dynamic. He considers "Jesus as a necessary but not the only necessary element of the Christ dynamic," the shape of which is "socio-cultural dynamic of 'reconciliatory emancipation.'" For Taylor, Jesus' role in the christic gestalt or socio-cultural dynamic of reconciliatory emancipation is like that of a leaven in relation to the dough. As a leaven, "Jesus is a necessary fermenting ingredient in the divine gestalt in history," but other ingredients are also necessary.[60]

Now, how about men? Can a male savior save men? This has to be asked, for not to do so is to presume a male savior is only problematic for women. A Jesus seen through the patriarchal culture, an incarnation of a patriarchal God whose divinity was largely a "phallic definition" of a self-sufficient, all-powerful, and impassionable God, cannot be liberating for men either.[61] Thus, Jesus must also be liberated from our patriarchal lenses so that we can see Jesus, not just as a "combination" of masculine and feminine fixed traits, but as sexually whole, one who is fully in touch with his phallic energy. James Nelson is very articulate on this point:

> What is to be a man? To be fully masculine is one of the two ways given to humanity of being fully human. To be fully masculine does not mean embracing something of gender foreignness, strange to our own male bodily experience. Rather, it means embracing the fullness of the revelation that comes through our male bodies. There is good phallic energy in us which we can claim and celebrate. It is the earthy phallus: deep, moist, and sensuous, primitive and powerful...It is soft, vulnerable, and receptive. It is a peaceful power. It knows that size is not merely quantitative; more truly, it is that strength of mutuality which can be enriched by other life without losing its own center.[62]

### Integrated and Liberated Womanity/Humanity

Revisioning a liberated humanity and, more particularly, liberated womanity, involves transgressing images of the self constructed under the cross of patriarchy and sexism. I travel along with feminist interpreters who raise questions about the common assumptions we make regarding characteristics we label inherently male or inherently female. Many of the characteristics we so label are developed through socialization in a patriarchal and sexist society. Biology certainly plays an important part. Women's menstruation and reproduction remind us of this. But many of the dimensions of gender that cause people suffering are human social constructions.

In a context in which the self develops and gets defined in binary opposition with the other, reimagining the new self requires the reclamation of those aspects considered as the natural possession of the other. Androgyny, I believe, is not the solution. Instead, I go along with those theologians who espouse the idea that women and men, even in their literal biological differences, have the capacity for wholeness. Women are not only relational but are also capable of rational modes of thought, just as men are capable of intimate mutual relationship and relational modes of thought. It appears to me, as suggested by others, that the direction is toward the development of an "integrated self and an integrated social order."[63] I will develop this idea of an integrated self and an integrated social order in chapter 8.

## Resistance: Living and "Singing for Our Lives"[64]

The journey toward a new humanity liberated from the evil of sexism is long and arduous. Sometimes we experience setbacks and at other times breakthroughs. Either way, we are not alone. Stories of courage abound that can help sustain and inspire us. In these stories we see a new humanity coming to expression. We see this new humanity coming to expression among women who, in the face of seemingly insurmountable odds, sing over and over again in rallies a song composed by Naomi Littlebear:

> You can't kill the spirit.
> It's like a mountain.
> Old and strong, it lives on and on.[65]

We can discern this new humanity coming to expression among women who, after years of oppression, finally stood their ground with a thunderous cry: "We cannot live without our lives." There are many women who "still feel uneasy about uttering that cry aloud," says Barbara Deming, but "that is what women now are going to keep on crying: 'I cannot live without my life! I cannot live without my soul!'"[66]

We can see this new humanity coming to expression among women who continue to laugh and sing for their lives in the face of the durability of the forces of closure. Singing has frequently been used by women throughout the world to mourn, strengthen solidarity, articulate grievances, and sometimes to pass on secret information. One powerful example happened in Nigeria. In November 1929, Nigerian women streamed into Oloko, Nigeria, from throughout Owerri Province. Word was sent via the Ibo women's network that it was time to "sit on" Okugo, the arrogant warrant chief of the Oloko Native Court during the British colonial rule of Nigeria. "Sitting on a man" is a figurative expression of a traditional process of punishment during which women gather in front of a man's home to present their grievances through songs, dances, and chants. After several days of protest, Okugo was arrested, tried, and convicted. News of this victory spread through women's networks and inspired other women throughout the region to organize "sit-ons" against their local warrant chiefs.[67]

Around forty years after the "sit-on" in Oloko, Nigeria, Vietnamese poet Hien Luong described the use of songs for solidarity and defiance. In 1969, Hien Luong was one of the female political prisoners at Con Son Island. The treatment of the prisoners was terribly inhumane. They were kept in "tiger cages" that, if they survived, would paralyze them for life. Hien Luong and other women defied their jailers by singing songs of struggle and liberation. The guards would beat them, demanding to know who among the women were singing. But the women continued singing with even stronger voices and sweeter harmony. Even Hien Luong marveled at "such a power in such frail bodies."[68]

Stories of courage, ultimate defiance, and hope are growing in number everyday. These stories are rising from the soil fertilized by women's experience of oppression all over the world. They are poignant as well as empowering in their honesty. We need to hear these stories, says Alice Walker, "because the times are so hard and anger is so deep, our sorrow so pervasive, and our patience so thin."[69] These stories are snapshots of slow miracles that surround us everyday. They are testaments of a new humanity struggling to be born.

## Notes

[1]Mark Kline Taylor, *Remembering Esperanza: A Cultural-Political Theology for North American Praxis* (Maryknoll, N.Y: Orbis Books, 1990), 111.

[2]Aruna Gnanadason, *No Longer a Secret: The Church and Violence Against Women*, revised ed.(Geneva: WCC Publications, 1997), 9–10.

[3]Joan D. Chittister, *Heart of Flesh: A Feminist Spirituality for Women and Men* (Grand Rapids, Mich.: William B. Eerdmans Publishing Company, 1998), 25.

[4]M. Shawn Copeland, "The Interaction of Racism, Sexism, and Classism in Women's Exploitation," in *Women, Work, and Poverty*, Concilium, ed. Elisabeth Schüssler Fiorenza and Anne Carr (Edinburgh: T. & T. Clark, 1987), 21.

[5]Allan G. Johnson, *The Gender Knot: Unraveling Our Patriarchal Legacy* (Philadelphia: Temple University Press, 1997), 5.

[6]Ibid., 6–7.

[7]See Chung Hyun Kyung, *Struggle to Be the Sun Again* (Maryknoll, N.Y.: Orbis Books, 1990), 24–25.

[8]Zillah Eisenstein, *Hatreds: Racialized and Sexualized Conflicts in the 21st Century* (New York: Routledge, 1996), 151.

[9]See Nawal El Saadawi, *Memories from the Women's Prison* (Berkeley, Calif.: University of California Press, 1983), cited in Eisenstein, *Hatreds*, 137–170; Juliette Minces, *Veiled Women in Islam*, trans. S. M. Berrett (Watertown, Mass.: Blue Crane Books, 1994).

[10]Christine Smith, *Preaching as Weeping, Confession, and Resistance* (Louisville: Westminster/John Knox Press, 1992), 68.

[11]Delores Williams, *Sisters in the Wilderness: The Challenge of Womanist God-Talk* (Maryknoll, N.Y.: Orbis Books, 1993).

[12]Nancy W. Gabalac and Mary Ballou, *A Feminist Position on Mental Health* (Springfield, Ill.: Charles C. Thomas Publishers, 1985), 79–97.

[13]Herb Golberg, cited in Taylor, *Remembering Esperanza*, 96–97.

[14]Warren Farrell, *The Myth of Male Power* (New York: Berkeley Books, 1993), 18, cited in Johnson, *Gender Knot*, 175.

[15]Johnson, *Gender Knot*, 175.

[16]Mark Gerzon, *A Choice of Heroes: The Changing Faces of American Manhood* (Boston: Houghton Mifflin Company, 1982), 126–127.

[17]Robert Strikwerda and Larry May, "Male Friendship and Intimacy," in *Rethinking Masculinity: Philosophical Explorations in Light of Feminism*, ed. Larry May and Robert Strikwerda (Lanham, Md.: Rowman and Littlefield Publishers, Inc., 1992), 103.

[18]Chittister, *Heart of Flesh*, 27.

[19]Sharon Ringe, "Reading from Context to Context: Contributions of a Feminist Hermeneutic to Theologies of Liberation," in *Lift Every Voice: Constructing Christian Theologies from the Underside*, ed. Susan Brooks Thistlethwaite and Mary Potter Engel (San Francisco: Harper and Row, Publishers, 1990), 286.

[20]Tertullian, *De Cult. Fem.*, 1.1. See Rosemary Radford Ruether, *Sexism and God-Talk: Toward a Feminist Theology* (Boston: Beacon Press, 1983), 167.

[21]Ruether, *Sexism and God-Talk: Toward a Feminist Theology*, 95.

[22]Linda Maloney, "The Argument for Women's Difference in Classical Philosophy and Early Christianity," in *The Special Nature of Women*, ed. Anne Carr and Elisabeth Schüssler Fiorenza (London: SCM; Philadelphia: Trinity Press International, 1991), 45.

[23]Martin Luther, *Lectures on Genesis*, Gen. 2:18, in *Luther's Works*, vol. 1, ed. Jaroslav Pelikan (St. Louis: Concordia Publishing House, 1958), 115.

[24]See Jane Dempsey Douglass, *Women, Freedom, and Calvin* (Philadelphia: Westminster Press, 1985), 24–41; Ruether, *Sexism and God-Talk*, 98.

[25]Hedwig Meyer-Wilmes, "Woman's Nature and Feminine Identity: Theological Legitimations and Feminist Questions," in *Women, Work, and Poverty*, 97.

[26]Ruether, *Sexism and God-Talk*, 126.

[27]Johnson, *Gender Knot*, 30.

[28]Christine Smith, "Sin and Evil in Feminist Theology," *Theology Today* 50/2 (July 1993): 208–19.

[29]Valerie Saiving, "The Human Situation," in *Womanspirit Rising*, ed. Carol Christ and Judith Plaskow (San Francisco: Harper & Row, 1979), 37.

[30]Judith Plaskow, *Sex, Sin and Grace: Women's Experience and the Theologies of Reinhold Niebuhr and Paul Tillich* (Washington: University Press of America, 1980).

[31]Mary Potter Engel, "Sin, Evil, and Violation of the Vulnerable," in *Lift Every Voice*, 152–64.

[32]See Dorothee Sölle, *Thinking About God: An Introduction to Theology* (Philadelphia: Trinity Press International; London: SCM Press, 1990), 148.

[33]Beverly Wildung Harrison, "The Power of Anger in the Work of Love," in *Making the Connections: Essays in Feminist Social Ethics*, ed. Carol S. Robb (Boston: Beacon Press, 1985), 14.

[34]Ibid., 14.

[35]Engel, "Sin, Evil, and Violation of the Vulnerable," in *Lift Every Voice*, 164.

[36]Katherine Zappone, "'Woman's Special Nature': A Different Horizon for Theological Anthropology," in *Special Nature of Women*, 91.

[37]See Taylor, *Remembering Esperanza*, 99.

[38]Audre Lorde, *Sister Outsider: Essays and Speeches* (Freedom, Calif.: The Crossing Press, 1984), 115.

[39]Chittister, *Heart of Flesh*, 148.

[40]Susan Wendell, *The Rejected Body: Feminist Philosophical Reflections on Disabilities* (New York and London: Routledge, 1996), 166–170.

[41]Charlotte Bunch, "Women's Rights as Human Rights: Toward a Revision of Human Rights," in Charlotte Bunch and Roxanna Carillo, *Gender Violence: A Development and Human Rights Issue* (Rutgers, N.J.: Center for Women's Global Leadership, 1991), 8, cited in Eisenstein, *Hatreds*, 144.

[42]Kathleen Barry, cited in Alison M. Jaggar, *Feminist Politics and Human Nature* (Totowa, N.J.: Rowman and Allanheld, 1983), 265.

[43]Wendell, *Rejected Body*, 179.

[44]See Donna Haraway, *Simians, Cyborgs, and Women: The Reinvention of Nature* (New York: Routledge, 1991); and Haraway, "A Manifesto for Cyborgs: Science, Technology, and Socialist Feminism in the 1980s," in *Feminism/Postmodernism*, ed. Linda J. Nicholson (New York: Routledge, 1990), 190–233, cited in Wendell, *Rejected Body*, 169.

[45]Susan Bordo, cited in Wendell, *Rejected Body*, 169.

[46]Mary McClintock Fulkerson, "Contesting the Gendered Subject: A Feminist Account of the *Imago Dei*," in *Horizons in Feminist Theology: Identity, Tradition, and Norms*, ed. Rebecca S. Chopp and Sheila Greeve Davaney (Minneapolis: Fortress Press, 1997), 114.

[47]Ibid.

[48]Catherine Keller, *From a Broken Web: Separation, Sexism, and Self* (Boston: Beacon Press, 1986).

[49]*The Confessions of St. Augustine*, trans. Rex Warner (New York: New American Library, 1963), Book 1, Chapter 4.

[50]Søren Kierkegaard, *Concluding Unscientific Postscript*, trans. D. Swenson and W. Lowrie (Princeton, N.J.: Princeton University Press, 1941), 122. Also see Keller, *From a Broken Web*, 35.

[51]Ibid.

[52]Keller, *From a Broken Web*, 38.

[53]See Christie Neuger, "Feminist Pastoral Theology and Pastoral Counseling: A Work in Progress," *Journal of Pastoral Theology* 2 (Summer 1992): 53, for the relationship between image of God and self-understanding and its application for pastoral counseling.

[54]Elizabeth Johnson, *She Who Is: The Mystery of God in Feminist Theological Discourse* (New York: Crossroad, 1992), 73.

[55]Cf. Robert Allen Warrior, "A Native American Perspective: Canaanites, Cowboys, and Indians," in *Voices from the Margin: Interpreting the Bible in the Third World,* ed. R. S. Sugirtharajah (Maryknoll, N.Y.: Orbis Books, 1991), 287–95.

[56]John A. T. Robinson, *Truth Is Two-Eyed* (London: SCM Press, 1979), 104, 120, cited in Paul Knitter, *Jesus and the Other Names: Christian Mission and Global Responsibility* (Maryknoll, N.Y.: Orbis Books, 1996), 74.

[57]Rita Nakashima Brock, *Journeys by Heart: A Christology of Erotic Power* (New York: Crossroad Publishing Company, 1988), 52.

[58]Ibid., 105–6.

[59]Peter Hodgson, *Winds of the Spirit: A Constructive Christian Theology* (Louisville: Westminster John Knox Press, 1994), 250–55.

[60]Taylor, *Remembering Esperanza,* 151, 172.

[61]See James Nelson, *The Intimate Connection: Male Sexuality, Masculine Spirituality* (Philadelphia: Westminster Press, 1988), 109.

[62]Ibid., 110.

[63]Ruether, *Sexism and God-Talk,* 113.

[64]See Pam McAllister, *You Can't Kill the Spirit* (Philadelphia and Santa Cruz, Calif.: New Society Publishers, 1988).

[65]Ibid., 16, citing Naomi Littlebear.

[66]Ibid., 149, citing Barbara Deming.

[67]Ibid., 121–24.

[68]Ibid., 131.

[69]Ibid., back cover endorsement.

# CHAPTER 6

# Reimagining Anthropology in Response to Racism

## Encountering God in One's Racial Identity

Intertwining with classism and sexism is racism. Like classism and sexism, racism has been with us so long that it has acquired the status of the always-already-there. Our perception of its being always-already-there may have been deepened by our encounter with the resiliency of racism even after many years of struggle to dismantle it. Like a virus, it is hard to beat racism because of its ability to adopt different expressions. Moreover, it is entrenched in our habits of thinking and in our institutions. One shot won't kill the virus of racism. But neither would new and stronger medicine guarantee the death of the racist virus.

The virus of racism is not only getting smarter or becoming cure-resistant, it is on the offensive, assaulting old gains and strengthening racist structures and practices. The tide of racism is not only rising in the U.S. against people of color, but against the Turks in Germany, Polish miners in France and Belgium, Surinamese and Indonesians in the Netherlands, Afro-Caribbeans and Asians in Great Britain, North Africans and Africans from Sub-Saharan Africa in France, and Asians in Australia.[1] As the dominant race feels increasingly threatened by the growing number of the racial others and the influx of new immigrants and refugees into previously white enclaves, more brutal expressions of racism are to be expected.

### When Our Faces Are at the Bottom of the Well:[2] Realism, Hope, and Ultimate Defiance

When in spite of many years of struggle, racism seems to have not gone away, it is easy to become discouraged, pessimistic, or cynical. In my own life, I have experienced those moments when I feel like the writer of Ezekiel; my "bones are dried up" and my "hope is lost" (Ezek. 37:11). Racism has been with us, and it is difficult not to believe in its permanence. We must face the durability and pervasiveness of racism squarely. This is a bitter pill that we must swallow, if we are to take full account of our hopes and struggles. Derrick Bell articulates this bitter pill in reference to blacks in the U.S.:

> Blacks will never gain full equality in this country: Even those Herculean efforts we hail as successful will produce no more than temporary "peaks of progress," short-lived victories that slide into irrelevance as racial patterns adapt in ways to maintain white dominance. This is a hard-to-accept fact that all history verifies. We must acknowledge it, not as a sign of submission, but as an act of ultimate defiance.[3]

Acknowledging the durability and pervasiveness of racism is not intended as a note of pessimism, as Bell points out, but as a note of resistance or of ultimate defiance. Like Korean women who are forced to wait but have transformed waiting into an act of resistance, so too, says Bell, is recognizing the fact of the pervasiveness of racism is an "act of ultimate defiance." More specifically, Bell wants us to see that involvement in the struggle is a victory in itself. In his words, the "essence of life fulfilled–a succession of actions undertaken in righteous causes–is a victory itself."[4]

Shawn Donaldson, interpreting Bell, speaks of struggling for the sake of struggle, or making the "struggle as an end rather than a means to an end."[5] I am sympathetic to Donaldson's interpretation that struggle should not be viewed as a means, but I have a different nuance. Instead of an either-or approach, which puts struggle as a means to an end or as an end in itself, I see the relationship of means and end as constitutive of each other. The struggle is not simply the process that is directed toward the goal (liberation), but the process is constitutive of the goal. The struggle itself is an experience of victory–of liberation–and the experience of liberation is expressed through the struggle.

As previous generations did, we must continue to sing "We Shall Overcome." I would suggest that this song is not so much about landing someday in an Edenic place, but an expression of ultimate defiance and ultimate hope. We must be grateful for the accomplishments of the past, but we can only be truly grateful to the monuments of the past by turning these monuments into movements–movements of resistance and transformation against racism. The struggle must continue!

## "I Don't See Color": Denying Racism

"I don't see color" is a statement we often hear from people who belong to the dominant racial group of any society. This statement, while appearing innocent and most often expressive of good intentions, shows that the speaker belongs to the dominant color of society. His or her skin color has not been the occasion of the pain of racism. For those who are victimized by racism, as in the case of people of color in the United States, color is a category they have to deal with every day of their lives, and white society always reminds them of that. They cannot choose not to deal with the issue of color, because they are confronted with it whether they like it or not. There is no choice.

Not seeing color in a racist society is itself an expression of the reality of racism. Its denial is itself a proof of its existence. In white America it is a mark of white privilege. One may say, "How can it be a mark of privilege when I do not even feel that I am privileged?" Precisely! Privilege becomes truly a privilege when we do not notice it or, in a much sharper way, when we do not have to assert or claim it. Robert Terry puts it pungently: "To be white in America is not to have to think about it."[6]

Even those whites who have chosen to think about racism and who actively participate in the struggle against it do so from the vantage point of white privilege. "White privilege," argues Shelley Park, "also extends to the ability to choose when, where and how to fight racism and who to 'invite' into the struggle."[7] Whites even dictate the manner and tone in which they will listen to the testimony of a person of color. Several times in courses I have taught, I assigned readings from African American authors that express the fire of anger. My purpose was to let my students know how deeply hurt black people are. But, some of my white students chose not to listen to the deep pain the authors shared because it was expressed in an angry tone. White students who do not want to deal with the materials may even decide to drop the course. They would listen only if blacks would express their pain over racism in a nice and gentle way. Unlike whites, people of color do not have the luxury of choosing when and where to fight or not fight against racism. They live with the pain of racism running through their blood vessels, as when a boy, with a look of innocence and curiosity, asked me: "Is your blood brown?" With quickness borne out of my few years of struggle against racism in the "land of the free and home of the brave," I retorted: "How about you? Is your blood white?"

Noncognizance of the color dynamics that affect relationships between human beings is not a simple matter of forgetting, but a deep-seated social disease. It is about the colonization of one's social consciousness by the virus of racism. The virus of racism has made whites "color-blind." White racism, according to Eugene Victor Wolfenstein, is a

> mental disorder, an ocular disease, an opacity of the soul that is articulated with unintended irony in the idea of 'color blindness.' To be color blind is the highest form of racial false consciousness, a denial of both difference and domination. But one doesn't have

to be color blind to be blinded by white racism...Black people see themselves in white mirrors, white people see black people as their own photographic negatives.[8]

"Color-blindness" is a denial of difference and domination. Not seeing color in a white racist society is not simply a matter of being neutral or apolitical; it both partial and political. It is partially and politically tilted in favor of the ruling racial group. It attempts to portray a neutral playing field in a society that fosters asymmetrical relationships along racial lines. "Color-blindness" not only denies the relationship between race and the social conditions that exist in society, it acts as a form of race subordination by its denial of the context of white domination and the subordination of people of color. "Color-blindness" is whiteness that assimilates, appropriates, and devours racial others, excreting that which it cannot digest.

Not seeing color is an attempt to portray an image of impartiality (whiteness) but, ultimately, says Paul Kivel, "this disclaimer prevents us from taking responsibility for challenging racism because we believe that people who see color are the problem."[9] Part of dismantling racism and white privilege in the U.S. is for whites to realize their "color-blindness" and to take full responsibility for their whiteness.

### Racism Is More than Prejudice: That's Not All There Is to It

The pervasiveness of racism and its connections with other "isms" suggest that it is more than prejudice or bigotry. All of us have prejudices. By prejudice, I mean the distorted ideas and attitudes we hold in relation to other groups even when they are contrary to facts. To be prejudiced is to oversimplify the complex traits of certain groups in order to catalog them into our frame of mind. It may often appear in negative stereotypes, but even when it takes a positive tone (i.e., "Black women are strong"), prejudice is still dangerous.[10] One may further classify bigotry, as Sharon Welch has done, as a form of extreme prejudice.[11] Through bigotry, a certain group entertains a condescending attitude and even a deep hatred against certain racial groups; nevertheless, bigotry is not the same as racism.

"Racial prejudice," says Barndt, "is transformed into racism when one group becomes so powerful and dominant that it is able to control another group and to enforce the controlling group's biases."[12] Simply put, prejudice plus power equals racism. More appropriately, following Welch, prejudice plus "collective and structural power" equals racism.[13]

The power to enforce a racial group's biases or prejudices needs to be understood not merely as a naked imposition of force from above, though it certainly includes this. This power is always a collective and structural power, and it works through societal institutions, involving economics, politics, and culture. Through societal institutions and mechanisms, the dominant group codifies, perpetuates, and imposes its biases and prejudices.

Through its cultural machineries, this group assigns values to real or imaginary differences in order to justify its privileges. Often, through "visceral taxonomy" and on grounds of "putative biological inferiority," it elevates and justifies its experiences, judgments, and behavior over others.[14]

When we construe racism in this fashion, it simply does not make sense to talk about "reverse discrimination" or "reverse racism" against the dominant race. Yes, all have prejudices, whether one belongs to the dominant group or to the marginalized groups. Nonetheless, while all have prejudices, it is not true that all have the same power to oppress and exploit systemically. To say that people of color are just as racist as whites in the United States is a denial of racism. It is an attempt to deflect attention away from the perpetrators by leveling the racial field. African Americans, Hispanics, Native Americans, and Asian Americans cannot be racist even as they have prejudices against whites and other people of color, because they do not have the systemic power to carry out their prejudices against the white populace *as a group*.[15] This does not mean that they do not manifest forms of racist behavior–a behavior they have internalized from white racism and primarily directed toward other people of color. However, even though one group of people of color may express racist attitudes and practices toward other people of color, it does not have the power to systematically oppress the other.

People of color cannot be racist in a white society: They cannot systematically oppress whites because they do not have the systemic power to impose their prejudices. This point seems very clear to me, yet it is difficult for most whites to understand. I do not suggest that whites are not intellectually capable of understanding that people of color do not have systemic power to oppress whites *as a group*, but it is difficult for most whites to grasp this point because it threatens their security. Poignantly, bell hooks raises the point:

> Why is it so difficult for many white folks to understand that racism is oppressive not because white folks have prejudicial feelings about blacks (they could have such feelings and leave us alone) but because it is a system that promotes domination and subjugation? The prejudicial feelings some blacks may express about whites are in no way linked to a system of domination that affords us any power to coercively control the lives and well-being of white folks. That needs to be understood.[16]

Collective, structural power working through established social institutions transforms bigotry into racism, a systemic disease. It is not a simple imposition of power by one group of individuals over another. Racism creates a built-in system of privilege for some but a built-in system of disadvantage for others. And, because of its systemic character, it means that eliminating racism requires a radical change in our institutions, our ways of thinking, and our ways of dwelling.

As a structural disease, racism is beyond the purview of good intentions. A white person in the U.S. may have good intentions or may even be active in the struggle to dismantle racism; still, as a white person, he or she benefits from racism. We have been led to believe that racism refers to particular discriminatory acts or acts of violence. While it certainly includes these aspects, Peggy McIntosh demonstrates that certain white privileges are not even thought of as such by whites.[17] Racism affects every aspect of our lives, all the time, wherever we are, whether people of color are present or not.

### The Social Construction of Racism and Its Many Faces

Racism's always-already-thereness makes it seem completely natural. It is pervasively present, surreptitiously effective, and nefariously ruthless. In spite of its natural appearance, racism is a social construct. This means racism can also be deconstructed and dismantled, though the process is terribly exacting and never ending. We continue the struggle against racism not only as an act of defiance, but also because we understand that racism is a social construct; it is not something innate in human beings. Though it seems to be always-already-there, it is a product of history.

Racism is a historic and cultural belief, says Benjamin Bowser, which is "learned, justified, and reinforced by cultural and institutional practices."[18] Without this tri-level organization, individual racist acts would not be perpetuated over time. Racism is a socially derived and learned behavior constructed in response to specific conditions and circumstances, often to promote the interest of the dominant racial group. Racism has developed into its complex form because it has served the interest of the dominant racial group: It has obscured the dominant group's privileged position and redirected the people's attention to the racial others as the problem. If racism evolved in response to various factors and circumstances, its dismantling would involve a whole range of historical factors.

In the case of Europe, racism developed and was refined in the context of a "Fortress Europe." Louis Kushnick asserts that Europe, particularly the countries identified with the European Community (EC),

> has been constructing a new European identity while it has been constructing the barriers of Fortress Europe. This new identity is a racialized identity. Europe is being defined in terms of its imperialist past, with its civilizing mission in opposition to the Third World and the countries of the periphery, and in terms of Christianity in opposition to Islam.[19]

This racist ideological construction has its concrete expression in racially discriminatory policies and practices involving such matters as immigration, police, the criminal justice system, health, education, and housing. Kushnick names this as "state racism." What is happening at the state level (state racism) resonates with "popular racism" or with increasing discrimination and violence perpetrated by people of the dominant race against the perceived racial others. State racism and popular racism mutually reinforce each other. Popular racism is validated by state racism. Under the validation of the state, racism, in the words of A. Sivanandan, is the "seed-bed of fascism."[20]

Adaptations of racism abound. At a more general and global level, racism, Bowser notes, has appeared in such forms as paternalistic racism, competitive racism, and postmodern racism.[21] These forms are all shaped by, or are adaptations to, the changing global sociopolitical and economic milieu. Paternalistic racism covers from the time of African and Indian slavery and direct colonialism through the 1950s. Racism found expression in a direct paternalistic form because it corresponded to the level of social and economic development of that particular period. But, as the world system and global economics changed into competitive economics triggered by booming industrialization, a direct form of racism became a liability rather than an asset. Responding to the transition into an industrial economy while continuing to exploit the economically and racially marginalized, industrialized countries (e.g., Germany, the United Kingdom, Canada, the U.S., and Australia) encouraged massive immigration to provide competitive wage labor.

Again another global transformation is underway, which is also changing the face of racism. Slavery is outmoded and offensive to the new sensibilities, and immigration to the industrial North is no longer the preferred option. One of the cues to this transition to postmodern racism is the phenomenon of "jobs flight." Jobs are moving from the industrialized North to the struggling South as transnational corporations seek "favorable investment climate." By favorable investment climate I mean fat tax breaks, low wages, no insurance and Social Security benefits for the workers, no labor unions, and less governmental regulation regarding environmental safety. Experiencing the erosion of their economic base, people of the affluent North have found an easy scapegoat in migrant workers, refugees, and immigrants.

Much as we celebrate the anti-racist opposition in South Africa that resulted in the dismantling of the apartheid regime, it is also to our benefit to acknowledge that the abolition of apartheid was triggered by a changing global economic system. According to Bowser:

> The recent dismantling of apartheid is not due to White South African altruism or to mounting anti-racist opposition. It is a strategic move acknowledging that sufficient economic barriers are already in place to keep Black South Africans subordinate and

140
# Reimagining the Human

to maintain general White privilege…Dismantling apartheid acknowledges that the economy and the media are the primary institutions that define and control society, not the state.[22]

The development and construction of racism in the U.S. has also evolved in response to the confluence of various factors throughout history. It is an integral part of nation building, economic development, and the colonization of other people. Like its European counterpart, U.S. racism developed as part of a national consciousness defined by the notion of "manifest destiny"—a destiny to civilize, christianize, and colonize, as well as to extract wealth and cheap labor from other lands for the emerging powerful nation. U.S. racism was born at the nexus of capitalism, colonial rule, and the emergent relationships between ruling and subordinate groups.

Joel Kovel takes account of the changing faces of racism in the U.S.[23] Kovel identifies these faces as dominative racism, aversive racism, and metaracism. Dominative racism can be classified in the global framework of paternalistic racism. It is characterized by outward and direct physical oppression and exploitation of, and violence against, the racial others. If dominative racism is characterized by direct physical oppression, aversive racism, as the term implies, shies away from physical contact but is just as strong as the dominative form. The aversive racists turn away and insulate themselves from people of color by relying on cultural patterns. This racism is the form prevalent in the northern part of the U.S. The third form, which is more abstract, but very pervasive, elusive, and effective, is what Kovel calls metaracism. It is a form of racism diffused throughout the late capitalist system, which closely corresponds to the postmodern racism identified by Bowser.

Racism is not a fixed arrangement handed down from Mt. Olympus by the gods, but a historical product and a confluence of various forces. It changes in appearance as other factors change. We must take into consideration that changes in racial dynamics are, to a certain extent, the result of changing dynamics in the geopolitical economy. This is not to say that our efforts to confront racism are useless, but to realize that what we often extol as "victories" are also the "adaptations" of racism; thus, we are called to make a sustained critique of racism.

## Racism as a Question of Anthropology

If I was able to say in the previous chapter that there is no economic talk that is not anthropological, the same could be said with regard to racism. One cannot talk about racism without getting involved in anthropological talk. Racism, in Audre Lorde's words, "is the belief in the *inherent* superiority of one race over all others and thereby the right to dominance. Sexism, the belief in the *inherent* superiority of one sex over the other and thereby the right to dominance. Ageism. Heterosexism. Elitism. Classism."[24]

Racism undergirds a certain way of construing and constructing the human. In this regard, racism is a question of anthropology, of who we are in relation to others. Racism involves our deepest beliefs about the human, beliefs that have often acquired the status of essentiality and eternality. In spite of the claim that certain attributes are inherently human, the inherently human we often refer to is actually the result of a long process of social and cultural evolution.

In particular, racism shapes a way of construing and constructing the human through the primary category of racial differentiation, even as other categories are implicated as well. If René Descartes' *cogito ergo sum* ("I think, therefore I am")[25] has transmuted into "I conquer, therefore I am," "I discover you, therefore you exist," "I possess, therefore I am," and "I consume, therefore I am," the karma of Descartes' *cogito ergo sum* has also been reincarnated in the form of "I am the racial norm, therefore I am superior," or "I am the racial norm, therefore you are a deviant."

Racism involves defining one's group identity in diacritical relation to another racial group, or a way of deriving one's identity by subordinating another racial group. Whites define their identity in diacritical relation to people of color, and people of color who have experienced racial colonization see themselves only in relation to the image and glory of whites. As young whites feel insecure about their future, a fear that neo-conservative politicians are fanning and riding, many of them have found security by defining their identity along racial lines.

Identity in a racist society is a racialized identity. Among whites, this racialized identity takes the form of defending "whiteness." Whiteness is a discursive regime of truth that whites have constructed to justify their superiority and the marginalization of racial others. This discursive regime, backed up by nondiscursive practices, invests whiteness with normativity and relegates blackness and brownness to signifiers of deviancy. Whiteness is an identity defined in oppositional terms and expressed through the consumption, appropriation, and excretion of the other. What cannot be digested is excreted. The superego's incarnation in whiteness demands that color–the wild and dirty–be excreted or repressed.

The racial others, considered deviant and dirty by normative whiteness, also find their identities defined in racial terms according to the standard of whiteness. As racial others, there is no other way for them to step out of the totalizing gaze of whites except by dealing with the white gaze head-on. No one escapes the racialization of identities in a racist society.

Our ability to deal effectively with racism is tied to our ability to critique, transgress, and reconstruct our racialized identities. We must constantly ask the question: In what way are our identities shaped by racial categories? People of color, or the racial others in any society, must look closely at how their identity has been defined as a function of their subordinated race. Whites in a white racist society must forever ask themselves to what extent their identity is a function of whiteness. This may entail, for their liberation from white racism, going against the regime of whiteness.

## Theology in Relation to Race and Racism

As in other fields of discourse, the dominant theological discourse has been oblivious to racial categories, even as its hermeneutical eye is infected by the virus of the "color line." This should not surprise us anymore after our critique of whiteness, for the dominant theology is basically dominated by white episteme. The dominant theology as basically white European American theology is "color-blind"; therefore, it does not factor race into the theological equation. While the dominant theologies of the West have affirmed the relativity of faith in history, white theologians have rarely applied this insight to the "color line." With rare exceptions, and with due respect to some white theologians, James Cone is right in saying that white theologians have done the business of theology as usual, from Jonathan Edwards to Schubert Ogden, by being silent about the fact of racism, segregation, and discrimination.[26] White dominant theology has been imprisoned, says Cone, by a certain "mental grid" that excludes the datum of race.

In a racist society, authentic and liberating theological reflection has to deal with the matter of race. Race has to be dealt with because, whether we like it or not, it is a mental grid that colors our theological interpretation. A grave distortion of our construal of race, racism can only be dealt with adequately by raising a hermeneutic of suspicion on the racial color of our theological interpretations. Theological reflection and construction that takes racism seriously must engage the task of exposing racist theological constructions that have infected our Christian heritage, deconstructing interpretations that masquerade as racially neutral, and constructing alternative theologies that promote the well-being of all races.

## Theological Excretions from the Bowels of Racism

Racism, like any other form of oppression, is not bereft of theological undergirding. It is undergirded by racist discourse, both subtle and obvious, crude and sophisticated. Christian theological heritage and symbolism throughout the ages has been infested and infected with racist interpretations.

In its more obscene form, devotees of the idol of racism have made direct use of theological sources to support their ways of thinking and acting. For those who have been shaped by the Christian worldview, scriptures and traditions have been used to support racist practices. Some of the most banal and hackneyed examples are the "curse of Ham" in Genesis 9:25–27 and the notion of the "chosen people" or the "chosen race." "Christians who are caught in the obsessive duality of understanding Black people as property rather than as persons," Katie Geneva Cannon argues, "concurred with both faulty exegesis and social pressure that depicted people with Black skin as demonic, unholy, infectious progenitors of sin, full of animality and matriarchal proclivities."[27]

The notion of the chosen people or chosen race has been used to undergird racist practices. In the history of Western conquest and colonization, the notion of the chosen race has been part of the colonizers' racist discourse. Snatching the notion of a chosen race from the Israelites, the colonizers considered it their manifest destiny to conquer and civilize racial others.

There seems to be nothing inherently wrong in the notion of a chosen people, but, when distorted, it offers a potent ideology supporting domination. As a hermeneutic lens, it has produced biblical interpretations that fail to see the plight of the nonchosen, and it has taken for granted or whitewashed the atrocities committed by the chosen people simply because they are God's elect. We may take the case of the Palestinians and other persons in the biblical narrative whose plight did not really matter to most biblical interpreters, because they were considered mere foils in the unfolding drama that revolved around the "elect" (Israelites) and their God.

It is only in recent years that the hermeneutic framework of the chosen race and its accompanying exodus-conquest-slave-master narrative have been questioned. There are certainly some aspects in the exodus narrative that are of value to oppressed communities, such as the experience of release from an oppressive power (Pharaohs of Egypt), the acquisition of the promised land (Palestine), and the mighty liberating hand of Yahweh. This liberating narrative, however, is simultaneously a "text of terror" or a "narrative of terror" or an exodus-conquest narrative, for the acquisition of the promised land comes by way of the conquest of a people (Canaanites), through the help of Yahweh the liberator-turned-conqueror.[28] Even when this narrative of terror is as blatant and nauseating as are the conquest of Canaan and Yahweh's command to annihilate its inhabitants (e.g., Joshua 1:1–9; 6:20–21; 8:24–29; 11:10–15), most readers simply push this aside without any compunction because the well-being of the nonelect Canaanites counts only to the extent that they serve as instruments for the benefit of the elect.[29]

Naim Stifan Ateek and Metri Raheb point out that Palestinians find reading of the exodus narrative to be extremely disturbing.[30] When they read the exodus narrative, they do not identify with the conquering Israelites but with the Canaanites. Exodus, for them, mirrors their oppression and attests God's identification with their oppressors. For Palestinians, exodus is about conquest, not liberation. For them, the exodus narrative is a narrative of terror.

Resonating with the Palestinians, Allen Warrior argues that American Indians identify with the biblical Canaanites, not with the conquering Israelites in the exodus-conquest-elect narrative.[31] Like the biblical

Canaanites, the American Indians suffered conquest and genocide at the hands of those who escaped from the "Old World" and laid a claim on the promised land ("New World"). For American Indians, the exodus narrative is a narrative of terror; it is the narrative of their conquerors.

In a slightly different vein, womanist theologian Delores Williams notes that African Americans identify with the slave Hagar, not the slave masters Sarah and Abraham. This is not surprising because the plight of Hagar mirrors their own plight. Unlike Sarah and Abraham, Hagar was a victim of the exodus-conquest-election-slave-master narrative. The exodus-conquest-election-slave-master narrative cannot be the narrative of a people who suffered slavery.[32] Of course the exodus narrative has been used in the black churches to support liberation, but contemporary black theologians and biblical scholars are cognizant of its other side: it is simultaneously a narrative of conquest.

In a painful and challenging tone, Warrior points out that no amount of excellent biblical scholarship can change the elect's narrative, such as in Norman Gottwald's *Tribes of Yahweh*.[33] "People who read the narratives," argues Warrior, "read them as they are, not as scholars and experts would *like* them to be read and interpreted. History is no longer with us. The narrative remains."[34]

The notion of the chosen race and its attendant exodus-conquest-election-slave-master narrative fits well the European American experience more than it does the struggling people of the Third World and racial/ethnic minorities living in the belly of Uncle Sam. In fact, no other race in our time has played the exodus-conquest-election-slave-master narrative so well as the European Americans. European Americans made an exodus from the "Old World" into the "New World" by way of conquest of the American Canaanites–the American Indians. Oppressed people, however, cannot fully identify with the exodus-conquest-election-slave-master narrative because they have not conquered a nation; instead, they are the conquered ones.

Under the canopy of racism, the exodus-conquest-election-slave master narrative has served to distort historical interpretation, as when European American historians take account of the conquest of American Indians. "Native American victories," as Robert Moore has pointed out, "are invariably defined as 'massacres,' while the indiscriminate killing, extermination and plunder of Native American nations by Euro-Americans is defined as 'victory'. Distortion of history by the choice of 'loaded' words to describe historical events is a common racist practice."[35]

When we consider the New Testament, we find it has also not escaped being used as a tool to support racism. Missionaries and evangelists have sought the "cultural circumcision" of people of color before they view them as fully Christian. Attempts by people of color to indigenize and contextualize the Christian kerygma often meet stringent resistance in the rhetoric of faithfulness to the gospel. The specter of syncretism always hangs over the heads of those who want to contextualize the gospel. Though we must be vigilant in our faithfulness to the gospel, the issue of syncretism has often been raised against the practices of people of color and hardly ever against the practices of European Americans. In short, allegations of syncretism often have a racist underpinning.

Most of the racist theological discourse in our modern world no longer makes any direct appeal to the biblical account. Except for the unpolished racist, the old hackneyed theological motifs no longer make sense. Instead, the trend of white interpreters has been to downplay the significance of color distinction and to argue for a transcendent God–a God that is colorless and "color-blind." This, they believe, is the way to find theological healing from racism. Theologians of color, in general, believe otherwise. This theological approach by white theologians is, for them, an expression of the theological genius of racism.

### Interpreting Sin in Light of the Evil of Racism

Though many of us do not realize it, "the heart of the issues of racial and ethnic diversity in the United States," says Fumitaka Matsuoka, is "theological in character." It is theological in character because "matters of race, culture, and ethnicity in this society are fundamentally the theological concerns of idols and of the One who confronts them with the claim of ultimacy."[36] Racism, in particular, is deeply theological because it is a prime instance of idolatry; it is, to use Eugene Victor Wolfenstein's term, an instance of "epidermal fetishism."[37]

Peter Hodgson in *Winds of the Spirit* resonates with Matsuoka's point on the idolatrous character of racism. Racism, for Hodgson, is a prime expression of idolatry: It is the deification of one's race and the marginalization of other racial groups. He speaks of racism as

> a prime instance of idolatry, for it entails the apotheosis of one's own race and the negation of others; its logic is genocide although its practice is usually segregation. It is an extraordinarily resistant ideology because it is so deeply rooted in the archaic consciousness of light-skinned peoples: the association of darkness with stain, evil, malevolence...Like all the -isms, it is driven by the fear of otherness, difference, and the desire to secure ourselves as the sole center and criterion by which everything is measured.[38]

Black theologians speak as well of the sin of racism as "idolatry." Racism is more than a question of rationality or irrationality. It is, for James Evans, "suprarational": It is an act of faith in the superiority of one's race.[39] In short, racism is an expression of idolatry. It means worshiping a human construction in which the dominant race has a vested interest.

In the U.S., this idol of racism is invested in the construction of whiteness. The sin of white people, for Cone, "is the definition of their existence in terms of whiteness. It is accepting the condition that is responsible for Amerindian reservations, black concentration camps, and the rape of Vietnam."[40] White sin is the elevation of whiteness to the status of normativity, and the relegation of other colors to deviancy.

How is the sin of racism experienced by people of color? How do we interpret the victimization of people of color in theological terms? Speaking in particular about the experience of African Americans, Cone is emphatic in saying that the sin of blacks is the "desire to be white." This means a loss of identity, a refusal to accept who blacks are. "It is," Cone continues, "saying yes to the white absurdity–accepting the world as it is by letting whites define black existence."[41]

Desiring to be white is an experience of alienation; it is a manifestation of internalized racism. It is not only a loss of identity or an expression of confused identity; it results, in Yamato's account of her own struggle, "in my acceptance of mistreatment, leads me to believe that being treated with less than absolute respect, at least this once, is to be expected because I am Black, because I am not white."[42]

Evans has a distinct way of articulating sin in relation to racism, but the main thrust is similar to Cone's. Sin, in light of blacks' experience of racism, is explained by Evans in terms of "dislocation" and "fallenness." Instead of focusing, as traditional theology does, on the distortion of human rational and moral capacity, Evans interprets the fall as an experience of dislocation that African Americans suffered because of their separation through abduction and slavery from the place they call home.[43]

## Toward a Humanity Delivered from the Thrall of Racism

Racism distorts the humanity of the dominant as well as the subordinated race, though this distortion is experienced differently. Since racism is experienced by the dominating race and the dominated race differently, deliverance from the clutches of racism must take different, though converging, routes.

### *Exorcising the Demon of Racism*

The demon of racism needs to be exorcised if we are to experience liberation from its grip. What comes easily to the popular mind when we speak of exorcism are horror movies, such as *The Exorcist.* There is a time for Hollywood movies, but my interest in dealing with exorcism is to link it with racism. Racism is an expression of idolatry: It involves raising the self-interest, security, and worldview of a particular race or people to a position of ultimate concern while relegating others to the margin. Racism's destructive power is far greater than we can imagine possible with individual demon possession. Its expressions are visible from the outside, but its control is lodged deep in the individual and collective psyche. Like an idol that feeds on the blood of the conquered, colonized, and exploited, racism must be exorcised.

Walter Wink, in *Unmasking the Powers*, provides an extensive account of exorcism and its relevance for contemporary issues from a theological angle.[44] "Exorcism in its New Testament context," notes Wink, "is the act of deliverance of a person or institution or society from its bondage to evil, and its restoration to the wholeness intrinsic to its creation."[45] The evil condition is not only purged, it is going to be replaced with a new way of life. In other words, it means liberation for those who have been possessed by the powers of death and restoration to a liberated life. Wink points to Jesus's act of cleansing the temple (Mk. 11:11, 15–19) as the paradigmatic act of collective exorcism in the New Testament. Wink argues that what made Jesus' acts of exorcism powerful and frightening, especially for the guardians of the reigning order, was the integration of his acts of exorcism into his proclamation of the inbreaking of the new order–the kingdom of God.[46]

### Encountering God in One's Race

"Trying hard to be an American," but still "falling short" of the normative American (the European American), is the plight of people of color in the U.S. "I have been four years in America," a Filipino immigrant from California expressed with a tone of sadness, "and I am still a stranger. It is not because I want to be. I have tried to be as 'American' as possible. I live like an American, eat like American, and dress the same, and yet everywhere I find Americans who remind me of the fact that I am a stranger."[47] Many young people of color, in an effort to be as American and cool as possible, even deny their cultural and ethnic identity and, at times, even blame their parents for their physical features. They want to be just like any white youth because that is the basis for getting out of the hell of nonacceptance. Whites, often with the intention of being nice, say: "We consider you to be just like us. You don't seem Asian."[48]

Not even the children and grandchildren of people of color have found full acceptance as Americans in white America. For white Americans, Asian Americans are always *Asian* Americans and African Americans are always *African* Americans, whereas whites are simply Americans. When a second generation Filipino American boy was asked by a white boy where he came from, he simply said, "Minnesota." This got him into trouble. The white boy forcefully insisted: "*Where* are you *really from*?" Confronted by this situation, many young Asian Americans have learned to answer the question by stating their parents' country of origin, which does not accurately say who they are. But this too invites trouble, for this is often interpreted by whites as a stubborn refusal of Asian Americans to be fully American. And when an Asian American responds, in essence, that he or she belongs to the Third World in the heart of America, more trouble is coming. The most likely verbal attack is: "If you don't like it here, why don't you go back to where you came from!"[49]

No matter how hard people of color try to be Americans, they cannot be Americans if the normative American is the European American. They will forever fall short of the norm; they will remain aberrations, forever "missing the mark" (sinners). Falling from this norm is like falling from grace; outside of this norm is hell, a place where an encounter with God is seen as impossible. The liberation of people of color cannot be found in trying to deny their identity by becoming white.

In the theological discourse of people of color, the question of color has been considered an inevitable part of one's identity. It is the locus of one's search for identity, and it is the locus for understanding God. Manas Buthelezi, like Elizabeth Tay and Matsuoka, gives focus to the issue of racial/ethnic identity in theology. He raises the question: "'Can I realize my authentic humanity in the medium of my blackness?' Is my blackness some fatalistic road-block in life or a context within which God has made it possible for me to be an authentic man?"[50] After being told for years to despise one's race, questioning whether one's race is a fatalistic road-block is not only understandable, but an act of demystification and an act toward liberation.

For the people of color who have been victims of racism under a white dominant society, the question of what it means to be human cannot be divorced from the question of what it means to be black (African Americans), *mestizo* (Hispanic), or red (American Indian). Cone argues that the fundamental datum of black theology is not only experience in general but black experience of racism in particular.[51] Evans, like Cone, underscores the point that what it means to be human cannot be divorced from the question of what it means to be black in a white-dominated culture.[52]

Similar concerns have been raised by other people of color as they struggle to liberate themselves from the imposed white identity. We can take, for example, second generation Puerto Ricans. Puerto Ricans find it impossible to be simply "Puerto Ricans" in a society that demands categories based on black and white. Considering the status of Puerto Rico in relation to the U.S., which one critic says is a "perfume colony," Román López Tames has likened the plight of Puerto Ricans to that of bats who are "rejected by birds and rodents, belonging to neither family in any concrete way, who [are] condemned to live a solitary life between the two worlds, misunderstood by both." Their Latin American cousins consider them as "Americanos" and the "Americanos" classify them as "Latinos." They are forever asking the questions: "What am I"? ("Que Soy?"), and "What are we?" ("Que somos?").[53]

"I encountered God in my ethnicity" is a succinct but deep statement that comes from the mouth of Elizabeth Tay.[54] How else could it be? It cannot be otherwise, especially if one's race has been a factor that has brought so much suffering. In a society in which people of color have suffered because of their racial identity, the way to their liberation requires an encounter with a God who affirms their race and with the message that points to self-identification as a precondition for experiencing the gospel. This point is articulated well by Matsuoka: "Self-identification of each racial and ethnic group is necessary, for the task of self-identification is a precondition to acknowledge the very nature of the gospel."[55]

### *In the Image of a Color-loving God*

Tay, who said she encounters God in her ethnicity, also helps us see the other side of her statement: "My identity as an Asian American woman who has been marginalized in American culture shapes, propels and is analogous to my understanding of God."[56] When God encounters us in our ethnicities or race, we are led to see who God is for us. This shows us the theological character of our search for identity and the anthropological character of our understanding of God. "In a racist society," Cone strongly asserts, "God is never color-blind."[57] If, as Alice Walker wrote, God would be "pissed-off" when we pass obliviously by the color purple, likewise God would be pissed-off at the notion of a "color-blind" God.[58] God would just go berserk when labeled "color-blind." A "color-blind God" (white God) has no place for people who suffer because of their color. People of color do not need a "color-blind" God. What they need is a God who sees and loves color.

"In the eyes of God, color does not matter" are words often heard from our pulpits. "Don't worry, brother; don't worry, sister; after all, we are equal in the sight of God" is commonplace pulpit rhetoric. No matter how good the intention is, I believe that it is counterproductive to preach as if color does not matter to God. The idea that color does not matter to God does not deal with the unchangeable reality that we have different colors. This approach continues to devalue the color of people and fails to criticize our ideological distortion: that the problem is not our differences but how we interpret our differences.

Instead of saying that color does not matter in the eyes of God, I say that color matters in the eyes of God because God loves color. To say that color does not matter in the eyes of God does not show impartiality to all colors, but obliterates other colors in favor of whiteness (noncolorness). God transcends colors not by becoming colorless and "color-blind," but by becoming colorful and color-loving. God transcends colors by loving colors—not by ignoring colors—and becoming thoroughly immersed in the various colors of the universe.

If God transcends color by becoming colorful, color-loving, and immersed in the various colors of the universe, then God could find Godself incarnating in particular colors. "God is black," claims the black theologian

Cone. The blackness of God is the key to blacks' understanding of God and also the way to understanding themselves. It means that God has accepted the blacks' condition as God's very own.[59] In the face of the denigration of their race, black Christians have stood on the solid conviction that God has become one with them, and that they are God's children, with dignity that is no less than whites'. This is not an assertion of racial or moral superiority but simply an assertion of their humanity. A black God, Linda Thomas and Dwight Hopkins assert, "enhances the psychological self-empowerment" of the black people.[60]

If we can say God is black, can whites equally say that God is white? Of course whites have already affirmed the whiteness of God, even if they do not intentionally say that God is white. Even in saying that God is "color-blind," they are already in effect saying that God is white, because only a white God in a white racist society can be "color-blind." For whites to affirm God's whiteness is merely to reaffirm what has been going on all the time. Explicit affirmation by whites of God's whiteness would not make white privilege more potent. After all, white privilege works precisely and more effectively because it is not asserted. Ontologically, one can say that God is white as God is black, but this onto-rhetoric does not have the effect for whites that it has for blacks. For whites to affirm that God is white is simply to perpetuate white supremacy; whereas, for blacks to speak of a God who is black, after many years of internalizing a white God, is an act of liberation. Whites do not need a white God for their own liberation; they need a God who condemns the white god—the idol.

### Jesus as a Person of Color Who Struggles for a Colorful Society

Since God, for Christian theology, has revealed Godself in the gestalt of the human Jesus of Nazareth, which his followers have proclaimed as the Christ, it follows that what racially oppressed people perceive as God's important attributes in relation to their plight are also seen in Jesus. Jesus helps them understand who God is as well as what being human is all about. Here is revealed to us the anthropological character of the christological quest.

If, for black theologians, God is black, they also affirm that Jesus is black. If God affirmed blacks' humanity by becoming black, then Jesus—God's incarnation—must be black. The blackness of Jesus is an affirmation that God is in solidarity with them. Cone has again articulated this point emphatically:

> The black community is an oppressed community primarily because of their blackness; hence the christological importance of Jesus must be found in his blackness. If he is not black as we are, then the resurrection has little significance for our times. Indeed, if he cannot be what we are, we cannot be who he is.[61]

To say that God in Jesus has become black is a precious affirmation for blacks who have been trampled upon by whites because of their blackness. "In a society that defines blackness as evil and whiteness as good," Cone can only say that "the theological significance of Jesus is found in the possibility of human liberation through blackness. Jesus is the black Christ."[62]

Hispanic theologians, in resonance with black theologians, also see God in the particularity of Jesus of Nazareth. If for blacks Jesus is black, for Hispanics Jesus is a *mestizo* (racial mixture). This is a way of interpreting christology that comes out of what Hispanics call the *mestizaje* perspective, or the perspective that comes out of their experience of being *mestizos* and *mestizas*. Out of this perspective, Virgilio Elizondo interprets Jesus' life and ministry in a new way.[63] Elizondo interprets Jesus' program of liberation in three geographical stages of his life, each of which refers to a corresponding theological principle: (1) Galilean principle, (2) Jerusalem principle, and (3) resurrection principle. The Galilean stage gives rise to the message of inclusion that breaks down barriers (social, economic, cultural/religious). In the Jerusalem principle, Jesus confronts the powers of his society and exposes the idolatry of the system, which leads to his murder. Finally, the resurrection principle speaks of the breakdown of exclusions and his message is spread throughout the world. This is the message of inclusion and rejoicing in the kingdom of God. The kingdom of God is *mestizo* and the future is *mestizo*.[64]

Asian theologians have also articulated a christological anthropology that sees Jesus as one who affirms their condition and their struggle for liberation. Theologizing out of the Philippine context, Edicio de la Torre claims that "[Jesus] must be a Filipino, if Filipinos are to be Christians."[65] C.S. Song, another Asian theologian, speaks broadly of Jesus as the crucified people of our time.[66] Through his "people hermeneutic," Song helps us move beyond the double impasse of the sterile, traditional academic quest for the once-upon-a-time historical Jesus and the disembodied Christ of electronic evangelists to a Jesus who can be discerned in the emaciated and mangled bodies of society's victims, in the struggles of people against the forces of death, and in the dreams and hopes of the crucified people. If we want to know God, we must know Jesus; if we want to know Jesus we must know the people. Jesus is the crucified people of Manila, Yangoon, Calcutta, Managua, and other places.

If blacks, Hispanics, and Asians speak of Jesus as black, *mestizo*, and Asian, respectively, are whites not entitled to speak of a white Jesus? Of course whites can speak of a white Jesus and, in fact, the dominant theology has been saturated with a white Jesus. People of color have, for too long, lived with a white Jesus. They have found it hard to imagine a Jesus who could be otherwise. I, myself, have grown up believing in a white Jesus. My own children have grown up believing in a white Jesus. We do not need more of this white Jesus stuff: People of color do not need it, and white people who seek liberation from white idolatry do not need it. We should be sick and tired of this white Jesus. We need a Jesus who affirms our various colors, and who proclaims judgment against the idolatrous construction of whiteness.

### What about the Dominating Race? Transgressing Whites' Racialized Identity

The struggle against racism is not only a struggle to restore the humanity of the racialized others; it also points to the new humanity of the dominant race. If the racialized others have grappled with the question of identity in their search for a liberated humanity, members of the dominant race must, likewise, grapple with their identity. Those who belong to the dominant race must continue to ask themselves to what extent their identity is a function of their race. Whites, in particular, must constantly ask themselves to what extent their identity is a function of whiteness and what choices they are going to make to escape from the prison of whiteness in order to become a "new white people." A people, says Barndt, "whose identity is not based on privilege and power."[67]

But whites cannot be a "new white people" apart from their solidarity with people of color. There is no path to becoming a "new white people" that bypasses the way of the people of color. The liberation of whites, for Cone, is bound with whites' "becoming black with God." This means, he argues, since God has come to blacks in God's blackness, "to receive God's revelation is to become black with God by joining God in the work of liberation."[68] Becoming black, brown, and red with a God who has incarnated in such marginalized colors, and working for racial liberation, is the way to becoming a "new white people."

Whites do not need a white God, neither do they need a white Jesus for their liberation. On the contrary, they need to kick out the white God and white Jesus; they need to burn the white God and white Jesus in the alchemical fire so that they will be free to worship the God who is not a white fetish. This means that whites must betray the white God and exorcise its demon. Of course, this does not happen by mere faith in whites of goodwill, but requires that whites and people of color work together to devise discursive and nondiscursive strategies that undermine racism.

### O God, Don't Make Me White on the Day of Resurrection

From the pain of those who have been victimized by racism and from wrestling together against the idol of racism comes a new understanding of ourselves and what we can become together. This new understanding does not lie on the erasure or the melting of all colors—which, in a white racist society, simply means the whitening of all—but on the flowering of various colors in which people do not establish their identities in diacritical superior-subordinate racial relations.

In the context of the United States, where race is an issue of intense contestation, the idea of a new person takes various shades. For the white person this means a new self-understanding and identity that is not a function of white privilege, but one that is founded on racial equality. I know it is painful for whites to lose this white privilege, but it is the only way for whites to be truly human. When a white person can stand with others not on the basis of his or her race but in mutual respect and recognition, he or she is on the road to being a liberated white person. This metamorphosis into a new person may mean the acceptance by white-skinned people that whiteness is not an absence of color but one among the many colors. White is a color, and white people are as colorful as the so-called people of color.

In the context of people of color in the U.S., the notion of a new person also assumes distinctive shapes. The new person of color requires a new self-understanding and identity that is not a reflection of the white image. This new identity, for people of color, would be an expression of a decolonized self that has gained the courage to say, in contrast to Revelation 7:9–17: "O God, don't make me white on the day of resurrection." Not even with the "blood of the Lamb" would they want to be "made...white"(v. 14). They just want to be whole and be included in the heavenly banquet. If ever they expect a transformation to happen on the day of resurrection, it is not that they want to become white or colorless, but that their respective color has a distinct place among others.

Moreover, for people of color in the U.S., the new self is not simply defined by its negation of whiteness. Asian Americans or African Americans must preach not only what it means to be an *Asian* American or an *African* American, but also what it means to be an American or, more appropriately, a citizen of the United States of America.[69] European Americans should not be left with the task of defining what it means to be an American. Let us be clear on this: European Americans do not have the exclusive right to define what it means to be an American.

Shifting to the global level, where the category of race cannot be separated from imperialism, I say that the new Third World person is one who is undergoing decolonization toward becoming a postcolonial subject. This new person is one who has learned to see her or his racial-ethnic identity as equal to others. And for a person who is located in the more economically affluent countries, this new person is one who has exorcised racial superiority and has learned to place his or her ethnic-racial identity in right relation with others. Moreover, I must say that the new global person experiencing liberation from racism is one who is acutely aware of his or her racial-ethnic identity and specific geo-political location, while firmly committed to racial justice and the flowering of all.

## Expressions of Ordinary Courage:
## A New Humanity Is Being Born

A new humanity liberated from racism is still in the making. While there are no human beings who are totally beyond the grip of racism, we see expressions of a new humanity experiencing liberation from racism among those who are struggling to live in nonracist ways and in communities striving to dwell differently despite various odds. We see embodiments of a new humanity in the making even among those individuals who resist simply because there is no other recourse but to resist. There is no heroism invoked here.

We do not need to look at archetypes of heroism in order to see the embodiments of a new humanity in the making. We just need a different lens to help us see a new humanity emerging in the ordinary courage of daily living and in the ordinary gestures of human thoughtfulness. When Rosa Parks refused to give her seat to a white man on a bus, she did not imagine making a heroic statement to the world. She was simply sick and tired of sitting at the back of the bus. But her act became a momentous one, for it inspired the Civil Rights Movement and the ensuing generations.

Desmond Tutu tells a similar story of an ordinary human gesture that drew him to the Christian faith and informed his commitment to uphold human dignity. Tutu once remarked that he became a Christian on the day Father Trevor Huddleston passed his mother on the street and Father Huddleston "tipped his hat."[70] Not a heroic act by the standard of this world, but a truly significant one in a society that dehumanizes others by virtue of their race. When we are no longer beholden to the archetypes of heroism that our society has taught us for so long and can see embodiments of a new humanity in ordinary people, we have experienced the birthing of a new humanity in our own selves. A new humanity is birthing in our very being because we have reclaimed power in ourselves and have regained the courage to live differently in the midst of a world torn apart by racial categories. Listen! The borning cry of a new humanity is getting louder.

## Notes

[1]Louis Kushnick, "Racism and Anti-Racism in Western Europe," in *Racism and Anti-Racism in World Perspective*, Sage Series on Race and Ethnic Relations, vol. 13, ed. Benjamin P. Bowser (Newbury Park, Calif., London and New Delhi: Sage Publications, 1995), 182.

[2]This heading is from Derrick Bell's work, *Faces at the Bottom of the Well: The Permanence of Racism* (New York: Basic Books, 1992).

[3]Ibid., 14.

[4]Ibid., xi.

[5]Shawn Donaldson, "When Our Faces Are at the Bottom of the Well," in *Everyday Acts Against Racism: Raising Children in a Multiracial World*, ed. Maureen T. Reddy (Seattle: Seal Press, 1996), 101.

Robert Terry, "The Negative Impact on White Racism," in *Impact of Racism on White Americans*, ed. Benjamin Bowser and Raymond Hunt (Newbury Park, Calif.: Sage Publications,

1981), 120, cited in Joseph Barndt, *Dismantling Racism: The Continuing Challenge to White America* (Minneapolis: Fortress Press, 1991), 56.

[7]Shelley Park, "Mothering Across Racial and Cultural Boundaries," in *Everyday Acts Against Racism*, 226.

[8]Eugene Victor Wolfenstein, *Psychoanalytic-Marxism: Groundwork* (New York and London: Guilford Press, 1993), 334, cited in Peter McLaren, *Revolutionary Multiculturalism: Pedagogies of Dissent for the New Millennium* (Boulder, Colo.: Westview Press, 1997), 269.

[9]Paul Kivel, *Uprooting Racism: How White People Can Work for Racial Justice* (Gabriola Island, B.C.: New Society Publishers, 1996), 15.

[10]Sharon Welch, "Human Beings, White Supremacy, and Racial Justice," in *Reconstructing Christian Theology*, ed. Rebecca S. Chopp and Mark Lewis Taylor (Minneapolis: Fortress Press, 1994), 173; Karen Baker-Fletcher and Garth Kasimu Baker-Fletcher, *My Sister, My Brother: Womanist and Xodus God-Talk* (Maryknoll, N.Y.: Orbis Books, 1997), 148.

[11]Welch, "Human Beings, White Supremacy, and Racial Justice," 173.

[12]Barndt, *Dismantling Racism*, 29.

[13]Welch, "Human Beings, White Supremacy, and Racial Justice," 173.

[14]M. Shawn Copeland, "The Interaction of Racism, Sexism, and Classism in Women's Exploitation," in *Women, Work, and Poverty*, Concilium, ed. Elisabeth Schüssler Fiorenza and Anne Carr (Edinburgh: T. & T. Clark, 1987), 21.

[15]Barndt, *Dismantling Racism*, 35.

[16]bell hooks, *Black Looks: Race and Representation* (Boston: South End Press, 1992), 15.

[17]Peggy McIntosh, "White Privilege and Male Privilege: A Personal Account of Coming to See Correspondences through Work in Women's Studies," in *Race, Class, and Gender: An Anthology*, ed. Patricia Hill Collins and Margaret Andersen (Belmont, Calif.: Wadsworth Publishing Company, 1992), 70–81.

[18]Benjamin P. Bowser, "Racism in the Modern World," in *Racism and Anti-Racism in World Perspective*, 285.

[19]Kushnick, "Racism and Anti-Racism in Western Europe," in *Racism and Anti-Racism in World Perspective*, 182.

[20]Ibid., 184, citing A. Sivanandan, "Racism: The Road from Germany," in *Race and Class* 34 no. 3 (January–March 1993): 69.

[21]Bowser, "Racism in the Modern World Community," in *Racism and Anti-Racism in World Perspective*, 287–307.

[22]Ibid., 298.

[23]Joel Kovel, *White Racism: A Psychohistory* (New York: Pantheon, 1970).

[24]Audre Lorde, *Sister Outsider* (New York: Crossing Press, 1984), 115. Emphasis added.

[25]René Descartes, "Discourse on the Method of Rightly Conducting the Reason and Seeking for Truth in the Sciences," in *Descartes Selections*, ed. Ralph Eaton (New York, Chicago, and Boston: Charles Scribner's Sons, 1927), particularly 1–37.

[26]James Cone, *God of the Oppressed* (New York: Seabury Press, 1975), 45–53.

[27]Katie Geneva Cannon, "Slave Ideology and Biblical Interpretation," in *The Recovery of Black Presence: An Interdisciplinary Exploration*, ed. Randall Bailey and Jacquelyn Grant (Nashville: Abingdon Press, 1995), 121; also Barndt, *Dismantling Racism*, 125.

[28]See Phyllis Trible, *Texts of Terror: Literary-Feminist Readings of Biblical Narratives* (Philadelphia: Fortress Press, 1984).

[29]See my article, "Exodus-Toward-Egypt: Filipino Americans' Struggle to Realize the Promised Land in America," in *A Dream Unfinished: Theological Reflections from the Margins*, ed. Eleazar S. Fernandez and Fernando Segovia (Maryknoll, N.Y.: Orbis Books, 2001), 167–81.

[30]Naim Stifan Ateek, *Justice, and Only Justice: A Palestinian Theology of Liberation* (Maryknoll, N.Y.: Orbis Books, 1989); also Mitri Raheb, *I Am a Palestinian Christian* (Minneapolis: Fortress Press, 1995). See also Marc Ellis, *Toward a Jewish Theology of Liberation: The Uprising and the Future* (Maryknoll, N.Y.: Orbis Books, 1989).

[31]Robert Allen Warrior, "A Native American Perspective: Canaanites, Cowboys, and Indians," in *Voices from the Margin: Interpreting the Bible in the Third World*, ed. R. S. Sugirtharajah (Maryknoll, N.Y.: Orbis Books, 1991), 287–95.

[32]Delores Williams, *Sisters in the Wilderness: The Challenge of Womanist God-Talk* (Maryknoll, N.Y.: Orbis Books, 1993); also Renita J. Weems, *Just a Sister Away: A Womanist Vision of Women's Relationships in the Bible* (San Diego: LuraMedia, 1988).

[33]See Norman K. Gottwald, *The Tribes of Yahweh: A Sociology of the Religion of Liberated Israel, 1250–1050 B.C.E.* (Maryknoll, N.Y.: Orbis Books, 1979).

[34]Warrior, "A Native American Perspective," 280.

[35]Robert B. Moore, "Racist Stereotyping in the English Language," in *Racism and Sexism: An Integrated Study*, ed. Paula Rothenberg (New York: St. Martin's Press, 1988), 269–75; also Moore, "Racist Stereotyping in the English Language" in *Race, Class, and Gender: An Anthology*, ed. Margaret Andersen and Patricia Hill Collins (Belmont, Calif.: Wadsworth Publishing Company, 1992), 317–329.

[36]Fumitaka Matsuoka, *Out of Silence: Emerging Themes in Asian American Churches* (Cleveland: United Church Press, 1995), 125–26.

[37]Wolfenstein, cited in McLaren, *Revolutionary Multiculturalism: Pedagogies of Dissent for the New Millennium*, 270.

[38]Peter Hodgson, *Winds of the Spirit: A Constructive Christian Theology* (Louisville: Westminster John Knox Press, 1994), 226–27.

[39]James Evans, *We Have Been Believers* (Minneapolis: Fortress Press, 1992), 105.

[40]James Cone, *A Black Theology of Liberation*, Twentieth Anniversary Edition (Maryknoll, N.Y.: Orbis Books, 1990), 107.

[41]Ibid., 108.

[42]Gloria Yamato, "Something about the Subject Makes It Hard to Name," in *Race, Class, and Gender: An Anthology*, 67.

[43]Evans, *We Have Been Believers*, 116.

[44]Walter Wink, *Unmasking the Powers: The Invisible Forces That Determine Human Existence* (Philadelphia: Fortress Press, 1986).

[45]Ibid., 59.

[46]Ibid., 58.

[47]Ronald Takaki, *Strangers from a Different Shore: A History of Asian Americans* (New York: Penguin Books, 1998), 316.

[48]Grace Sangkok Kim, "Asian North American Youth: A Ministry of Self-Identity and Pastoral Care," in *People on the Way: Asian North Americans Discovering Christ, Culture, and Community*, ed. David Ng (Valley Forge, Pa.: Judson Press, 1996), 203.

[49]Nobuko Joanne Miyamoto, "What Are You?" *Amerasia* 1/3 (1971), cited in Fumitaka Matsuoka, *Out of Silence: Emerging Themes in Asian American Churches* (Cleveland: United Church Press, 1995), 109–10.

[50]Manas Buthelezi, "The Theological Meaning of True Humanity," in *The Challenge of Black Theology in South Africa*, ed. Basil Moore (Atlanta: John Knox Press, 1974), 93, cited in Evans, *We Have Been Believers*, 114.

[51]Cone, *A Black Theology of Liberation*, 84.

[52]Evans, *We Have Been Believers*, 99.

[53]Samuel Betances, "Race and the Search for Identity" in *Race, Class, and Gender: An Anthology*, 277–78.

[54]Elizabeth Tay, "I Encountered God in My Ethnicity," *In God's Image* 11/3 (1992): 13. Cited in Matsuoka, *Out of Silence: Emerging Themes in Asian American Churches*, 133.

[55]Matsuoka, *Out of Silence*, 133.

[56]Tay, "I Encountered God," p. 13.

[57]Cone, *Black Theology of Liberation*, 6.

[58]Alice Walker, *The Color Purple* (New York: Washington Square Press, 1978), 178.

[59]Cone, *Black Theology of Liberation*, 6.

[60]Dwight Hopkins and Linda Thomas, "Womanist Theology and Black Theology: Conversational Envisioning of an Unfinished Dream," in *A Dream Unfinished*, 80.

[61]Cone, *Black Theology of Liberation*, 120.

[62]Ibid., 121.

[63]Virgilio Elizondo, *The Galilean Journey: The Mexican-American Promise* (Maryknoll, N.Y.: Orbis Books, 1983).

[64]Virgilio Elizondo, *The Future Is Mestizo: Life Where Cultures Meet* (Bloomington, Ind.: Meyer-Stone Books, 1988).

[65]Edicio de la Torre, *Touching Ground, Taking Root: Theological and Political Reflections on the Philippine Struggle* (Quezon City, Philippines: Socio-Pastoral Institute, 1986).

[66]Choan-Seng Song, *Jesus, the Crucified People* (Minneapolis: Fortress Press, 1996).

[67]Barndt, *Dismantling Racism*, 162.

[68]Cone, *Black Theology of Liberation*, 66.

[69]Jung Young Lee, *Korean Preaching: An Interpretation* (Nashville: Abingdon Press, 1997), 118.

[70]Donald Shriver, Jr., "The Taming of Mars: Can Humans of the Twenty-First Century Contain Their Propensity for Violence?" in *Religion and the Powers of the Common Life*, ed. Max Stackhouse with Peter Paris (Harrisburg, Pa.: Trinity Press International, 2000), 150.

# CHAPTER 7

# *Reimagining the Human in Light of the Travail of the Ecosystem*

The ecosystem is in travail; it is groaning. It is not in pain simply because of natural evolution, but because of the destructive acts of human beings who have experienced alienation from their bodies, who are estranged from their fellow human beings, made into commodities by the market, and shortsightedly focused on immediate material gains and the pursuit of power. An ailment in the souls of individuals and society redounds to the destruction of the ecosystem.

For a long time we have continued to destroy the ecosystem, ignoring its cry. It is easy for us to turn away from the deterioration of the ecosystem, for its gradual destruction may often appear imperceptible. It often requires some major catastrophic event–a *force majeure*–or what insurance industries call "acts of God" before people come to their senses about the ecological disaster. But even with the occasional catastrophic events, people are quick to go back into their ecological stupor.

Still, an ecosystem in pain finds a way to get back at the perpetrators. It may absorb our abusive behavior for a time, but it has its carrying capacity or limit. What we do with it, often in the name of growth, has limits. The rapid rate of air pollution is already beyond the capacity of the earth's atmosphere to absorb and purify; the destruction of the earth's forests and other vegetation has resulted in global warming; the hamburgerization and bananazation of huge tracts of land, including tropical forests, has led to soil erosion, flash floods, and the extinction of some species of plants and animals; the pollution of the lakes, rivers, and seas has made them uninhabitable for some species; and the food supplies that come from these areas have become highly toxic for human consumption. If we continue our ecocidal acts, we will leave a devastated ecology for our children. We must realize that "we no longer inherit the earth from our parents, we borrow it from our children."[1]

This is a sobering statement; my heart is heavy. Even within my own lifetime I have seen that, indeed, I no longer inherit the earth from my parents, but borrow it from my children. Many of the fish and other marine life that once flourished in the sea of my childhood home in Leyte, Philippines, are no longer there for my kids to see. I thought I could still take my children to that place and have them taste what I experienced as a young boy, but that is no longer possible. Of course, the local population has increased, but the main factors, I believe, are destructive fishing methods and agricultural practices. Agricultural chemicals from the rice field flow to the river and, finally, to the ocean.

Just as classism, sexism, and racism provide ideological undergirdings for the oppression of people on the basis of class, gender, and race, so the destruction of the ecosystem is undergirded by the ideology of naturism. Naturism is a way of thinking and dwelling that places the human species at the top of a hierarchy in which other species are relegated to the status of objects to be exploited. In the hierarchy of being, the human being is at the top of the holy order and other objects are assigned meaning only as they serve the purposes of human beings. Naturism is the ideology that undergirds our genocidal acts against nature.

## Naturism's Interlocking with Other Forms of Oppression

It is crucial that we understand naturism in relation to other forms of oppression if we are to do justice to it, and if we are not simply to broadly condemn our general human culpability while overlooking our various locations and varying levels of responsibility in relation to the ecological crisis. We need to understand how forms of oppression interlock, because the interrelationships affect our experience of the ecological crisis. Just as womanists emphasize the interlocking character of the "triple jeopardy" of racism, sexism, and classism, the ecological crisis should be viewed in a "nonadditive" framework. Ecological crisis is experienced simultaneously along with the other forms of oppression.

If women are raped, nature—which is closely identified with women—is also raped. If "human others" have suffered dehumanization and exploitation, nature, which is placed at the bottom of the hierarchy of being, has certainly absorbed the onus of all forms of oppression. Where there is classism, sexism, and racism, there is ecocide. In the lives of the poor we can discern the interweaving of naturism and classism; in environmental racism we can discern the link between naturism and racism; in the exploitation and rape of women's bodies we can discern the interlocking of naturism and sexism.

The longtime controversy between social justice activists and ecologists conveys the importance of seeing the interlocking forms of oppression.

Like many ecologists today, I affirm the intrinsic connection of our struggles for justice and ecological well-being. However, because I am taking the experience of the struggling poor of the Third World with utmost seriousness, I engage ecology with a distinct emphasis.[2] This, for me, generates an approach to ecology that takes the issue of class seriously, which is distinct from those ecological approaches that start from the experience of privilege. I argue that the experience of the poor provides a persuasive entry point for understanding the interlocking connection of naturism with other forms of oppression.

Thomas Berry states that "when nature goes into deficit, then we go into deficit...Neither economic viability nor improvement in the life conditions of the poor can be realized in such circumstances."[3] General statements such as Berry's easily get a nod of approval from many people. It is true, indeed, that when nature goes into deficit, all go into deficit. But what appears unequivocally clean at an abstracted and generalized level has flaws when analyzed closely through the lens of the interlocking forms of oppression. I hope that we have not forgotten that the poor were living in deficit long before the elites realized that when nature goes into deficit a worse catastrophe is going to happen and affect all.

Similarly, it has been argued that bread cannot be shared with the poor if wheat cannot be grown. When wheat or other sources of flour cannot be grown, there is no bread. We cannot share what we do not have. That is a brutal reality. This statement, I believe, is not meant to disregard or minimize the severity of the plight of the poor, but to underscore the crucial nature of ecological concern. However, this statement needs to be qualified because its logic dangerously levels our different experiences of the ecological crisis.

We cannot deny that bread cannot be shared if wheat cannot be grown, but it does not necessarily follow that bread *will* be shared because wheat *is* grown. We must remember that the poor have suffered long from the lack of bread, even when they have broken their backs toiling to grow the amber waves of wheat. In terms of ontological priority or the "order of being," growing wheat takes precedence over sharing, but under an unjust social reality—a reality in which many starve to death while the few wallow in luxury—the crucial issue is not simply growing wheat but *sharing.* Social justice is the crucial issue here.[4] How many times have peasants been promised that once the bountiful harvest comes they will have something to fill their crying stomachs? How many times have landlords promised that if there is a good harvest the tenants will have enough food and some cash to buy the most basic necessities in life? How many times have the promises been broken?

Another argument used to buttress an ecological sensibility is related to nuclearism. It has been rightly argued that while "death cuts off life," nuclear extinction "cuts off birth."[5] When everything and everybody is made extinct, all issues vanish: The poor will not inherit the earth and their revolutionary struggles will be in vain. The problem with this argument is that in an effort to make this *the* problem of the world, we forget that even before the nuclear destruction that ends all, millions of people have already experienced destructions, perpetrated mostly by wealthy nations and individuals backed up by their sophisticated and destructive technology.

While it is true that nuclear annihilation is a problem that ends all problems, it does not necessarily follow that it is considered *the* problem by the starving poor. The poor are far more preoccupied with their uncertainty over the next day's meal than they are with nuclearism. They may be shortsighted, but this is only because they have been dehumanized by the destructive forces, and they are focused on the need to survive. The shortsightedness of those who continue to devastate the ecosystem for enormous wealth is a different story. The experience of the poor requires them to prioritize basic needs; this does not mean that nuclearism is not an important matter.

We have all suffered from ecological crisis and we are all responsible for this crisis, but we have suffered unevenly, and our participation in the destruction of the ecosystem is likewise uneven. The repugnant irony is that those who are most responsible for ecological devastation are also those who have suffered the least from its effects. They have the means to cushion the impact of ecological disaster on their plush neighborhoods, and to insulate themselves when possible. When events of cataclysmic proportions visit their neighborhoods, they can underwrite these risks through what the insurance industry calls "umbrella policies." Oppressed communities suffer most, and they were suffering long before ecologically sensitized wealthy individuals realized there was a problem. Unlike privileged communities, poor communities have no means of insulating themselves from environmental destruction. More often than not, their communities have been used as dump sites.[6]

While it is true that the choice between ecology and justice is a bad one to have to make, given the chance to choose, the poor would surely choose combating hunger as a budgetary priority over combating the greenhouse effect. Choosing between ecology and justice is bad, but in the context of grave poverty the poor have made the correct choice, if they are to survive *for a while.* But the reality is that the poor do not often have a choice. They would rather die slowly of toxic contamination than die instantly of hunger. These are the parameters of their choice: to die slowly or to die instantly. In fact, poor people more often are forced to go to places where there are serious health hazards to scavenge something for immediate survival value. They know that their lives are in danger, but they have no choice. Their choice of food, over and against a wider and longer term ecological concern, is the correct choice in a context in which there are no good choices. The worst choice is made when the powerful elites continue to amass wealth but do not care for the earth.

Because they do not treat ecology as a separate issue, poor people are sometimes thought to be silent about ecology. However, when the poor begin to articulate their understanding of ecology, it carries with it a certain depth, militancy, and passion: It is the depth of interdependence, the militancy of protest, and the passion for life. The poor, particularly the indigenous people, do not speak of ecology as a separate issue because in their daily experience they know that their existence and identity depend on the blessings of nature, particularly the land. A cry from indigenous people in the Philippines conveys this deep connection: "Our lands are marked for destruction, and we with them. To defend our lives, we have to defend our lands!"[7]

The land, for indigenous people, is not a simple piece of property to be owned and disposed. It is foundational to their existence, identity, spirituality, and sense of meaning. This is the context in which native Hawaiians (*Kanaka Maoli*) speak of love of the land (*aloha 'āina*).[8] Among indigenous people of the South Pacific, this deep connection with the land is reflected in the identical word for land and womb, or placenta: *fanua* (Samoan), *fonua* (Tongan), *fenua* (Maohi Nui or Tahitian), *whenua* (Maori), and *vanua* (Fijian). To be evicted from one's land is not simply to lose a property, but to be "cut off from one's source of life: one's mother at it were."[9] To be evicted from one's land is death in its most comprehensive form: obliteration of a people.

It is, however, different for those people who have been uprooted from nature and have waged war on nature; those who work in well-furnished offices and only get exposed to "nature" from time to time during tanning sessions; those who live on processed, ready-to-eat microwavable foods. Their daily experience does not tie them to the ground, to the soil, to the source of life. This alienation from nature has produced an army of ignorant children and a calloused generation. Jack Nelson has not failed to take note of the shocking and shameful truth that "[m]illions of our [North American] children grow up believing that the origin of food is the supermarket."[10]

We need to tell our children that every time we eat ham, beefsteak, and lamb stew, we are eating pig, cow, and sheep, respectively. We must help our children understand that thousands of pigs, cows, and sheep are slaughtered every day for us to have tasty ham, steak, and stew. We must eat with the full awareness and responsibility of our deep connections in the web of life. It is only in this manner that we can celebrate and enjoy our eating. Aboriginal Australians show us the responsibility as well as the delight of eating in a poem, "Barra and Turtle":[11]

> Barramundi
> And short necked turtle
> Move free and easy
> And the water—it's theirs.
> You can catch them
> With a fishing line or spear,
> But only take what you need
> So there's more next time.
> They're very good eating,
> Especially when barbecued in the coals
> And shared with everyone...
> We enjoy the togetherness.

The devastation of the earth and the oppression of marginalized people (the poor, women, people of color, and indigenous people) suggest a framework for understanding naturism as well as the possible approaches for reconstruction. If naturism is connected with socio-economic exploitation, then it is not sufficient to struggle for ecological well-being without struggling for justice. Likewise, if naturism is linked with sexism, the struggle against naturism must be a struggle against sexism. And, if naturism is structurally linked with racism, then the struggle against naturism must also be a struggle against racism.

The use of the term "eco-justice" conveys a meeting of minds, after many controversies, between human rights activists and ecologists that justice and ecology are intertwined. The term suggests that one cannot be a liberationist without being concerned with nature's liberation, and vice versa. There is "no sustainability without justice, and no justice without sustainability."[12] Likewise, one cannot be a feminist without also being an ecofeminist. If it is true that feminists agree, in spite of their differences, that the domination of women and the exploitation of nature are connected, then to be feminist, as Anne Clifford argues, is also to be an ecofeminist.[13] The acknowledgement of this interweaving has crucial bearings on our theological reconstructions.

## Toward a New Sensibility/Worldview

Our dominant worldview is not only patriarchal, racist, classist, and sexist, it is also anthropocentric. As the term implies, anthropocentrism is a worldview that makes human beings the center of the universe, and relegates other creatures to subordinate positions. Anthropocentrism operates on the notion of a hierarchy of being, with human beings on top.[14] Of course, human beings do not have equal position to each other on the pyramid, but in relation to other species, human beings occupy the top of the pyramid.

The classical formulation of anthropocentrism is the statement of Protagoras of Abdera (ca. 485–10 B.C.E.): "The human being is the measure of all things."[15] When viewed in relation to women, whom the patriarchal society has identified with nature, this anthropocentrism is basically androcentric. The human being who is the measure of all things is the human being with male gonads. If Protagoras' apothegm represents the classical statement of anthropocentrism, Descartes' *cogito ergo sum* expresses the modern transmutation. The "I" of Descartes' "I think, therefore I am" is the "I" that has claimed to be the center of the world and whose aim is the *dominium terrae*, the dominion and conquest of the earth.

Anthropocentrism undergirds and finds expression in naturism, for in making human beings the center and pinnacle of creation, it renders other beings as adjuncts and instruments for human benefit. When the worldview is anthropocentric, naturism follows. Where there is naturism, there is anthropocentrism. They cannot be separated. Other living creatures are denied any integrity of their own; they exist only to serve instrumental functions for human beings. Naturism's connection to anthropocentrism makes clear that naturism is an anthropological question.

The papal bull *Romanus Pontifex* illustrates the connection between anthropocentrism and naturism. Pope Nicolas VI (1447–1455) promised the Portuguese monarchs rule over the earth in these terms:

> We, giving due consideration to each and every one of the things indicated, grant full and free authorization to invade, conquer, battle, defeat, and subject any Saracens, pagans, and other enemies of Christ, wherever they may be, and the kingdoms, duchies, principalities, dominions, possessions and the fixed and moveable property as they have and possess; and to reduce to perpetual servitude their persons, and to set apart for themselves and their successors, and take possession of and apply for their own use and utility and that of their successors, their kingdoms, duchies, principalities, dominions, possessions and property. Having obtained this power, King Alfonso accordingly justly and legitimately possesses the islands, lands, ports and oceans which correspond and belong by right to King Alfonso and to his successors.[16]

If naturism is intertwined with anthropocentrism, we cannot unshackle ourselves from naturism without doing the same with regard to anthropocentrism. It is in this regard that a call for a new paradigm, worldview, or cosmology makes sense. Naturism, which is undergirded by an anthropocentric worldview, necessitates a call not merely to a sense of responsibility within the old paradigm, but to a new paradigm, a new sensibility. We are not simply called to a new lifestyle within an old framework, but toward a different framework for understanding ourselves in relation to the cosmos. What we need is an overarching worldview, a new cosmology, and a new sensibility that will inform our dream of a "new creation." What is demanded of us is to "think differently" so that we may "behave differently."[17] It is only in this context of a call to a new sensibility that a call to a new sense of responsibility makes sense. Without a new sensibility, the call to responsibility only scratches the surface of our ecological crisis.

The call to a sensibility beyond anthropocentricism is a radical one. This has to be, for we cannot fully speak of a life-centered way of relating under a paradigm that is anthropocentric, patriarchic, hierarchic, dualistic, mechanistic, deterministic, atomistic, individualistic, androcentric, phallocentric, homophobic, and xenophobic.

### Theological Anthropology and Naturism: The Ambiguous Promise of Christian Theology

The ecological promise of Christianity is ambiguous, says Paul Santmire in his work *The Travail of Nature*.[18] To say this is to at least entertain the possibility that there is something in Christianity, no matter how ambiguous, that can be of service to ecological healing. On the other hand, there are those who would say that Christianity is irredeemably patriarchal, and therefore irredeemably anti-ecological. In line with Santmire and others who have remained within the Christian tradition, I still entertain the possibility of the ecological promise of Christianity.

It is unfair to put all the blame on Christianity for our recent ecological crisis, but it has played an important role in the exploitation of nature. In what has become a classic article, Lynn White, Jr., strongly argues that Christianity, especially in its Western form,

> is the most anthropocentric religion the world has seen... Christianity, in absolute contrast to ancient paganism and Asia's religions (except, perhaps, Zoroastrianism), not only established a dualism of man and nature but also insisted that it is God's will that man exploit (exercise dominion) nature for his proper ends.[19]

The creation accounts in Genesis 1–3 have been used often as "archetypes" to justify the exercise of "dominion" over nature.[20] Scholarly arguments have been made asserting that dominion does not mean domination or the subduing of other living creatures. Richard Clifford, for example, argues that God's command to "subdue" in the Genesis account does not mean to dominate or exploit. Rather, it means to inhabit the land that God gives, making it into a home in which godly life can be lived. In his words, to subdue "does not mean to exploit but rather to receive it as a gift and live on it."[21]

Etymological and exegetical studies are helpful here. Nevertheless, it appears that people habitually equate dominion with the practice of domination.[22] Even with regard to Clifford's exegetical study, what unfortunately sticks in the minds of many readers is not his reinterpretation of the word *subdue*, but people's association of the word *dominion* with the word *domination*, or, in a more concealed and refined way, management of the natural resources.[23]

What this unfortunate habit of thinking suggests to me is that a larger challenge needs to be addressed: the issue of worldview. When the worldview is anthropocentric, or even theocentric, dominion can only mean in practice the domination of nature; dominion justifies human control of nature. Exegesis of biblical texts must be seen as part of the whole project of worldview critique and the articulation of an ecological worldview.

When we examine theological ideas, especially those of the theological giants of our Christian faith, we can also discern the ambiguous ecological promise of Christianity. Santmire, who has done an extensive study of the works of major theologians such as Irenaeus, Origen, Augustine, Aquinas, Bonaventure, Dante, Francis of Assisi, Luther, Calvin, Barth, and de Chardin, points to this ambiguous ecological promise.

Santmire identifies three metaphors he considers useful in evaluating the ecological bearings of the ideas of some of our theological giants: (1) the metaphor of ascent, (2) the metaphor of fecundity, (3) the metaphor of migration to a new land. The metaphor of ascent, for Santmire, falls under the "spiritual motif," while the metaphor of fecundity and the metaphor of migration to a new land fall under the "ecological motif." The metaphor of migration to a new land is ambiguous but, as Santmire contends, it does not relinquish the idea of being rooted to the land because the metaphor continues to speak of a new land. In Santmire's categorization, the spiritual motif, which is focused on the redemption of the human being, is ecologically problematic; whereas, the ecological motif, which underscores human relatedness and destiny in relation to the rest of creation, offers a positive ecological promise. Hence, the ambiguous ecological promise of Christianity.

Given Santmire's interpretive categories, some theologians fall heavily on the spiritual motif and others on the ecological motif. Origen, for example, because of the dominance of the metaphor of ascent and the striking closeness of his theological ideas to those of the Gnostics, is classified under the spiritual motif. While not explicitly Gnostic, Santmire interprets Origen as coming "strikingly close to the apperceptions and the sensibilities of Gnosticism."[24] In this case, Origen is ecologically problematic because he sees human life in nature as something to be overcome in order to be with God in eternity. On the other hand, Irenaeus, for Santmire, is ecologically promising because of his stance against the Gnostic heresy of his time and because he did not see God and the human as ontologically set apart from nature.

Augustine, a major theologian whom we cannot ignore, receives a more positive assessment from Santmire. In contrast to Origen, Santmire contends that though Augustine was deeply steeped in Platonism, he did not develop a doctrine of God that is essentially defined as over against the world of nature. Because the metaphor of migration to the good land and fecundity are visible in the theological ideas of Augustine, Santmire believes that Augustine's theological position "represents the flowering of ecological promise of classical Christian theology."[25]

Aquinas receives a more sobering assessment from Santmire than Augustine. The celebrated Thomistic principle that grace does not destroy nature but perfects it, is, for Santmire, narrowly anthropocentric, because what is perfected by grace are the spiritual creatures, not plants, animals, and other bodies. This is sobering given the enormous influence of Aquinas on Christian thought, especially in Roman Catholic theology.

How about the Protestant Reformers? In another essay, "Healing the Protestant Mind: Beyond the Theology of Human Dominion," Santmire makes the point that those who follow the traditions of (Reformers) Luther and Calvin are ill-equipped to deal theologically with the global ecological crisis.[26] "The Protestant mind," he says, "has become fixed, not to say fixated, on what Karl Barth called 'the-anthropology,' the doctrine of God and humanity."[27] This "the-anthropology" is fixated on the God-human relationship, while relegating the world of nature to a "staging" area in the unfolding drama of human sinfulness and God's redemptive act in Christ. Assigned no inherent value, except an instrumental one, the world of nature becomes simply an object waiting for human beings to use and dominate. This way of thinking, Santmire argues, must be healed so that it can respond adequately to the ecological crisis of our time.

I agree with Santmire that the ecological promise of Christian theology is ambiguous, although there are dimensions we can retrieve and reinterpret. On the other hand, I would like him to be more critical in his assessment. Santmire's interpretive categories, it seems to me, prevented him from questioning in a radical way the anthropocentric and patriarchal undergirding of the theologians he examined. Even if some classical theologians (Irenaeus) moved into "theocentrism," this kind of theocentrism, no matter how modified, falls under the anthropocentric framework. Creation, though not solely for human use, continues to be treated instrumentally—for God's sake or as an avenue for human beings to reach God. The main difference between this kind of theocentrism and anthropocentrism is that in this theocentrism the main "user" is God. But to say that the main "user" is God is de facto the instrumentation of nature by human beings in the name of glorifying God. For in real life, it is human beings, not God, who must use the natural world. Just as my spouse would feel demeaned and dehumanized if I say, "I love you for God's sake," so it is no less demeaning and exploitative to use nature even for the glory of God or for God's sake. I know that this way of thinking goes against the grain of our common Sunday school view of stewardship. But, for heaven's sake, let us stop using creation for God's sake.

Even as we entertain the possibility that we can retrieve and reappropriate those aspects of our biblical and theological heritage that are ecologically promising, let us not forget the dominant worldview overarching our biblical and theological heritage. Many feminist and ecologist theologians have made us aware of the anthropocentric worldview undergirding classical and modern theologies, even under the appearance of theocentrism. From Augustine to the Reformers, argues Sallie McFague in *Super, Natural Christians*, nature generally falls into the role of a backdrop, or it serves as a stage for God's more important work: redemption.[28]

Frederick Ferré, in his work *Hellfire and Lightning Rods: Liberating Science, Technology, and Religion*, shares his own assessment:

> I find it a significant weakness in mainstream Christianity that all values in nature are merely extrinsic and derivative. Humankind stands accountable, true, but only to God, not to the vulnerable earth. God's absolute monopoly of first-order being and worth leaves the world around us with only surrogate status.[29]

## Rethinking Sin in Light of Naturism

Like other forms of oppression, naturism is sin in its radical form. There is, however, a qualitative difference when we think of sin in light of naturism. While the victims of other forms of oppression are all participants in the sinful structure, the main victims of naturism—the whole ecosystem—cannot be charged with complicity with regard to the sin of naturism. Nature absorbs and suffers from our sinful acts against it, but we alone—self-reflective human beings—can sin. If there is one stark distinction between us and other creatures, it is that we alone can sin; we alone can wantonly destroy the earth, including ourselves. Other creatures can be destructive, but not in the sense of extending themselves beyond what is needed for living. Only human beings can be destructive with intentionality and severity.

The ecological crisis calls for a major rethinking of how we view sin. We cannot continue to hold an anthropocentric or theocentric view of sin, and hence, of grace and salvation, if we are to respond adequately to our ecological crisis. In the early part of this book I pointed out, following Suchocki, that sin is a violation of creation's well-being. Creation is not limited to human beings, but includes the whole cosmos. We sin not only against fellow human beings but against the world of nature through our anthropocentric and, consequently, dominative and consumeristic acts. In light of our ecological crisis, Matthew Fox says that sin means "injuring creation and doing harm to its balance and harmoniousness, turning what is beautiful into what is ugly."[30]

Reappropriating the Christian tradition, McFague speaks of sin as "living a lie" in relation to God, self, fellow human beings, and other creatures. Living a lie means our "refusal to accept our place in the scheme of things."[31] More particularly, it involves claiming to be the center of creation and relegating others to the margins for our own purposes. It means our refusal to accept that we are one among other beings in the universe and that our uniqueness does not justify our claim to superiority over others. It also means denial and usurpation of the place of other beings in the scheme of things.

We are reminded here that sin is a relational concept, and it is always a breach of right relation. There is no sinful act that does not harm the self and others: It is always and necessarily social. McFague identifies three dimensions in which we need to view sin from an ecological perspective. For McFague, we live a lie in relation to other human beings ("us versus us"); we live a lie in relation to other animals ("us versus them"); and we live a lie in relation to nature ("us versus it").[32]

McFague's scheme is broad enough, yet it does not neglect the particularities. Sin includes the distortion of our relationship with the animal world ("us versus them") as well as a distortion of right relationship with nature ("us versus it"). To live a lie in relation to animals is to live as if we can dispose of them as we wish and to refuse to share with them the space necessary for their existence. To live a lie in relation to the world of nature is to objectify and commoditize it as well as violate its well-being.

Ecological sin is not only about the world of nature and animals around us, it is also about how we relate to other human beings, because human beings are part of the whole ecosystem. Sin, at the level of "us versus us," can be interpreted as the refusal to accept our place in the scheme of things by forbidding others to share space with us. But this is a naive generalization. As McFague is very well aware, sin is the refusal of the "haves" to share space and the basic ecological support system with the "have-nots."

All three dimensions of sin point to the interconnections of sin as well as to the interconnections of life. The life and well-being of human beings, animals, and nature depend on these interconnections. We may call these interconnections the web of life. In this regard, sin as refusal to accept our place in the scheme of things is an act of breaking the web of life.

A caveat here is appropriate. To speak of sin as refusal to accept our place within the scheme of things must always be put in the perspective of just relation, if it is not to perpetuate the reigning cosmology, and, hence, of unjust relation. In many instances, this understanding of sin has been used to perpetuate oppression. For years, marginalized groups have been told to accept their place in the name of the natural scheme of things. Those who have refused to accept their place within the scheme of things as defined by the powers that be have been declared sinners. In other words, acceptance of our place within the scheme of things can only be liberating and healing if the oppressive scheme of things is deconstructed and is replaced with a just scheme of things.

## Who Are We in the Scheme of Things?

Our critique of sin leads to the examination of our place in the scheme of things. Who are we in the scheme of things? Who are we in relation to the world around us? What is this rightful place that we have refused to accept? These questions call for an articulation of a cosmology or of a worldview.

There are several ways of responding to the questions I have posed regarding cosmology/worldview. Many ecologist-theologians of our time have found the ideas of postmodern science to be very promising in helping us understand our rightful place in the scheme of things. We may have come from different places in the world and from different traditions, but we have a "common creation story"–a common story not only among human beings but a common story with the nearest amoeba and the distant stars. This common story does not simply speak of a common journey between autochthonously self-contained beings, but a common journey among intrinsically related beings. According to Ian Barbour, "[T]he chemical elements in [our] hand and in [our] brain were forged in the furnaces of the stars."[33] This common story sheds significant light on who we are. We have common elements, a common beginning, a common plight, and a common destiny–hence, a common story.

The common creation story helps us see the larger scheme in which we belong and that there is an encompassing narrative of which we are a part–a cosmic narrative. Our story is a specific human story (and various human stories coming out of our specificities), yet our story is part of a much larger story. Although we often think and behave as if our story were the only story and the only one that matters, there is a much wider narrative in which we participate and in which our plight and destiny are bound. Part of our search for who we are involves finding our stories and weaving them into the wider story.

When we see ourselves in relation to the vastness of the universe, we are jarred from our usual habits of thinking that the earth is the center of the universe or that we are the center of the universe. In fact, the common story does not clearly point to where the center is, for every living being is at the same time centered and connected. Starting with the Copernican revolution, we have become aware that the earth is not the center of the universe, but we have continued to live as if we were the center of the universe, with the sun rising and setting over us. The common story continues to remind us to re-center ourselves, not as the center of the universe but as centered in being intrinsically one with the whole cosmos.

To say that we are one with the whole cosmos and that we were forged with the distant stars is awesomely revealing of who we are as embodied selves. To speak of being embodied is not only to speak about being attuned to our individual bodiliness, but to claim that the world is our body. We do not simply have or possess bodies, but we *are* bodies and the world is our body. We are specific bodies, which give physical shape to our centered selves, but our bodiliness is as wide as the world. The world's well-being is our well-being. Our common story reminds us that we need to change our notion that we can insulate ourselves from the destiny of the cosmos.

The common story also helps us understand that though we may be different, as others are different, we are also intrinsically related and interdependent. Individuality (particularity) is an important feature of this common story, but we are also connected to the whole. We are not "self-made beings," but we belong to the web of life. We cannot totally separate ourselves from the world of nature, and we do so only at our own peril. What happens to the world, happens to us, for the elements that are in the cosmos and the air that we breathe are connected with the elements of our bodies.

It is in the context of our interdependence that we must understand any discourse about intrinsic worth. Every being in the cosmos has intrinsic worth, but a worth predicated on an authentic individuality that is possible only in the context of interdependence. While many ecologist theologians stress notion of "value in itself" or "intrinsic worth," I want to claim the primacy of interdependence, bondedness, and solidarity. Given the individualistic predilection of the West, I am afraid the notion of "intrinsic worth" resonates with an anthropology that often starts with the intrinsic worth of the individual before moving to the social, rather than construing the individual in the social. To assert the intrinsicality or the intrinsic worthiness of something or someone is a necessary move against any form of instrumentation. However, it remains vulnerable to the "absolutization" of an individual entity by virtue of the claim to intrinsic worth. I propose intrinsicality in interdependence as a way to prevent, on one hand, any form of instrumentation, and on the other hand, the absolutization of intrinsic worth without interdependence.

Holmes Rolston III resonates with my position on this issue. Rolston sees the notion of intrinsic worth or "the for what it is in itself" as problematic in a holistic web, because it is too "internal" and because of its tendency to forget that something is "good" only "in a role, in a whole."[34] Individual mountains, animals, plants, and human beings have intrinsic value, but this value is inseparable from their being part of the whole ecosystem.

Under the canopy of anthropocentricism, we have learned to develop our identities as human beings through disconnection, rather than through connectedness and interdependence. Our way of relating to fellow human beings parallels our way of relating to other beings in the cosmos. We seek to disconnect ourselves because we want to establish our difference from other forms of life. But the difference that we seek through our acts of disconnection is an adjunct to our claim to superiority. We establish our difference through disconnection because we believe deep in our hearts that it is only in disconnecting ourselves that we can claim superiority.

Rather than seeing our difference and uniqueness as a reminder of our interdependence, we confuse our difference and uniqueness with superiority.[35]

Other beings are just as different as we are, and we should not confuse our uniqueness with superiority. If by superiority we mean that everybody and everything depends on us, we have failed to understand the web of relationship. There is not only a continuity between the simplest organisms in the cosmos and the more complex forms, like human beings; there is an inverse dependence of the so-called complex forms of life on the simple forms. This reality is difficult to accept because we have lived as if we were self-made beings, independent from other creatures. There is interdependence among living beings, but we are inversely dependent on the simpler forms of life. This does not only apply to our relationship with the natural world, but to our relationship with fellow human beings. The affluent class lives as if the lower income people are dependent, if not parasitic, on them; instead, it is the other way around. Their wealth is an outcome of a parasitic relationship with lower paid workers. This way of construing our relationship to the simple forms of life should strip us of our arrogance and de-center us from the anthropocentric scheme of things as well as the scheme of things defined by the power wielders.

If the cosmos is our context, then we can say that we are citizens of the cosmos. Our citizenship is a universal citizenship. More particularly, we are citizens of the planet Earth; we are "earthlings." We are not fit to live elsewhere. We are not simply sojourners or tourists on this earth, though we continue to behave as such; the earth is our home. We must stop treating this earth as a hotel that we can just leave after using its amenities. This is the only home we have, so let us stop entertaining the idea that we can put our eggs in another basket (e.g., the planet Mars).

To say that we are earthlings does not mean that we forget the particularities of our citizenship. I believe it is necessary to be reminded of this if, in our efforts to expand our citizenship to the wider cosmos, we do not forget the unequal privileges we have received by virtue of our national citizenship. People who have suffered because of their national citizenship know that the rhetoric of planetary citizenship may serve to mask the power imbalance among nations and the privileges that citizens of affluent nations, no matter how ecologically sensitive they are, have accrued from the unequal relationship between countries.

## Image of God: Imaging Ourselves

The common creation story is one story, though a significant one, for understanding ourselves and our place in the cosmos. Our biblical heritage also offers a story, a creation story in which we may see ourselves. The Genesis creation account says that human beings are created in the image of God. As in the chapter on sexism, I must again remind us that before we make the claim that we are created in the image of God we should clarify first what our image of God is and the relationship of this God with the world. Let us first scrutinize our image of God; otherwise we will end up imaging ourselves to a God who continues to perpetuate naturism. What is the image of this God to whom we have to image ourselves? What kind of God do we want to be an image of? How does this image of God inform the way we relate to the ecosystem? These questions are crucial, because the way we understand the God-world relation serves as a model of how we relate to the world of nature. In other words, our views of God and God's relationship with the world shape the way we relate to the world. We imitate God's way of relating as we construe it.

Some theologians, including McFague, Barbour, and Claude Stewart, have identified several models of God-world relation that have shaped and expressed the ways we relate to the world of nature.[36] There are basically five proposals: (1) deistic, (2) dialogic, (3) monarchical, (4) agential, and (5) processive-organic.

In the deistic model, the relationship between God and the world is analogous to that of the relationship between the clockmaker and the clock. After the initial burst of God's creativity, God remains inactive and detached. God's care for the cosmos is expressed through the overall design and efficiency of the created world. God intervenes only if there is something wrong with the system. This model supports the notion of an interventionist, God-of-the-gaps view of divine reality.

The dialogic model views the relationship between God and the world (here, human beings) as analogous to the relationship between one person and another person. In contrast to the impersonal character of the deistic model, the dialogic model underscores the interpersonal and covenantal relationship between God and human beings. Its main weakness is that it focuses on the relationships between God and humans and between human beings. Nature, here, is merely a stage in the unfolding drama of God's interaction with the world.

In the monarchical model, the relationship between the world and God is analogous to that of the king and his subjects. The king is almighty and all-knowing, controls everything, demands absolute obedience from his subjects, and predestines their future. Disobedience is the greatest sin. Though the king is an absolute monarch, he is also construed as a loving and compassionate father.

The agential model of God-world relation is analogous to the agent and his or her action. If there is an action, there is an actor: action and actor are inseparable. Human action is taken as a model of divine action. If human intention is expressed through human actions, God's intentions can also be discerned through God's actions in the overall cosmic drama. God, the agent, is understood to act in and through nature and history.

The organic-processive model of God-world relation implies an intense organic interrelatedness. It may take the analogy of the relationship between an individual to a community of which the individual is organically related, or it may take the analogy of the world as God's body, as McFague does. God is affected by the world, suffers with the world, and changes with the world. Between God and the world there is interdependence and reciprocity, though the relationship is not fully symmetrical. God's power, unlike the hierarchical model, is a power of persuasion.

Barbour, Stewart, and McFague take various positions in relation to the models cited above. Barbour advances the process-organic model as the most viable model for our times. Stewart argues for the agential model. He believes that the agential model "performs more of the functions requisite to an adequate theology of nature, with fewer liabilities, than any other models of the God-world relationship."[37]

McFague combines the agential and organic model. This combination, for her, opens the possibility of speaking of God's immanence and transcendence as two facets of one reality. It is through the agential model that God's transcendence or distinction from the world is affirmed, and it is through the organic model that God's immanence is maintained. The deistic, dialogic, monarchical, and agential models underscore divine transcendence at the expense of divine immanence, while the organic model puts more stress on divine immanence. With the agential and the organic models combined, McFague argues, it becomes possible to speak of transcendence in an immanental way or to speak of immanence as the other side of transcendence.

All these models shape the way we image ourselves and promote certain attitudes toward the way we relate to other beings. What attitudes or sensibilities are encouraged by the above models of God-world relation?

The deistic model promotes a mechanistic attitude that shapes our ways of relating to other human beings and to the world of nature. When we model ourselves to a machine-God, we also behave like machines in relation to others. The deistic God is a detached God who cannot provide comfort or companionship to the afflicted, especially when a promised quick fix does not materialize.

The dialogic model, with its preoccupation with the human and the internal dimension of human existence, does not address the issue of ecological crisis. It is not only silent, but promotes a sensibility that treats the natural world instrumentally. It fosters the belief that the world of nature is simply there for human satisfaction, adhering to a view of nature as a staging place for communion with God. Its focus on the inner self as the space of encounter between God and the individual promotes a privatistic Christianity, and it pushes under the rug the issue of social transformation, which is constitutive of the divine-human encounter. This model tends to promote the dichotomy of body and soul, nature and history, with soul and history on top of the dualism. It also encourages a privatistic-otherworldly salvific thrust.

Regarding the monarchical model, its royalist and triumphalist metaphors promote anthropocentric, androcentric, totalistic, imperialistic, militaristic, dualistic, and hierarchical ways of thinking and relating. The God of the monarchical model is a powerful and interventionist being who encourages passivity among his subjects and obedience to the divine command. Disobedience is the major category of sin in this model. Even if the monarch is a benevolent father, the form of relationship that it generates is paternalistic.

Of these models the monarchical and deistic models have the greatest liabilities. Imaging ourselves in the image of God based on these models only perpetuates ecological devastation. While the dialogic model can be modified from an exclusive focus on human beings to include a dialogue with other beings, it appears inadequate to usher us toward an ecological sensibility.

It appears to me that the agential and processive-organic models offer more fruitful images of God, because they point to our deep connections and rightful place in the created universe. These models offer an image of a God who does not ask us to exploit nature even for God's sake. It is not for God's sake, because God is embodied in the world. This God is not a being out there, shaping nature and historical events from the outside, but a God who is inseparable from the cosmos. This is the God to whom we must image ourselves, for this is the image that is truly in us if we only have the eyes to see.

## Anthropology, Christology, and Ecology

If we must deal with the question of God's image itself even before we can begin to understand what it means to be created in God's image, we must likewise deal with the image we have of Jesus. The Christian understanding of God's image is historically mediated through Jesus of Nazareth, whom we call the Christ. What kind of God do we see in Jesus? How does Jesus reflect the image of God? How is his imaging of the divine relevant to our ecological crisis and our attempt to reconstruct an ecologically sensible anthropology? How do we interpret christology in relation to our ecological crisis and our vision of ecological well-being?

Of fundamental importance to any christological claim, which I also believe is of ecological significance, is the notion of the incarnation. God was incarnate or became flesh in Jesus. This is a radical claim in a context in which God is thought of as impassionable, never changing, and removed from any association with something bodily. In the incarnation, we see a God who affirms and redeems the body from the gnostic/docetic idea that the body is a prison house. Incarnation affirms the sacredness of the body: We can encounter God in and through our bodies as well as the cosmic body.

With our awareness of our common creation story and our knowledge that the elements of our bodies contain particles of the distant stars and the nearest amoeba, we should be able to extend our understanding of God's incarnation to the world of animals and nature around us. God incarnates Godself in the whole cosmos, and as Christians we see this clearly in both the life of Jesus of Nazareth, our paradigmatic figure, and the christic communities that supported Jesus. The world is God's incarnation. We can discern God's incarnation through the web of life that sustains us as well as in the lives of people who are seeking to affirm life amidst the forces of death.

The classical formula regarding the divinity and humanity of Jesus also comes to a new light once we have acquired an ecological eye. Against odds and controversies, the early church affirmed that Jesus is truly human/ truly divine (*verus homo/verus Deus*). It is difficult, if not impossible, to think of Jesus as truly human and truly divine under the old framework in which God and human being are as far apart as the most distant star and the nearest bacteria. Many of the attempts to articulate Jesus' dual nature (human and divine) have ended up stressing the divine at the expense of Jesus' humanity or Jesus' humanity at the expense of Jesus' divinity.

But our ecological eyes have shown us that we need not see Jesus' humanity and divinity as either/or, nor even as a "combination" of two extrinsic substances. In Jesus, we have the intrinsic connectedness of humanity and divinity raised to a significant height. Jesus is one who fully embodies divine-human communion. Jesus' life not only raises the divine potential of the human, it also embodies the integration of the divine and the human.

Jesus was not only the Christ-*bearer*, says James Nelson, but the "Christ-*barer*." Jesus bares the possibilities of the integration of the human and the divine, of our wholeness. Jesus does not simply "combine" humanity and divinity; he bears the intrinsic connections between divinity and humanity and, in bearing so, he also bares to us our own possibilities. "To be fully human," writes Nelson, "is to know the Christ—not as supernatural invader but as that reality truest to our own natures, and as that reality which intimately connects us with everyone and everything else."[38]

The integration of the human and the divine in Jesus overturns the hierarchical dualism between the spiritual and the material. But it also points to the constructive side: that our aim is for wholeness and connection, that the spiritual is truly material, and that the material is truly spiritual. They belong together as facets of the whole human being. The unity of the spiritual and the material in Jesus is an expression of the redemption of the material from its subordination to the spiritual.

If the human Jesus—whose origin was forged with the stars and the amoebas and whose elements and possibilities are also ours—struggled against various life-negating elements, healed the sick, and prophetically proclaimed the reign of God's shalom, his life and ministerial acts are also ours and on behalf of the ecosystem. If we truly know and live our intrinsic connections with the distant planets and the nearest beings, we cannot speak, witness, or dream about our individual selves without thinking of beings other than ourselves on whom we are largely dependent. Jesus' ministry of healing, feeding, and idol-smashing extends to the whole web of life.

### Human Salvation, Ecological Salvation: Shalom in a "Biocratic" Cosmos

"What has not been assumed cannot be restored; it is what is united with God that is saved," says Gregory of Nazianzus in relating christology to salvation.[39] Christ has to be human in Jesus to save humanity, for he cannot save what he has not "assumed." Within an anthropocentric milieu, this statement was clearly concerned with the salvation of humanity. But a christology rooted in an ecological consciousness and the insights from our common creation story understands that Christ in Jesus "assumed" not only humanity, but the whole cosmos. As the whole cosmos is "assumed" in Christ's incarnation, so the whole created universe is given the offer of salvation. This does not mean that Jesus is the "totality" that "assumes" the cosmos, but that we see the "whole" through the particular. This is one of the ways to reappropriate the classical formulation. What is crucial here, whether one tries to reappropriate the classical formulation or not, is that the whole cosmos is the locus of salvation.

In the incarnation and the unity of the divine and the human in Jesus we also see the direction, place, and scope of salvation. McFague asserts that salvation is the direction of creation and creation is the place of salvation and to whom it happens. And the scope of salvation is the whole of creation, for God cannot save a fragment without saving the whole. In McFague's words, "creation is not one thing and salvation something else; rather, they are related as scope and shape, as space and form, as place and pattern. Salvation is for all creation."[40] We do not need to be transported somewhere to the seventh heaven to meet God, for being with God means being with the world and being true to ourselves.

Recognizing the whole of creation as the locus, scope, and recipient of salvation, we need to expand the framework of our notion of societal dwelling from a concept of democracy to one of biocracy. It is in the context of the cosmic web of life that we must interpret what we mean by shalom, right relation (justice), and harmony (ecological interdependence). There is shalom in our societal dwelling when there is justice and harmony. But the justice and harmony I speak about are not limited to the relationship between human beings; rather, justice and harmony refer to just and harmonious relations among all beings.

Larry Rasmussen's notion of justice strengthens the point I am making. He says, "*Justice*, biblically, *is the rendering,* amidst limited resources and the conditions of brokenness, *of whatever is required for the fullest possible flourishing of creation.* That which makes for wholeness in nature, psyche, and society is 'just.'"[41] Justice and harmony in the created cosmos are not only intertwined but inextricably bound, for one cannot really speak of justice without some notion of harmony and cosmic order, whether it is acknowledged or not. Justice (right relation) is the foundation of cosmic harmony, and justice is justice only if there is cosmic harmony. A harmonious order is a just order, a just order is a harmonious order.

Douglas Knight's study of Hebrew cosmogony illuminates my point:

> YHWH created the world according to *sedaqâ*, "righteousness," a principle of moral and cosmic orderliness…When *sedaqâ* prevails, the world is at harmony, in a state of well-being, in *salôm.* An act of sin in the religious sphere or injustice in the social sphere can inject discord and shatter *salôm.* It then takes a decisive act of *mispat,* "justice," to restore the *salôm* and reestablish the *sedaqâ.*[42]

### A New Sense of Worldliness, a New Spirituality

All the major insights I have woven together in this chapter point to a new sense of worldliness, a worldly spirituality. What is this life that is lived under the influence of the spirit and fully cognizant of the indwelling of the spirit? Is this life different from our life here on earth?

No! The new life that the spirit brings is not different from this life here; rather, it is the power that makes our life here different. It is an earthly life lived differently while we have life. It is a life lived differently because of our experience of the transforming power of the spirit.

When the spirit dwells, says Jürgen Moltmann, life "wakes up" and "becomes wholly and entirely living, and is endowed with the energies of life."[43] This indwelling of the spirit is not the indwelling of something outside of us or in other beings. Instead, it is the coaxing of the spirit that is in us by the universal spirit of the cosmos, and the discovering inside ourselves of the bubbling energies that seek and affirm life. Our own vitality is an expression of this universal vitality, and the universal vitality is an expression of the interweaving of various vitalities.

The indwelling of the spirit enables us to live differently, a life liberated into a new sense of earthiness and sensuousness. Contrary to the understanding that we become otherworldly when we become spiritual, we become truly earthly and we acquire a new sensuousness when we recognize the indwelling of the spirit. Life in the spirit does not abolish bodiliness; it renews it for eternal livingness. When the spirit dwells in us we are reminded that we are earthlings, citizens of this earth. The world around us is not an obstacle to a life in the spirit. It is only because of the world and through it, not in spite of it, that life in the spirit is realized. This spirit keeps us in touch with our bodies, thinks through our bodies, and experiences God's spirit through the sight, smell, and caress of other bodies, in both the human and the natural world.

When the spirit wakes us up and coaxes our own spirit, scales fall from our eyes and we start to see the world not simply as a machine or a natural resource, but with enchantment. This is not a simple romantic enchantment, but an enchantment that leads to celebration and thanksgiving. "Enchantment with nature," writes Leonardo Boff, "opens us to our specific mission in the universe, that of being priests celebrating and giving thanks for the grandeur, majesty, rationality, and beauty of the cosmos and everything in it."[44] We are not simply managers or even stewards, but cobeings with other beings and cocelebrants with them.

Enchantment and thanksgiving come along with the understanding that life is a gift. Life is not our own possession, neither are we the originators of our own lives. We start in life not as "self-made men" or "self-made women" but as dependents and receivers. We have received life from the web of life, from plants, animals, from our parents, and from society as a whole. Life is a gift to us that we must not take for granted, but for which we can only be grateful. Those who live in homes where water always runs through the spigots or faucets are most likely to take water for granted; in the same way, those who have reliable and comfortable income are most likely to take their next meal for granted. We should not take life for granted, not even breathing itself, for death reminds us that we cannot take it for granted. As the air and water become polluted, we can no longer take them for granted. We should not take the world that sustains us for granted, because it is a gift from the web of life–God.

With our ecological eyes we have been led to see that life is a gift we have received from others, for which we should be thankful. But receiving and thanking are not the only modes of relating to the web of life that sustains us. Throughout our lives we are guests–guests of the community that sustains us, and guests of God's good creation–but guesting is not the only mode of living. Guests must also become hosts if guests are not to become parasites. I agree with Matthew Fox who says that, "in addition to thanking by receiving, there exists thanking by sharing or hosting. The guesting is to feed the hosting...We host because we have first been guests."[45] Hosting or serving is that dimension of thanksgiving that is oriented to the well-being of others.

In a world in which the universal culture of death reigns, life under the impact of the spirit finds expression in prophetic worldliness. "If spirit is life," contends Boff, "then the opposite of spirit is not matter but death, and the realm of death includes all the processes that lead to breakdown and prepare the way for death."[46] These processes include oppression and exploitation of marginalized human communities as well as the desecration, destruction, and exploitation of the ecosystem. These forces of death that destroy the web of life must be denounced with courage and determination.

When the universal spirit ignites our spirit, we experience a new life. The spirit of life breaks through the indifference of our hearts, our inner numbness, and our emotional frigidity. From calloused hearts of stone, we acquire the hearts of flesh, with undivided love for life and sharpened senses. With the spirit rousing our vitality, we can cry out again, weep again, laugh and dance again. And we can be outraged again, outraged at the wrongs being done against the whole of creation, outraged because we care and because we hope. The spirit of life transforms us into true ecological beings, consciously living interdependently with other beings, celebrating, and courageously defending the web of life. This is who we are in the whole of creation, this is what we are called to become, and this is how we are called to act.

## Ecological Actions by Ecological Human Beings

"If you think your actions are too small to make a difference, you've never been in bed with a mosquito."[47] It is easy to feel small and powerless against the destructive power of naturism, much more so when we feel disconnected from each other. As new ecological beings we know deep in our hearts, however, that we are interconnected, and that our actions, wherever we are, may have impacts even beyond our immediate neighborhood. The rubber tapper movement in the Amazon and the Chipko (tree-hugging) movement in the Himalayas offer insightful and empowering testimonies.

Somewhere in the obscure river town of Zapuri in Acre, Brazil, lived Francisco "Chico" Mendes Filho.[48] Mendes, a rubber tapper by trade, organized and mobilized three hundred thousand rubber tappers and a million farmers and hunters, all victims of World Bank and Brazilian government-supported cattle ranching and hydroelectric projects that had stolen and destroyed their lands. An alliance was also forged with Brazilian NGOs and First World allies. Mendes and representatives of indigenous, environmental, and human rights organizations traveled to the United States and lobbied the U.S. Congress and the World Bank. They demanded the creation of "extractive reserves" under the management of local rubber tapper communities. On December 22, 1988, Mendes was murdered. But the struggle for extractive reserves went forward. The Brazilian government finally created nineteen extractive reserves covering nearly three million hectares of rainforest.

The Chipko movement offers another empowering story. It started in the Himalayas in 1973 as a nonviolent movement against the large-scale felling of trees. It received its inspiration from the old legend of Amrita Devi and her Boshnoi friends, who died hugging trees in an attempt to prevent their destruction. From its small beginning, the Chipko movement has spread all over India and has been effective in its campaign against the felling of thousands of trees. It has also inspired various people's movements around the world.

In one incident in 1977 the forestry department planned to cut 640 trees in Tehri Garhwal. At a public hearing intended to address the issue, the forestry officer lost composure and shouted: "'You foolish village women, do you not know what these forests bear? Resin, timber and therefore foreign exchange!'" And the women replied:

> Yes we know.
> What does the forest bear?
> Soil, water and pure air,
> Soil, water and pure air
> are the basis of life.[49]

The birth of the Chipko and rubber tapper movements embody a fundamental belief in our deep connections and the power of our concerted actions. Their presence is a testimony that a new human being, an ecologically conscious and politically active one, is in the making. We can discern the birthing of this new humanity among individuals who embody ecological sensibility, and in movements for ecological well-being.

## Notes

[1]R. B. J. Walker, *One World, Many Worlds: Struggles for a Just World Peace* (London, U. K.: Zed Books; Boulder, Colo.: Lynne Rienner, 1988), 101.

[2]See Eleazar S. Fernandez, "People's Cry, Creation's Cry: A Theologico-Ethical Reflection on Ecology from the Perspective of the Struggling Poor," *Tugón* 12/2 (1992): 277–94.

[3]Thomas Berry, *The Dream of the Earth* (San Francisco: Sierra Club Books, 1988), 71–72. The context of this quote (Chapter 7, "Economics as a Religious Issue") offers an insightful view of how economics is to be construed in a new way that is in consonance with the ecological sensibility. Berry wants his readers to speak of economics not simply in the language of "deficit expenditure" or "income does not balance outflow," but in terms of earth economics, that is, an economics integrated with the processes of nature. This is the economics that promotes a sustainable society.

[4]See T. J. Gorringe, *A Theology of the Built Environment: Justice, Empowerment, Redemption* (Cambridge: Cambridge University Press, 2002), 250–52.

[5]Jonathan Schell, *The Fate of the Earth* (New York: Avon Books, 1982), 117.

[6]Art Meyer and Jocele Meyer, *Earth-Keepers: Environmental Perspectives on Hunger, Poverty, and Injustice* (Waterloo, Ontario, and Scottsdale, Pa.: Herald Press, 1991), 59–63; Grace Thorpe, "Our Homes Are Not Dumps," in *Defending Mother Earth: Native American Perspectives on Environmental Justice*, ed. Jace Weaver (Maryknoll, N.Y.: Orbis Books, 1996), 47–58.

[7]I cannot trace the precise source, but my memory goes back to a poster in support of the struggle of indigenous people in the Philippines.

[8]*He Alo A He Alo: Hawaiian Voices on Sovereignty* (Honolulu: American Friends Service Committee–The Hawai'i Area Office, 1993), vii.

[9]Ilaitia S. Tuwere, *Vanua: Towards a Fijian Theology of Place* (Suva, Fiji: Institute of Pacific Studies of the University of the South Pacific and College of St. John the Evangelist, 2002), 36.

[10]Jack Nelson, *Hunger for Justice: The Politics of Food and Faith* (Maryknoll, N.Y: Orbis Books, 1980), 155.

[11]Christine Rowan, "Barra and Turtle," in *Earth Revealing, Earth Healing: Ecology and Christian Theology*, ed. Denis Edwards (Collegeville, Minn.: Liturgical Press, 2001), 68.

[12]Gorringe, *Theology of the Built Environment*, 251, paraphrasing Rosa Luxemburg.

[13]Anne Clifford, "When Being Human Becomes Truly Earthly: An Ecofeminist Proposal for Solidarity," in *In the Embrace of God: Feminist Approaches to Theological Anthropology*, ed. Ann O'Hara Graff (Maryknoll, N.Y: Orbis Books, 1995), 176. Also, see Lois K. Daly, "Ecofeminism, Reverence for Life, and Feminist Theological Ethics," in *Liberating Life: Contemporary Approaches to Ecological Theology*, ed. Charles Birch, William Eakin, and Jay B. McDaniel (Maryknoll, N.Y: Orbis Books, 1990), 93.

[14]See Kathryn Tanner, "Creation, Environmental Crisis, and Ecological Justice," in *Reconstructing Christian Theology*, ed. Rebecca Chopp and Mark Lewis Taylor (Minneapolis: Fortress Press, 1994), 99–123.

[15]Protagoras, *Fragment 1*, in H. Diels, *Die Fragmente der Vorsokratiker* (Hamburg, 1957), 121, cited in Leonardo Boff, *Cry of the Earth, Cry of the Poor*, trans. Phillip Berryman (Maryknoll, N.Y.: Orbis Books, 1997), 71.

[16]See Paulo Suess, ed., *A Conquesta espiritual* (Petrópolis: Vozes, 1992), 227, cited in Boff, *Cry of the Earth, Cry of the Poor*, 69–70.

[17]Sallie McFague, *The Body of God: An Ecological Theology* (Minneapolis: Fortress Press, 1993), 202.

[18]Paul Santmire, *The Travail of Nature: The Ambiguous Ecological Promise of Christian Theology* (Philadelphia: Fortress Press, 1985).

[19]Lynn White, Jr., "The Historical Roots of Our Ecological Crisis," in *Western Man and Environmental Ethics: Attitudes Toward Nature and Technology*, ed. Ian Barbour (Boston: Addison-Wesley, 1973), 25.

[20]Elisabeth Schüssler Fiorenza makes a distinction between archetype and prototype. While both denote original models, archetype suggests an unchangeable ideal, while prototype suggests a model that is open to new possibilities. See her *Bread Not Stone: The Challenge of Feminist Biblical Interpretation* (Boston: Beacon Press, 1984), 61.

[21]Richard Clifford, "Genesis 1–3: Permission to Exploit Nature?" *Bible Today* (1988): 136, cited in *In the Embrace of God*, 184.

[22]See Frederick Ferré, *Hellfire and Lightning Rods: Liberating Science, Technology, and Religion* (Maryknoll, N.Y: Orbis Books, 1993), 154.

[23]John B. Cobb, Jr., *Sustainability: Economics, Ecology and Justice* (Maryknoll, N.Y.: Orbis Books, 1992), 95.

[24]Santmire, *Travail of Nature*, 52.

[25]Ibid., 73.

[26]H. Paul Santmire, "Healing the Protestant Mind: Beyond the Theology of Human Dominion," in *After Nature's Revolt: Eco-Justice and Theology*, ed. Dieter Hessel (Minneapolis: Fortress Press, 1992), 57–78.

[27]Ibid., 57.

[28]Sallie McFague, *Super, Natural Christians: How We Should Love Nature* (Minneapolis: Fortress Press, 1997), 58.

[29]Ferré, *Hellfire and Lightning Rods*, 153.

[30]Matthew Fox, *Original Blessing: A Primer in Creation Spirituality* (Santa Fe: Bear and Company, 1983), 119.

[31]Sallie McFague, "Human Beings, Embodiment, and Our Home the Earth," in *Reconstructing Christian Theology*, 152.

[32]Sallie McFague, *Life Abundant: Rethinking Theology and Economy for a Planet in Peril* (Minneapolis: Fortress Press, 2001).

[33]Ian Barbour, "Creation and Cosmology," in *Cosmos and Creation: Theology and Science in Consonance*, ed. Ted Peters (Nashville: Abingdon Press, 1989), 147, cited in McFague, "Human Beings, Embodiment, and Our Home the Earth," 151.

[34]Holmes Rolston III, "Values in Nature," in *Environmental Ethics* 3/2: 113–28, cited in Jay B. McDaniel, *Of God and the Pelicans: A Theology of Reverence for Life* (Louisville: Westminster/ John Knox Press, 1989), 57.

[35]See Elizabeth Dodson Gray, *Patriarchy as a Conceptual Trap* (Wellesley, Mass.: Roundtable Press, 1982), 88–91.

[36]Claude Stewart, *Nature in Grace: A Study in the Theology of Nature* (Macon, Ga.: Mercer University Press, 1983), 255–81; Ian Barbour, *Religion in an Age of Science* (New York: Harper and Collins, 1990); Sallie McFague, *Models of God: Theology for an Ecological, Nuclear Age* (Philadelphia: Fortress Press, 1987).

[37]Stewart, *Nature in Grace*, 281.

[38]James Nelson, *The Intimate Connection: Male Sexuality, Masculine Spirituality* (Philadelphia: Westminster Press, 1988), 111.

[39]Cited in Walter Lowe, "Christ and Salvation," in *Christian Theology: An Introduction to Its Traditions and Tasks*, revised and enlarged edition, ed. Peter Hodgson and Robert King (Minneapolis: Fortress Press, 1985), 228.

[40]McFague, *Body of God*, 182.

[41]Larry Rasmussen, "Creation, Church, and Christian Responsibility," in *Tending the Garden*, ed. Wesley Granberg-Michaelson (Grand Rapids, Mich.: William B. Eerdmans Publishing Company, 1987), 121.

[42]Douglas A. Knight, "Cosmogony and Order in the Hebrew Tradition," in *Cosmogony and Ethical Order: New Studies in Comparative Ethics*, ed. R. Lovin and F. Reynolds (Chicago: University of Chicago Press, 1985), 149.

[43]Jürgen Moltmann, *The Source of Life: The Holy Spirit and the Theology of Life* (Minneapolis: Fortress Press, 1997), 11.

[44]Boff, *Cry of the Earth, Cry of the Poor*, 200.

[45]Fox, *Original Blessing*, 116.

[46]Boff, *Cry of the Earth, Cry of the Poor*, 191.

[47]Anonymous, cited in *Affluenza: The All-Consuming Epidemic*, ed. John de Graaf, David Wann, and Thomas Naylor (San Francisco: Berrett-Koehler Publishers, Inc, 2001), 191.

[48]See Jeremy Brecher and Tim Costello, *Global Village or Global Pillage: Economic Reconstruction from the Bottom Up*, 2d ed. (Cambridge, Mass.: South End Press, 1994), 92. Also, see Donald Messer, *A Conspiracy of Goodness: Contemporary Images of Christian Mission* (Nashville: Abingdon Press, 1992), 79–80.

[49]Cited in *Dare to Dream: A Prayer and Worship Anthology from Around the World*, ed. Geoffrey Duncan (London: HarperCollins Religious, 1995), 213.

# CHAPTER 8

# *Becoming a New Human Being in Right (Just) Relation*

The previous four chapters (chapters 4–7) introduced us to four ways of reimagining the human in response to four forms of oppression. In this chapter I intend to integrate the main insights of the previous chapters that point to the shape of a new human being and identify the primary category that weaves these insights together. At the outset, I say that this primary category is relationship: It depicts both our cosmic predicament and the possibilities for salvation.

Throughout this book I have spoken about the new human being as one who is becoming or struggling to be become human. Much as we desire to capture the being of the human, we are not going to seize it because being human is always a process of becoming human. Part of its elusive character is that the new human being is not a pure state after we have purged the old one. The new human being beyond classism, sexism, racism, and naturism is still the old human being struggling to be the new one. José Comblin sheds light on this:

> Old and new coexist for the time being, intimately conjoined, and Christians must live their humanness in the form of an ongoing struggle between the new and the old. Their new person must struggle if it is to exist, resisting the pressures of the old, striving to overcome the weight of the old, and creating a new reality with the materials left behind by the old.[1]

So, what I am articulating does not assume the character of a blueprint for what being human is or must be. Instead, it is an imaginative reconstruction of an alternative way of being human borne out of pain and the longing for greater well-being. I could have waited for some more years before making public my understanding of the human, but that is contrary to my understanding of scholarship as journey and exploration. The next section is my attempt to find the category that re-centers my exploration of becoming human.

### Finding Heart: The Centered Self as Self-in-Relation

Heart, like other rich metaphors, has been trivialized. In a world dominated by a materialist-calculative worldview, the heart metaphor is often relegated to the margins, while the mind (rationality) takes center stage. With this discursive subordination of the heart, it is not a surprise that the mind is identified with the powerful and the successful, while the heart–commonly perceived as the realm of the affective and the emotive– is stereotypically associated with the weak and marginalized members of society. I argue, however, that we need to reclaim the heart metaphor. Reappropriating the metaphor of the heart, I believe, is helpful in de-centering and re-centering what has been traditionally dualized and hierarchized.

In spite of the volumes of discourse against dualistic and hierarchical ways of interpretation, it is still jarring to imagine thinking through our hearts and feeling through our mental faculties. Yet this is precisely what we need to do: to think through our heart or to move our vision from our brain to our heart. This does not mean that we should stop thinking clearly, but to make the point that our brain must be congruent with our heart. This is in line with the admonition of the great spiritual leaders of the church who spoke of "keeping the mind in the heart." This means, following Tilden Edwards, keeping our "thoughts, feelings, bodies, actions, wills, and sense of identity connected with our spiritual heart day by day, moment by moment." Human "sanity and authentic discernment, love, and delight," Edwards continues, "depend on this connectedness."[2]

Only when our thoughts, actions, wills, and bodies are connected to our hearts can we maintain our sanity; for heart, both in Latin and French (*cor* and *coeur* respectively), means core or center.[3] The heart is the center or the innermost core of who and what we are. As the "center of all vital functions," says Rita Nakashima Brock, heart "is the seat of self, of energy, of loving, of compassion, of conscience, of tenderness, and of courage."[4] Heart, as a metaphor for center or core, unites body and spirit, reason and emotion, thinking and acting.

Is it not true that that which we know best, we "know by heart"? Is it not true that what we truly remember, we "remember by heart"? Is it not true that when we take something seriously, we "take it to heart"? Is it not true that when we speak with passion and honesty we speak "from the bottom of our hearts"? Heart to heart conversation means sincere and honest conversation. When one does something outrageously abhorrent, we say: "Where is your heart?" When we have gained courage we also have "found our hearts." When we are filled with joy, we feel it in our hearts. And, when we have learned by heart we act on what we know.

If heart is the center or the core, then to speak of finding heart is to speak of finding our center. Finding our center is an experience of becoming a centered self, which should not be confused with being self-centered. A self-centered person has the self as the center. Everybody and everything revolves around the self. The self-centered person has a bloated self. On the contrary, a centered self is a self that has come to the awareness of other selves or has come to the consciousness of a wider world in which it is a part. Instead of being closed off or self-obsessed, the centered self reaches out for relationship and finds the true self only in interdependence with other beings. It is aware that it can view the surrounding world only from the perspective of its own center, yet it sees its well-being only in relation to the well-being of others within the web of interdependent relations. It reaches out to the surrounding world without losing identity or dissipating one's energies.[5]

Looking back at what I have said in previous chapters, it has become clear to me that relationship is a primary category in this study. Relationship is constitutive of who we are and what we can become. Relationality, not rationality, is decisive for our humanity. Not all individuals have the ability to reason (at least in the way we commonly construe reason), as in the case of total mental disability, but we all relate to the web of life. Descartes' human being, defined primarily in terms of thinking (*Cogito ergo sum*),[6] must be transmuted into *Cognatus ergo sum* (I am related, therefore I am) and *Cognatus ergo summus* (I relate, therefore we are).[7]

*Cognatus ergo summus* finds resonance in Bantu cultures of Africa in the phrase *umuntu ngamuntu ngabantu* (I am because we are, and because we are I am). Desmond Tutu's "ubuntu" theology (plural rendering of the term "Bantu") is rooted in the proverbial Xhosa expression (Tutu belongs to the Xhosa people) *ubuntu ungamntu ngabanye abantu* (roughly translated, "each individual's humanity is ideally expressed in relationship with others").[8] Something similar is also found among the Sotho in South Africa: *Mothoke mmotho ka botbo babang* (a person is a person only through people).[9] These sayings from various cultures make the point that we can only be human through relationship with other human communities.

We need, however, to extend relationship to other species and the whole of the ecosystem. The common story I articulated in chapter 7 points to our intrinsic relationship with the ecosystem. The Lakota phrase *mitakouye oyasin* ("for all my relations") articulates in a profound way the intrinsic relationship of all creatures. The relationship is not simply extrinsic but intrinsic: The well-being of the ecosystem is our well-being not simply because we make use of the ecosystem, but because our very being is intrinsically one with the ecosystem. When we say we are because of our relationship, we should not forget, as George Tinker reminds us, our relationship beyond the two-leggeds, which includes the "four-leggeds, the wingeds, and the living-moving-things."[10]

If being in relation is what constitutes who we are, then it is also what makes us truly an image of God. Relationship is the primary lens through which we interpret the notion of the image of God. We image God most profoundly when our individual interactions, families, and communities— as well as our political, economic, and ecclesiastical structures—reflect life-giving relations. Conversely, the image of God construed in a relational framework presupposes what God is like: The very essence of God is "to be in relation." God is the term we use to refer to that source and power of life-giving relation. God is the web of life-giving relation. This recognition that God's very being is "to be in relation" challenges us to rethink seriously not only human beings but all of reality.[11]

## The Gestalt of Relationship: Right (Just) Relationship in the Wider Web of Life

We can find our humanity only in the context of relationship, not outside of it. Relationship makes us or breaks us. In this case, relationship as such is not sufficient category. We must articulate the gestalt or shape of the relationship that makes us truly human. What is the gestalt of this relationship? Broadly, relationship must take the shape of harmony, justice, and mutuality among intrinsically interdependent beings. These three qualities must be understood in relation to each other.

The term *harmony* suggests accord, agreement, compatibility, coordination, symmetry, unity, and peace. All these synonyms of harmony presuppose an overarching order or design. We appraise agreement, coordination, symmetry, unity, and peace only in relation to a certain design or order, whether it is social order or cosmic order. Thus any articulation of harmony begs the question: What is the order within which we must define harmony? Harmony in relation to what order or design? I will argue later that this order must be understood within the framework of a biocratic cosmos.

Just as harmony must be appraised in relation to the order it presupposes, so harmony and order must be examined in relation to the claims of justice. Harmony and order are predicated on just and mutual relationship. Without justice and mutuality there is no harmony; there is no peace. An unjust order is an order of dis-order. The *Kanaka Maoli* (native Hawaiian) word *pono* conveys in a profound way the meaning of harmony: justice, righteousness, balance, and right relation.[12] Harmony exists when there is justice or righteousness and mutuality (balanced relation) among creatures. Justice and mutuality are critical hermeneutical lenses through which we must view and evaluate harmony and order.[13] This is especially so under the present condition of unjust ordering, which is hierarchical, anthropocentric, androcentric, classist, and racist.

What does mutuality look like within this just order? What is mutual relationship among intrinsically interdependent beings? Mutuality is characterized by the mutual giving and receiving of self. This giving and receiving happens only in an atmosphere of openness, an openness to the gift of the other. In the mutual interaction, the participants come out affirmed and nourished. The individuality of each participant thrives in the process of mutual interaction. Each one becomes fully alive in the interactive process. Mutuality sustains life in a biocratic cosmos.

This articulation of relationship among beings in the web of life–taking the gestalt of justice, mutuality, and harmony–can be categorized under the notion of right relation, a term I used in the previous chapters. All forms of interlocking oppression dealt with in this work exhibit instances of a breach or violation of right relation. If the four forms of oppression are violations of right (just) relation, then liberation and healing must necessarily involve the righting of violated relation. Well-being is present only insofar as right relationship exists within the web of life.

The task of defining right relationship is a complex one. Right relationship must be viewed within a broad framework of relationships. In a cosmos made up of interconnections, there is no single happenstance that is not connected to the whole web of relationship. Both at the macro and the micro levels, relationship happens. Finding right relationship within the web of life requires us to place human beings within the wider scheme of things, or within the wider scheme of relationships. It is for this reason that a reconstructive synthesis must start with an ecological framework.

### An Ecological Being in an Ecological Household: Finding Our Place in the Wider Scheme of Things

While classism served as my entry point in the treatment of the interlocking forms of oppression, in this chapter I am going to recapitulate and synthesize the main insights from an ecological perspective. Using ecology as a wider framework to synthesize the main insights is not only appropriate but on target, because ecology, as its root suggests, refers to the "structure of the household." After dealing with the structure I am going to proceed to other dimensions that include the "rules of the household" (economics) and the dynamics of power relations in the household (politics).[14] This choice locates the constructive insights of the previous chapters within a more comprehensive worldview. Ecology sets the constructive insights in the much broader framework of cosmology. Ecological cosmology helps us to see and situate human beings within the wider web of relationships.

An adequate account of human beings can only happen within an ecological cosmology. Dealing with the rules of the household (economics understood in a limited sense) without dealing with the structure (ecology) is like rearranging the furniture in the living room without changing the house structure; changes may be visible but are not structural. If we are to speak of economics that moves beyond chrematistics, we must speak of ecological economics. If we are to speak of politics that moves beyond anthropocentric and androcentric politics, we must speak of ecological politics. And to make sure that politics and economics are not construed separately, as if there is pure economics without politics, it is fitting to speak of an ecological political-economy.

Insights from ecology tell us that the reigning model for construing the human is not congruent with the web of life. It is anthropocentric, hierarchic, dualistic, individualistic, atomistic, and necrophilic. Ecological sensibility questions this reigning notion, challenging us to de-center and re-center human beings. What is this re-centered human being? The re-centered human being is not the center or the apex of creation, but a vital participant within the cosmic symphony. The human being is centered in the cosmic web of life-giving relationship.

Interdependence characterizes human beings' relationship with the whole ecosystem, with human beings inversely dependent on other, less complex, beings. The common creation story tells us of a deeper dimension to this interdependence. Interdependence speaks of intrinsic relationship; it is not an interdependence of extrinsic beings. With the understanding that our bodies are forged from elements of the distant stars and the nearest bacteria, our notion of self is enlarged, along with our notion of bodiliness. We know that the world is our body because of our intrinsic connections and because we know that what happens to the world happens to us. Our well-being is not isolated from the well-being of the whole creation.

When we are de-centered and re-centered within the cosmic web of life, we become truly earthly, and we see ourselves as earthlings, citizens of the earth. This world is not simply a jumping stage to another world beyond the blue. We are not tourists in this world (though we behave as such), with the world as our hotel. God created and loved this world, and we belong to this world. This world is encompassed by the love of God, and whether in death or in life we belong to God and go back to God.

Unfortunately, we have been taught in our Sunday schools that we are denizens of another world and that this world is a backdrop to God's mighty action in history, which will involve snatching us away to a world beyond. Geiko Müller-Fahrenholz notes a historical shift from an "ecodomical" interpretation (the world understood as home) of the term *oikos* (household) by the early Christian communities, toward a construal of the term *oikos* as *paroikia*, which means "living away from home."[15] In the context of the persecution of the early Christian communities, the idea that Christians are aliens and exiles or "resident aliens" (*paroikoi*) in a hostile world and that their true home is in heaven was a very crucial one (compare 1 Pet. 2:11). It helped them hang onto their faith even in the face of persecution.

Even though the *paroikia* perspective can be helpful to the Christian communities, the "ecodomical" perspective needs to be retrieved. In the wake of our ecological crisis, the "ecodomical" perspective reroots human beings to the earth as home or place of refuge. In fact, earth is the only place of refuge. The world is not only a space but our place, and it is the only place where we are fit to live. But the *paroikia* perspective need not be totally discarded. The *paroikia* perspective can be interpreted as a transcendent prophetic principle: It underscores the critical nonconformist calling of faith communities. The faith communities are *in* this world, but they are not *of* this world.

## Making Our Hearts as Large as the World: Becoming Human in a Highly Globalized World

After locating human beings within the wider scheme of things or in the context of our biocratic cosmos, it is necessary to locate individuals and communities in relation to one another at the global level. Simply to locate human beings in the wholeness of the universe is to fail to take into account that they are located in a world in which geo-politics is a harsh reality for many. Human beings do not just exist as generic human beings in relation to the world; they are identified with certain geo-political regions of the world. This influences the way they live as well as how they treat and are treated by people of other nations.

As I noted in chapter 7, I am skeptical of those citizens of the so-called First World countries who readily call themselves citizens of the earth, but often fail to take note of their privileged earthly location relative to citizens of other nations. Their avowed claim to planetary citizenship often conceals their privilege to exploit the earth beyond their shores. Without critical scrutiny, the notion of planetary citizenship may just serve to support the "gobblelization" of the whole earth by the privileged planetary citizens of the affluent countries. In fact, this masking of privilege is already going on and has become more acute in this era of heightened globalization in which citizens of wealthy nations encounter less restriction of their acquisitive desires. Only when we acknowledge our uneven locations within the dynamics of global interactions can we articulate what it means to be a global person and community.

What does it mean to be a new global person? The new global person is not one who claims to view reality from the point of view of eternity, nor one who globalizes, christianizes, and civilizes the world. The new global person is neither one who consumes more global goods nor one who participates frequently in global travel tours. This new global person, I assert, is one whose heart is as large as the world.

At this juncture I would like to lift up a story to illustrate my point. A dialogue in John Drinkwater's work, *Lincoln: A Play*, helps convey my point and challenge. Mrs. Blow, a zealot for the Northern cause, asked President

Abraham Lincoln if there was any good news regarding the Civil War. Lincoln replied: "Yes, they lost twenty-seven hundred men and we lost eight hundred." Mrs. Blow was ecstatic, saying: "How splendid!" Registering a deep dismay, Lincoln retorted: "Thirty-five hundred human lives lost." But Mrs. Blow interrupted: "Oh, you must not talk like that, Mr. President. There were only eight hundred that mattered." With sadness, Lincoln spoke to Mrs. Blow with measured emphasis: "Madam, the world is larger than your heart."[16]

Obviously, her heart was small. The well-being of the other group was not held in the embrace of her heart. Her zealous identification with her group constricted her love, and she could not imagine being concerned with the plight and pain of the other group. In her fervent identification with her group, she constructed a wall of separation that prevented her from connecting with the other.

Literally, the world is larger than our hearts. Physically, a heart is but a small organ of our body, though a very important one. But metaphorically, it is not impossible to make our hearts as large as the world. Though the enlarging of our hearts does not come easily, it happens when we open ourselves to this possibility. In my decade of living in the U.S., I have seen this heart among people who truly love their country but still love global justice. They know that it is not a contradiction to love one's country and still love global justice. These are the people who have sustained me in my diaspora life, a life that is always longing for a home. Through my encounter with these people I have come to the realization that white North Americans do not look alike.

A heart as large as the world is a heart that sees the connections of our lives, wherever we are located on this planet Earth. It is a heart that knows that we live in the intersection of the global and the local, and that the global is lived locally and the local is lived globally. A heart as large as the world, especially in the era of globalization, knows that we share common vulnerabilities. Knowing that our worlds intertwine and that our existence lies at the nexus of the global and the local, we need to affirm with R. B. J. Walker that "behind the insistence on acting locally is a challenge to rework the meaning of human community in an age in which our vulnerabilities are indeed global in scale while our capacity to act is circumscribed by who and where we are."[17]

A heart as large as the world is a heart that experiences the pain of the world, especially the pain of those who have suffered the most. It is a heart that embraces the pain of the other, even the forces that are antagonistic to one's interest, for it knows that the pain of one is the pain of all. We may live in different worlds and different cultures, but at the most elemental level we connect with people in their joys and their sufferings.

It was disheartening to see some people in the Middle East dancing in the streets after the terrorists accomplished their dastardly acts on September 11, 2001. It was difficult for me to imagine how some groups could dance in celebration of that tragic event in which around three thousand people were buried under the rubble of the World Trade Center and a section of the Pentagon. Anger was my immediate reaction. But as I began to regain my senses, I was saddened at the human capacity to do such horrendous acts and to laugh at the tragedy that befalls others. Only those who have experienced acute disconnection from the human community can dance at the tragedy of others.

Having our attention focused on the terrorists and those who danced in the streets may prevent us from seeing our connections to the violence. Maybe we have forgotten that people in the United States have also danced at the tragedy of others. Not only that, the U.S. government has engineered the tragedy of others. This is not the place to recite the litany of terroristic acts that the U.S. has perpetrated all over the world, but it is important to cite one because it illustrates selective and organized forgetting to support narrow national interest.

What is perturbing is that so few, even among well-educated people in the U.S., know or remember what happened on September 11, 1973. What we also do not remember (or do not want to remember) is that, rather than the victim, the United States (a country that unabashedly claims to be the vanguard of democracy and freedom in the world) engineered an overthrow of the democratically elected government of Chile. It was on that day, September 11, 1973, that Salvador Allende died defending democracy in Chile. Imagine Santiago, Chile, on that fateful day:

> billowing smoke and raging fire, an apocalypse of destruction and terror, airplanes overhead attacking the Moneda, the symbol of Chilean democracy. And after the airplanes and the fire and the destruction came the disappearances and the tortures, the disbelief and the despair, the unspeakable.[18]

I want to point out that the violence of the terrorists and the laughter of their sympathizers in the Middle East are part of the whole cycle of violence in which the United States is not, to say the least, totally innocent. Difficult as it may be for us to hear, the act of the terrorists is a moral protest and a cry of desperation, even if it is morally indefensible. Knowing that terrorism is an expression of the global cycle of violence and an expression of a deep breach of human connection, we need to act in ways that break the cycle of violence and promote healthy relations among people of the world.

Let us not, however, forget that people from around the world were not indifferent to the cry of the victims of September 11, 2001 tragedy. People of the Third World felt connected with the U.S. tragedy because they have known for so long what it means to live under the reign of terror and to lose homes and loved ones. Even in the Arab world, the September 11 tragedy was not just perceived as a U.S. tragedy; it was a global, human tragedy. "Almost everyone I met in the Middle East over the years," says Dale Bishop, Co-Executive of Global Ministries (United Church of Christ, U.S.A., and Christian Church [Disciples of Christ]),

> made the distinction between me as an individual American and the policies and behavior of my government, and I think that this is why, aside from some isolated incidents among the Palestinians, there was an overwhelming sympathy for the losses sustained by American families in the attacks on New York and Washington. That doesn't mean that criticism of the United States will abate in the aftermath of these events, but it represents a basic belief that innocents should not suffer because their government makes bad decisions.[19]

For a few extremists, however, "a line has been crossed," continues Bishop, "and a whole society is regarded as fair game." By its very logic, terrorism does not make any distinction between civilians and combatants. It is meant to terrorize the whole society. How we respond to the challenge of the extremists is very critical. Bishop says:

> Our ability to distinguish between the relatively few extremists and our potential friends in the Middle East will determine whether al-Qa'ida is the wave of the future, or a passing, if horribly destructive, phenomenon. An American response that extends the circle of victimization is, most likely, the terrorists' real goal. One can only hope that our government will not follow the script that extremists have written for us.[20]

It is ironic that when we become imperialistic we are actually narrowing our worlds. Our hearts constrict. We do not hear the cry of others. We become self-centered. Because the divine call comes to us through the mediation of the world or through the cry of the people, it is not easy to discern and respond to the call unless we listen intently and carefully. We cannot hear the divine call through the world if we do not remove the obstructions that block our hearing. One of the biggest obstructions to our hearing is the fear for our own security. If the fear of God is the beginning of knowledge (Prov. 1:7), I would also say that the fear for our security is the beginning of idolatry. Feeling threatened, we construct high walls and narrow our world to protect ourselves even as we become more imperialistic in an effort to doubly secure ourselves.

Making our hearts as large the world requires a major reorientation, which involves the shattering of our narrow world and our redirection to a center that takes into account the well-being of the wider world. Making our hearts as large as the world involves finding a center that does not totalize or swallow others. It means becoming centered in the interconnections of communities around the world. While we are more inclined to value immediate relationships, we do not stop with our skin: We form, to use Marjorie Suchocki's words, "a network of connections spiraling out beyond ourselves."[21]

The church is not exempt from this challenge to widen our worlds. For the church, this means recovering its center in God's *basileia*, which embraces the universe outside of the parish. Though this may appear to be an exaggeration, there is a profound difference between a church-oriented people and a church oriented toward God's *basileia*. David Bosch puts rather clearly the kingdom-oriented church or the "regnocentric" church in contrast to the church-centered church:

> Kingdom people seek first the Kingdom of God and its justice; church people often put the church work above concerns of justice, mercy, and truth. Church people think about how to get people into the church; Kingdom people think about how to get the church into the world. Church people worry that the world might change the church; Kingdom people work to see the church change the world.[22]

Threatened by declining membership and with no clear options beyond survival, the pressing concern of church-oriented people is the attraction of new members by adopting a marketing strategy. With survival as the nagging concern, the "world is our parish" has become the "parish is our world."[23] This church exists simply for its own preservation; such a church has not carried out its reason for being.

Embracing the sensibility that makes our hearts as large as the world requires more than a trip to the library to find out that Jesus' preaching was centered on God's *basileia*. It requires locating ourselves in unfamiliar places, confronting our fears, and making ourselves porous to the revelatory encounter with the other. What drew Moses to the burning bush? As Aidan Kavanagh puts it: "It was Presence, not faith, which drew Moses to the burning bush. And what happened there was a revelation, not seminar."[24] A revelatory experience of transformation requires more than a series of consciousness-raising seminars.

In a Philippine exposure trip that I led, a revelatory event took place. In the house of one of the fisherfolks I noticed an aquarium with very small fish, like the size of a toothpick. I asked our hosts what kind of fish they were. The fisherfolks of Laguna de Bay started to tell our group that the fish in the wider lake (the siblings of the fish in the aquarium) already weighed around two pounds. There was a big difference in size between the fish in the aquarium and those that were out in the lake. Then I turned to my students and explained the parable: Just like the fish, if we stay within our aquariums we will not grow; our world will remain small and narrow.[25] But if we take the risk and venture into the wider world, we open ourselves to the possibility of making our hearts as large as the world.

And what does this venturing into the wider world and making our hearts as large as the world have to do with one's location and particular place of ministry in the world? I dare say, it has everything to do. T. S. Eliot's lines in "Little Gidding" are insightful here:

> We shall not cease from exploration
> And the end of all our exploring
> Will be to arrive where we started
> And know the place for the first time.[26]

It makes all the difference in the world to come back to where we started and know the place for the first time. It makes all the difference in our struggles and ministry to know that the world is connected to the local acts that we do, and what we do now has eternal significance. We do not only become effective concerned citizens or parish ministers in a globalized world, but we minister or act with integrity. We minister with integrity because we have taken into account that even our ability to do ministry is often subsidized by the cheap labor of crucified people in our cities and the Third World. We minister with integrity and effectiveness because we have taken into account the interweaving of our lives and the lives of others.

Becoming a new global person is a challenge. There are not only structures that pose obstacles at the global level, there are also interlocking forms of systemic evil that thwart our efforts toward becoming persons with hearts as large as the world. Becoming a new person requires the overcoming or breaking of the walls of systemic evil, walls like classism, sexism, racism, and naturism.

A story helps illustrate the emergence of a new person or a new community that embodies a heart as large as the world and, with it, the commitment to break boundaries of disconnection and unjust relations. This story happened during the First World War.

Soon after the devastation of the First World War, Quakers responded to the need of the impoverished people of Poland by distributing food and clothing. As the story goes, one relief worker contracted typhus and died within twenty-four hours. There were no other cemeteries, except that of Roman Catholics, and canonical law forbade burying anyone not of that confession in consecrated ground. So the deceased relief worker was buried in a grave outside the fence of the cemetery. But during the night the villagers moved the fence of the cemetery to include the grave.[27]

The new person is committed to a mission—not mission impossible—of moving fences. What do fence movers do? Fence movers dare to dream, dare to hope, dare to struggle to break idolatrous fences of divisions and dare to forge more just and inclusive communities. They are boundary crossers in the good sense, overcoming fences of race, class, and gender divisions. They dare to dream of a just, colorful, and sustainable tomorrow.

## Being Human Beyond the Class Lines

One obstacle toward becoming human with a heart as large as the world is the wall of classism. If classism manifests a global dimension in the name of imperialism or, more subtly and pervasively, globalization, any articulation of being human beyond class lines must take account of this global aspect. When I speak of human being beyond class lines, I do not envision a human being who is already outside of class lines. More appropriately, I speak of *being human* beyond class lines. The human being beyond class lines is one who is becoming human or struggling to be human. Put differently, the human being beyond class lines is one who embodies both the promise of being human and the struggle to be human.

Finding humanity beyond class lines involves a thorough unveiling of the many expressions of classism in both our private lives and the public sphere. It involves a struggle against classism and its various expressions. While the utopian classless society has, by and large, been discredited, it points to something positive: that a classist society is a social construct that privileges others at the expense of the many. As a social construct, it is alterable. Moreover, living beyond class lines calls us to share the various forms of wealth necessary for sustenance, and suggests that those who have more materially need not rule over others. Living beyond the class lines is a way to regain and reimagine our humanity.

Reimagining our humanity beyond the class lines calls for a major critique of our relationship to the material world and with one another. It involves a revaluation of life-giving material goods and reevaluation of our "material practice."[28] It also involves building and maintaining structures and promulgating policies that promote greater well-being for all, including nature. Put negatively, reimagining our humanity involves resistance against structural and institutional arrangements that maintain the classist system.

One major aspect of our relationships needing reevaluation and revaluation is human labor. We work primarily to address basic human needs, although our work is also an expression of our creativity and self-fulfillment. We derive dignity from our work. Yet for many, their work is an expression of their degradation and dehumanization. Many workers labor for nothing other than money needed to survive, and many of these laborers do not even receive livable wages.

Both work and workers need redemption. A radical transformation must happen in the way we think of work, the products that come from this work, and our relationship to one another. A work of transformation must take place in which new work arrangements are created and different criteria are established. If labor is an expression of who we are, it must be measured in terms of the well-being it provides to the worker and to the whole of society. Various types of human labor must be valued according to their contribution to the whole well-being of society, and not solely on the criteria set by those who control the capital. A new human community is in the making when labor does not live under the curse of capital, but finds its proper value in relation to the web of life. This new human community is birthing when laborers receive livable wages in return for their hard work, and when they find dignity in their work.

But work must be redeemed and redefined not only in relation to the life of the workers and the well-being of the whole society, but in relation to the world of nature. It must be redeemed from the kind of work that relates to nature at a merely instrumental level and exploits it for human ends, especially for the profit of the powerful few. Redeeming work in relation to the natural world means reconceiving work that embraces care and harmonious living with the rest of creation. The new human worker (*homo faber*) is one who not only transforms the world of matter into useful goods, but also relates to it with interdependence and care.

Once work is reevaluated and revalued, the same must be done with wealth and property. The Christian tradition offers insights into this task. There is no need to belabor the point that material goods are not only a requirement for our existence, they make us who we are. Wealth and property are not evil in themselves. Money, a form of easily exchangeable wealth, is not evil in itself either. In the words of Chrysostom, "money is called *chremata* [from *chraomai*, "I use"] so that we may use it, and not that it may use us. Therefore possessions are so called that we may possess them, and not they possess us. Why do you invert the order?"[29] Money exists for our use. The problem, however, is that we invert the order. Instead of using money, money uses us. Instead of possessing it, we are possessed by it. We become money possessed. Possessions possess us by defining us and making us into their own image. In the Pilipino language, the money-possessed person is one who is *mukhang pera* (literally a person whose face is money). This person sees himself or herself in relation to money and views the world in terms of money. The *mukhang pera* is a money-possessed person. The emergence of a new person can happen only when the money-possessed person is exorcised and reoriented toward the proper value of material goods.

Our relationship to material goods must be defined in terms of our use of them rather than our being used by them, but this norm is not adequate. More than seeing one's relation to material goods in terms of *chremata*, the early Christian theologians also employed the twin concepts of *autarkeia* (self-sufficiency) and *koinonia* (community). Clement says that properties are for our use and for the sake of *autarkeia* (self-sufficiency).[30] Self-sufficiency and self-reliance not only free us from being a perpetual burden to others, they are also marks of human dignity. But the quest for self-sufficiency may run amok if left by itself. The quest for self-sufficiency must be balanced by the quest for *koinonia*. As Charles Avila puts it: "[T]he purpose of property, and of wealth, is not only to achieve individual *autarkeia*, but also to attain *koinonia*," a fellowship that dismantles the death-laden differentiation between those who have more and those who have very little for survival.[31]

If we are what we are because of our relationships, we cannot be who we are as truly human when in our affluence others are deprived. In a covenanted community in which the journey toward an authentic humanity is a companionship, we can only find our humanity as real companions (*cumpanis*= *cum* [share with] + *panis* [bread]) who share bread as we journey together.[32] A new human being is in the making when we have learned to share bread and when we no longer use bread to elevate ourselves and exploit others.

*Chremata, autarkeia,* and *koinonia* are, however, not comprehensive enough in revaluing our relation to the world around us, especially with regard to the ecosystem. Ecological insights demand that we move beyond relating to the world of nature in terms of use, even for self-sufficiency and communal well-being. We must place *chremata, autarkeia,* and *koinonia* within the larger context of ecological right relation. The purpose of wealth and human knowledge is to promote just harmony and intrinsic interdependence. Wealth, which is derived from nature and human labor, must be used to promote the healing of nature. The classist structure knows no other way of relating to nature except through exploitation to promote and perpetuate hierarchical social classification.

The intertwining of classism and consumerism also informs us that our journey toward a humanity liberated from classism requires a fundamental reorientation of our relationship toward consumer goods, how we define our identity, and well-being. Against a classist-consumerist society that defines identity on the basis of consumption, constructing a new humanity beyond class lines requires that we stop judging persons' worth on the basis of their consumption. Since those who seek abstracted image or symbolic value find no satisfaction in them, a radical reorientation is needed to ground us in the legitimate use value of things. For us to be reoriented to the use value of goods, however, requires that we be fully attuned to the needs of our embodied selves and to the needs of the larger body of which we are an integral part.

The intersection of consumerism, nutrition, and ecology helps clarify what I mean about being attuned to the needs of our embodied selves. Under the shadow of classism, people do not always eat for the purpose of physical well-being, but for reasons dictated by class. This kind of eating habit puts a heavy load on the land and the animal population. The classist-elitist eating habit is conspicuously extravagant, lavish, and wasteful. The single serving size in North American restaurants is far larger than the physical requirements of a person. Even the matter of healthy diet that has become fashionable is tinged with classism and elitism.

When we look at the Third World, the classist impact on nutrition takes a different configuration. Because highly processed food items are associated with upper class status and the Western way of life, people dream of acquiring them. If we observe the eating habits of Third World people, we will notice that as their economic status gets a step higher, fresh vegetables and fruits slowly disappear from their tables in favor of white bread, hot dogs, bacon, ham, and canned fruits. This is a feat of class and nutritional distortion. Eating under the shadow of the class system is not marked only by the absence of food for the many and abundance for the few, it is also marked by distorted eating habits.

Once we understand the connection between classism, consumerism, nutrition, and ecology we see things from a wider perspective. Without doubt, the most basic and urgent need is to have food to eat, but this need cannot be divorced from questions about "what we choose to put into our mouths," "how we eat them," and "how we get them."[33] The new human being is one who not only has something to eat, but eats for the purpose of physical health and greater well-being for all, including the ecosystem.

Moving beyond class lines, elitism, consumerism, and commoditization requires a spiritual renewal. I say spiritual because consumer goods and commodities have been spiritualized or have been equated with the presence of the Spirit. Increased consumption of commodities and accumulation of properties is considered a sign of the Spirit's presence in one's life. Wanting more is a "sign that we are alive and more deserving than those with fewer needs."[34] In effect consumerism says that we are not human unless we have a highly consumptive lifestyle. The heart of this claim is spiritual: more particularly, a distorted spirituality.

Not only does this distorted spirituality or way of being human need to be exposed, there is also a need to articulate what being spiritual means in response to commoditization and consumerism. Instead of loading ourselves with things, which only "thingify" us, we need to be filled with the Spirit. And when we are filled with the Spirit, we bear "fruit of the Spirit," such as "love, joy, peace, patience, kindness, generosity, faithfulness, gentleness, and self-control" (Gal. 5:22–23). We are liberated from the identification of possession with being alive and we become truly alive in the Spirit.

Reimagining the human beyond class lines, as I argued earlier, entails more than reorienting some aspects of our lives; it must include our whole economic system. The current economic system does not only dehumanize human beings, it is also exploitative of nature. We need an economic system in which we participate with God, the economist, in creating an economic system that opens access to all those in need of life-giving resources. In the world of classism and the marginalization of the many, participation in the formation of the *oikonomia tou theou* (economy of God) means including in the household (*oikos*) those once victimized and marginalized by our current household. To be an image of God in relation to the political economy is to image ourselves in God the economist and become *homo economicus* with God.

## Integrated Self, Integrated Society: The New Male and Female

If human identity under the shadow of naturism is defined in relation to the subordination and instrumentation of other species, racialized in a racist society, and valued along class lines in a classist society, human identity is also sexualized and genderized in a sexist society. This is the kind of identity we have in a sexist society: It is a sexualized-genderized identity, an identity that follows the path defined by duality, hierarchy, and binary opposition of male and female categories, with the female relegated to the subordinate pole. This female subordination finds expression in the various forms of oppression women have experienced.

The patriarchal worldview must be deconstructed if a new human being is to be born. Likewise, sexist practices must be exposed and opposed whenever they show their ugly heads. Gender stereotypes must be transgressed. An identity must be articulated along nonsexualized lines, which involves the retrieval of those categories considered natural to the other sex. I am not suggesting androgyny, because androgyny still presupposes binary male and female categories and the subordination of the female. Also, androgyny presupposes an autonomous individual who possesses both male and female qualities. But we are not autonomous, as much as we like to believe we are, and we cannot be both even if we recover the parts of ourselves that have been alienated in a patriarchal and sexist society.

Instead of androgyny, what I am suggesting is an integrated individual. The notion of an integrated individual should not be confused with androgyny, because I am not putting the traditional male and female stereotypes into one person. For me integration refers to the human capacity of both men and women for wholeness. It refers to the human capacity of both men and women to embrace in some measure those qualities that are traditionally stereotyped as belonging to the other. It asserts that both men and women can make a connection with the experiences of the other. There is no suggestion being made here that an integrated self is complete and closed off. Instead, the integrated self holds an open posture.

With wholeness and openness to the gifts of the other as the main tenets of an integrated self, then a self is integrated only insofar as it is a self-in-relation. An integrated self is not realized individualistically but only in a community of persons, each of whom contributes their gifts and limitations to the community.[35] An individual may manifest an integrated self only insofar as she or he reflects the integration occurring in the community of persons. An individual experiences self-integration only because of the gifts of the community. Openness to the gifts of the other is a requirement for integration. With this move toward the communal demand of integration, any claim to an integrated self understood as autonomous, self-sufficient, and complete is occluded. One can say "I am" only because "we are."

Thus, any talk about integration must deal with the larger society or must lead to the affirmation of an integrated social order. Because dualism and hierarchies are not limited to gender and sexuality, but have been projected sociologically onto the wider society in the forms of class, race, and ethnic domination, the call for integration must include the social order. It is only in the context of an integrated social order that individuals and communities manifest self-integration. Since there are social forces that prevent this integration, a struggle to transform the social order becomes a necessity. The new integrated humanity is not so much an arrival as a painful process of giving birth.

A new humanity is in the making when we no longer see and treat people along genderized and sexualized categories; when men and women are struggling to transgress binary oppositional categories of the feminine and masculine; when women do not see themselves through the eyes of men or through the eyes of a male God; and when men do not see themselves through the eyes of the "self-made man." A new humanity is in the making when both men and women are able to live with their different physicality openly and reciprocally. And a new human being is born among those who are struggling to resist sexist practices at home, church, school, corporations, and government offices.

Because dualism and hierarchies of gender and sexuality are tied to the ways we have treated the whole ecosystem, an authentic experience of individual and social integration must include an experience of integration with the whole ecosystem. As in the case of social integration, there are also forces that prevent the integration of the natural world into the lives of human communities. Thus, the call for the integration of human and other living communities is also a call for the praxis of transformation.

### Being-in-Difference: Diversity in a Democratic Society and a Biocratic Cosmos

Being-in-difference is the term I use to express the point that at the very heart of our ontological existence is the reality of difference. Difference is a principle of existence. At the heart of our ecological life is diversity. Beings come in different sizes, shapes, colors, tastes, smells, functions, etc. Diverse beings form a web of relationships for life's flourishing.

Alienation from our identity as being-in-difference leads to fatal consequences. When we attempt to remove difference, the life support system collapses. We do this when we pollute the environment, make other species extinct, engage in indiscriminate logging, and adopt farming practices that are nonsustainable. What we do to the whole ecosystem is a mirror of who we are: Our destructive practices mirror our own alienation.

In the context of human society, we violate being-in-difference as a principle of life when we treat human differences with indifference. We treat difference with indifference when we dualize and hierarchalize differences. We treat difference with indifference when we co-opt differences deemed superior and destroy those considered inferior.

It is time for us to learn ways of relating across differences that promote greater well-being. It is not difference that causes separation but our views toward difference. Difference is taken seriously when the integrity of the particular and different is taken into account; when, in the effort to seek connections and commonalities, difference is not muted; when difference is seen as necessary for mutual fecundation and transformation; and when difference is considered as a necessary condition for interdependence. Difference necessitates that we live a life of interdependence.

Taking difference seriously is constitutive of our journey toward a new humanity. A new humanity is in the making when, through the eyes of our embodiment, we see difference as a principle of life and well-being for all and a condition for a life of interdependence. We can discern this humanity in the process of being born when whites no longer see other races through the lens of "whiteness," and when people of color no longer see themselves through the white normativizing gaze. We discern this new humanity bursting out in the world when people of color in a white-dominated society are no longer torn apart by the sense of "two-ness" warring inside their very selves, as W. E. B. Du Bois puts it, but experience the integration of their "double self."[36] With this new way of seeing, people of all stripes no longer see color as a means for exclusion, but as a gift that calls for celebration. The new white human being is no longer the one who sees his or her identity as a function of whiteness and in diacritical opposition to people of color. On the other hand, people of color experience liberation from dreaming of becoming whites on the day of resurrection.

The new human being is fully aware that identities are dynamic and changing, and that identities need not be conceived in purist either-or categories. In our highly globalized world it is more adequate to speak of "both-and" or "in-both" identities because people assume multiple identities.[37] Being a *mestizo* or a *mestiza* is not a form of deviancy, but an identity that embodies the rich possibilities of connection. The new society is inhabited by human beings who are experiencing liberation from the crucifying norm of pure identity. It is a society that embraces the presence of individuals with multiple identities, not as a problem to be solved but as an invitation to a richer life.

Our way out of racism into a new humanity requires naming our racial pains and burning the idol of racism. Like the early witnesses of the first Pentecost who had to break their silence and let loose their stammering tongues under the impact of the Spirit, we, too, must break our silence and go public with our colorful vision. Moreover, we who have been empowered by the spirit of Pentecost must engage in a conspiracy, transgressing racial divides and breaking hegemonic modes of thinking that we may reinvent ourselves in ways that are more humanly colorful and respectful of difference.

### Eucharist and the New Humanity: New Heaven and New Earth

The eucharist encapsulates a vision of a new humanity in the new heaven and the new earth. It points to the direction and shape of God's economy (God's household) and the demands of living in the present. It discloses the character of the reign of God or the *basileia tou theou*, the place of human beings, and the quality of relationships between beings.

Like other powerful symbols, however, the eucharist is an intensely contested one. It has been used as a symbol of exclusion instead of unity, and of domination instead of liberation. A symbol that points to the life of the crucified has been used to crucify, to fence rather than to embrace. For religious as well as lay communities of women, the eucharist has become a source of pain and anger. What has been considered a sacrament of grace and unity has become a symbol of sexual inequality. Yet even as the eucharist has been clouded by distorted interpretations, it continues to be a powerful symbol that invites us to imagine a different world of relationship.

There is no doubt that the eucharist points to the ugly reality of our world. The broken bread and the cup of wine symbolize what the forces of death can do. These forces of death are ready to crush those who resist the work of destruction and proclaim the path of life. Jesus of Nazareth was not spared by these forces of death when he witnessed to the coming reign of God. Many contemporary prophets have suffered a similar fate in their opposition to the forces of death. Bread broken and cup poured point to the reality of the breaking of the web of life; they point to the broken relations brought about by the evils of classism, sexism, racism, and naturism.

The message of the eucharist cannot be divorced from the reality of crucifixion. The crucifixion of Jesus is not absolutely unique. When we view it in an absolutely unique and surrealistic fashion, we rob it of its power. What the forces of death did to Jesus is symbolic of what they have done to many. It reminds us of the banality of daily crucifixions. Jesus represents the crucified people of Nicaragua, Philippines, East Timor, Mexico, and Lebanon. "[T]he Eucharist," says Winston Persaud, "*re-presents* the suffering of Jesus the Christ for the sake of the world and simultaneously *presents* the world of suffering in need of healing."[38]

Yes, the eucharist points to the world of suffering in need of healing or salvation. But while pointing to the world in need of healing, it also offers a vision of a healed world. Out of a broken body has emerged a vision of what a mended body is like. The broken body of Jesus, symbolized in the broken bread of the eucharistic celebration, is broken open for the many that all may experience healing and liberation. The body is broken open as a symbol of openness, service, and hospitality. Out of the broken body, ritualized in the eucharistic celebration, comes the invitation to dine at a common table.

The common table, particularly the meal table, is an important direction. As a symbol, the eucharistic table points to the common meal table of the household. M. Douglas Meeks pointed out that: "Like all households, God's household is structured around a table."[39] The meal table is central to the household. It is here that the members of the household are served, fed, and nourished. Important household conversations happen around the meal table.

Inasmuch as God's household is beyond individual households, it is fitting to speak of a meal table for the whole world. Instead of limiting our image to one of a single family sharing, serving, and feeding each other, we imagine a meal in which all are invited. Theologian C. S. Song renames the Last Supper as "people supper." It is a people supper prepared by the community for the whole community.[40] The community prepares and shares the meal. The people supper is a communal event.

I suggest that we interpret the eucharistic celebration in this way. In terms of its New Testament background, I suggest that we see it through the lens of the egalitarian meals Jesus did throughout his ministry (Mt. 14:13–21; Lk. 9:10–17; Jn. 6:1–14).[41] It was through one of these egalitarian meals that the people recognized the resurrected Jesus, as in the Emmaus story (Lk. 24:13–35). It was in the breaking of bread that he was recognized by his sorrowful followers.

Likewise, we recognize Jesus and recognize God wherever egalitarian meals happen. In egalitarian meals the crucified Jesus is resurrected, and in shared meals God's power is alive. As Jesus' presence is known in the breaking and sharing of bread, so we are known as disciples of Jesus and children of God whenever and wherever we celebrate egalitarian meals. "Were such an understanding of the eucharist to infiltrate Christian churches today," notes Sallie McFague, "it could be mind changing–in fact, perhaps world changing."[42]

Deepening the symbol of the eucharistic meal, Song suggests that the egalitarian people supper happened at a "round table."[43] The round table illustrates the egalitarian power dynamics, the positioning of all in relation to the food, the sharing of the meal, the communication that transpires among those around the meal table, and other related "table manners." In relation to ministry, Chuck Latrop has this to say: "Concerning the why and how and what and who of ministry, one image keeps surfacing: A table that is round."[44]

Letty Russell explores the rich ramifications of the image of the round table in thinking and imaging about the life of the church in her work on feminist ecclesiology.[45] The image of the round table, Russell suggests, reveals to us the nature of the church and what it is called to become; how it must construe power, church structure, "table talks," and leadership; the "table principles" to which it must adhere and be committed; and the way it must construe ministry in a world divided by various forms of oppression.

The people supper at a round table offers a lens for understanding power relations in God's household. There is no definite beginning and ending to a round table; no person can claim the beginning and another the ending. In fact, the circle around the table begins with any person, not with the chief or head of the household. We cannot fix the location of the elder at a round table, because there is no head of the table, as there is at a rectangular table. Each one sits at a significant location around the table, for all the locations at a round table are equally significant. If there is a preferred seating arrangement, the honor goes to the least of our brothers and sisters (Lk. 14:7–11).

Communication or conversation is also influenced by the circular shape of the table. Everyone is visible from one's location at the round table; therefore one does not strain one's neck trying to see others who are seated at the far end, as in the case of a rectangular table. Communication is not always directed to the one occupying the head of the table, as in the case of rectangular table. The round table provides a structural model of communication among members of the household.

The people supper at a round table manifests not just the presence of food, but the miracle of sharing. The food is located at the center of the table, within reach of each member. The round table shows us the positioning of persons in relation to the food: Everyone is located in a spot with direct access to the food. With each having direct access to the meal, the structure or system is already organized in such a way that sharing becomes possible. The giving and receiving of food circulates around the table. At the round table people supper, communion becomes a reality.

The people supper at a round table also points in the direction of hospitality. The round table is a "welcome table" to which those who have long been unwelcome are welcomed. At the welcome table we can discern the longing that those who have long been excluded will some day sit at the round table. At the round table those once excluded can dine, enjoy the banquet, and participate in the table talk. The African American church tradition gives us a glimpse of this passionate longing for the welcoming round table:

> We're gonna sit at the welcome table!
> We're gonna sit at the welcome table one of these days;
> Alleluia![46]

While hospitality is readily construed as something we offer to visitors and strangers, like offering a warm welcome and sharing what we have, it is also a matter of what we offer to ourselves. Hospitality requires creating a friendly space in our hearts and homes for others to feel at home, disarm themselves, listen to their own voice, and find their own center. Hospitality is the creation of a free space for a new and healthy relationship to grow. In other words, hospitality is about our openness and our receptivity to the presence and gift of others. Henry Nouwen asserts that hospitality is a "friendly emptiness where strangers can enter and discover themselves as created free; free to sing their own songs, speak their own languages, dance their own dances; free also to leave and follow their own vocations."[47]

The eucharist, interpreted through the lens of egalitarian meals, transcends the experience of hostility and becomes a symbol of hospitality. The body broken by hostilities has become a symbol of hospitality. Hostility is transformed into hospitality when we provide a space for others to find their voice, to sing their own songs, and articulate their narratives among us. Hostility is transformed into hospitality when we experience liberation from our preoccupation with ourselves, our security and comfort, and our idolatry expressed in classism, sexism, racism, and naturism.

A society where classism, sexism, racism, and naturism reign cannot be truly hospitable. In fact, all these "isms" are expressions of inhospitality, if not hostility. That the eucharist, against the background of egalitarian meals, has become an instrument of exclusion is a scandal, an example of "bad table manners." It has been used as an instrument of sexism, relegating women to the margin, because this powerful sacrament has been controlled by male clerics. What happens to women in relation to the eucharistic celebration mirrors their experience in the wider society. Thus, the restoration of the eucharist to its symbolic value of hospitality requires the overcoming of inhospitality in the form of sexism.

As the eucharist/people supper points to the overhauling of inhospitality because of sexism, it also does so in regard to racism. Racism is inhospitable to racial others; thus, the eucharist/people supper points to its dismantling. Hospitality can fully happen in a wider society only when the system of racism is overcome. There are, I believe, small communities that embody the spirit of hospitality in a profound way in midst of a racist society. But a racist society cannot be truly hospitable to racial others. In the U.S. context, hospitality happens when the dominant white race allows the creation of free spaces where racial and ethnic minorities can celebrate who they are and find their own center, not to be melted into the melting pot. The eucharist/people supper offers an alternative to the inhospitable melting pot. Which vision would we choose? We can put the alternatives in this stark way: "East is East, and West is West, and never the twain shall meet" (Rudyard Kipling's famous lines), or, following the words of the invitation to the Lord's supper—"People will come from east and west, and from north and south, and sit at table in the kin(g)dom of God."[48]

Egalitarian meals point to a community of people of various races and ethnicities coming together to share and celebrate God's blessings. The colorful future that eucharist/people supper points to is not merely pluralism or an affirmation of a multi-colored world, but a future in which image representations, differences, and power dynamics are taken into serious account. In contrast to the melting pot, another image has risen to prominence as a result of the burning of South Central Los Angeles, the "melting furnace." In the L.A. "pillar of flame" God's horrendous shape was present, making us realize that we are going to be consumed by the fire of racism unless it is shoved into the melting furnace. This melting furnace is not the melting pot of assimilation, but a furnace that burns our idols of death, purges us of our bigotry, and energizes us to continue struggling for a reconciled relationship.

The United States of America, with its multicultural demographic make-up, is faced with a painful choice. Alice Walker, when asked whether California (a multiethnic society) represents the America of the future, replied: "If that's not the future reality of the United States, there won't be any United States, because that's who we are."[49] America's recognition and acceptance of its multicultural self is a crucial step in the journey toward a colorful tomorrow.

People supper at a round table needs to be extended into a cosmic round table, in which hospitality is understood in the context of the interdependent web of life. Hospitality within the framework of ecological sensibility means allowing others to have spaces where they can live with integrity in relation to the overall harmony. Hospitality involves creating a home for each one to feel at home in the cosmos. This is in consonance with God's economy, in which God intends to make this world into a home for all.

People supper at a round table is a proleptic celebration of the promised future. It is a rich and deep symbol of who we are and what we are called to be. The bread and wine, produce of God's earth and products of human labor, come together in an act of communal liturgical celebration to reveal the interdependence and communion of God, humanity, and nature. The elements of bread and wine truly re-present the broken body of Jesus, because Jesus' broken body is one with the produce of the earth. In partaking of the elements we truly re-member the broken bodies throughout the ages because they live in us—the living—and are one with us in our experience of re-memberment (being made whole). Through the eucharistic/egalitarian meals we experience a glimpse and a foretaste of the richness of a liberated and healed community of interdependent beings in a cosmic body. The whole sacred celebration points to God's incarnation in the fullness of history and nature in which "God [will] be all in all" (1 Cor. 15:28) and human beings will truly embody the image of God.

### Notes

[1]José Comblin, *Retrieving the Human: A Christian Anthropology* (Maryknoll, N.Y: Orbis Books, 1990), 7.

[2]Tilden Edwards, "Living the Day from the Heart," in *The Weavings Reader: Living with God in the World,* ed. John S. Mogabgab (Nashville: Upper Room Books, 1993), 55.

[3]Rita Nakashima Brock, *Journeys by Heart: A Christology of Erotic Power* (New York: Crossroad Publishing Company, 1988), xiv; Clark Williamson, *Way of Blessing, Way of Life: A Christian Theology* (St. Louis: Chalice Press, 1999), 253.

[4]Brock, *Journeys by Heart,*, xiv.

[5]Williamson, *Way of Blessing, Way of Life,* 252–53.

[6]René Descartes, "Discourse on the Method of Rightly Conducting the Reason and Seeking for Truth in the Sciences," in *Descartes Selections,* ed. Ralph M. Eaton (Chicago, New York, and Boston: Charles Scribner's Sons, 1927).

[7]See Justo González, *Out of Every Tribe and Nation: Christian Theology at the Ethnic Roundtable* (Nashville: Abingdon Press, 1992), 74; also Robert McAfee Brown, *Persuade Us to Rejoice: The Liberating Power of Fiction* (Louisville: Westminster/John Knox Press, 1992), 65.

[8]Michael Battle, *Reconciliation: The Ubuntu Theology of Desmond Tutu* (Cleveland: The Pilgrim Press, 1997), 39.

[9]Karen Baker-Fletcher and Garth Kasimu Baker-Fletcher, *My Sister, My Brother: Womanist and Xodus God-Talk* (Maryknoll, N.Y.: Orbis Books, 1997), 137.

[10]George Tinker, "An American Indian Theological Response to Ecojustice," in *Defending Mother Earth: Native American Perspective on Environmental Justice,* ed. Jace Weaver (Maryknoll, N.Y.: Orbis Books, 1996), 158. Also see Clara Sue Kidwell, Homer Noley, and George Tinker, *Native American Theology* (Maryknoll, N.Y.: Orbis Books, 2001), 48–51.

[11]Mary Catherine Hilkert, "Cry Beloved Image: Rethinking the Image of God" in *In the Image of God: Feminist Approaches to Theological Anthropology,* ed. Ann O'Hara Graff (Maryknoll, N.Y.: Orbis Books, 1995), 200.

[12]See *He Alo A He Alo: Hawaiian Voices on Sovereignty* (Honolulu: American Friends Service Committee–Hawai'i Area Office, 1993).

[13]See José Miguez Bonino, *Toward a Christian Political Ethics* (Philadelphia: Fortress Press, 1983), 79–86.

[14]John B. Cobb, Jr., *Sustainability: Economics, Ecology, and Justice* (Maryknoll, N.Y.: Orbis Books, 1992), 56.

[15]Geiko Müller-Fahrenholz, *God's Spirit: Transforming a World in Crisis* (New York: Continuum; Geneva: World Council of Churches, 1995), 109.

[16]John Drinkwater, *Abraham Lincoln: A Play* (Boston and New York: Houghton Mifflin Company, 1919), 57; see also Donald Messer, *Contemporary Images of Christian Ministry* (Nashville: Abingdon Press, 1999), 175.

[17]R. B. J. Walker, *One World, Many Worlds: Struggles for a Just World Peace* (London, U. K.: Zed Books; Boulder, Colo.: Lynne Rienner, 1988), 102.

[18]Teresa Berger, "Fragments of a Vision in a September 11 World," in *Strike Terror No More: Theology, Ethics, and the New Order,* ed. Jon L. Berquist (St. Louis: Chalice Press, 2002), 112.

[19]Dale Bishop, "Who Are These People and Why Do They Hate Us So Much?" private publication.

[20]Ibid.

[21]Marjorie Hewitt Suchocki, *The Fall to Violence: Original Sin in Relational Theology* (New York: Continuum, 1994), 70.

[22]David Bosch, cited in Paul Knitter, *Jesus and the Other Names: Christian Mission and Global Responsibility* (Maryknoll, N.Y.: Orbis Books, 1996), 110.

[23]Donald Messer, *A Conspiracy of Goodness: Contemporary Images of Christian Mission* (Nashville: Abingdon Press, 1992), 22.

[24]Aidan Kavanagh, cited in Kathleen Norris, *Amazing Grace: A Vocabulary of Faith* (New York: Riverhead Books, 1998), 341.

[25]This happened in Laguna de Bay. The students who were with me when this insightful moment happened were Karen Aitkens, Sally Mann, and Daniel Narr.

[26]Cited in McAfee Brown, *Persuade Us to Rejoice,* 142.

[27]Douglas V. Steere, *Mutual Irradiation* (Pendle Hill, Pa.: Sowers Printing Company, 1971), 7, cited in Messer, *Conspiracy of Goodness,* 127.

[28]Mark Kline Taylor, *Remembering Esperanza: A Cultural-Political Theology for North American Praxis* (Maryknoll, N.Y.: Orbis Books, 1990), 233.

[29]Chrysostom, *Inscriptionem Altaris et in Principium Actorum,* 1, 2 , PG51:69, cited in Charles Avila, *Ownership: Early Christian Teaching* (Maryknoll, N.Y.: Orbis Books, 1983), 144.

[30]Clement, "The Educator," 2, 3, PG 8:436, cited in Avila, *Ownership,* 145.

[31]Avila, *Ownership,* 145.

[32]McAfee Brown, *Persuade Us to Rejoice,* 67.

[33]Michael Fox, *Eating with Conscience: The Bioethics of Food* (Troutdale, Ore.: New Sage Press, 1997), 126.

[34]M. Douglas Meeks, *God the Economist: The Doctrine of God and Political Economy* (Minneapolis: Fortress Press, 1989), 172.

[35]See Mary Aquin O'Neill, "Mystery of Being Human Together," in *Freeing Theology: The Essentials of Theology in Feminist Perspective,* ed. Catherine Moury LaCugna (New York: HarperSanFrancisco, 1993), 150.

[36]W. E. B. du Bois, *The Souls of Black Folk: Essays and Sketches* (Greenwich, Conn.: Fawcett Publications, Inc., 1961), 17.

[37]Jung Young Lee, *Marginality: The Key to Multicultural Theology* (Minneapolis: Fortress Press, 1995).

[38]Winston Persaud, "The Cross of Jesus Christ, the Unity of the Church, and Human Suffering," in *The Scandal of a Crucified World*, ed. Yacob Tesfai (Maryknoll, N.Y.: Orbis Books, 1994), 128.

[39]Meeks, *God the Economist*, 45.

[40]C. S. Song, *Jesus, the Crucified People* (Minneapolis: Fortress, 1990), 200.

[41]John Dominic Crossan, *Jesus: A Revolutionary Biography* (San Francisco: HarperSanFrancisco, 1994), 179–81.

[42]Sallie McFague, *Life Abundant: Rethinking Theology and Economy for a Planet in Peril* (Minneapolis: Fortress Press, 2001), 174–75.

[43]Song, *Jesus, the Crucified People*, 204.

[44]Chuck Latrop, "In Search of a Roundtable," cited in Letty Russell, *Church in the Round: Feminist Interpretation of the Church* (Louisville: Westminster/John Knox Press, 1993), 17.

[45]See Russell, *Church in the Round*.

[46]"Welcome Table," in *An Advent Sourcebook*, ed. Thomas O'Gorman (Chicago: Liturgy Training Publications, 1988), 50.

[47]Henry Nouwen, *Reaching Out: The Three Movements of the Spiritual Life* (New York: Doubleday, 1975), 51.

[48]Dana W. Wilbanks, *Re-Creating America: The Ethics of U.S. Immigration and Refugee Policy in a Christian Perspective* (Nashville: Abingdon Press, 1996), 109. Take note of my preference for the word *kin*dom.

[49]Reese Erlich, "Alice's Wonderland," an interview with Alice Walker, *Image, San Francisco Examiner* (July 19, 1992): 12.

# CHAPTER 9

# *The Eschatological People*

## Living the Promise of the Future in the Realities of the Present

In spite of our long history of struggle, the forces of death continue to dominate our world. Even as technological advancements have enhanced our ability to promote health, cure diseases, and prolong life, we are witnessing the increasing use of these technological advancements for the destruction of the entire planet. There have been times when I have felt discouraged by the turn of events. Many of those who have struggled are already dead, and many of those who are still breathing live as if they are already dead because they are losing hope. Are we condemned to carnival-like cynicism or hopelessness? What is the promise of the future? Is there any reason to hope? Where will we find the sustenance we need to live a life of integrity in the present? How do we muster courage when the forces of death are overwhelming? What about those who died struggling against the forces of death? Have they died in vain? What about those generations who are yet to come? What future do they have? And, finally, why bother? These are some of the questions that led me to explore the implications of eschatology in the quest to be human.

### Hermeneutic Lens for Reading Eschatological Discourse

*Eschatology* (doctrine of last things) is a dreadful theological word. I smell the death of civilization, hear the sounds of wars, and sense the specter of nuclear annihilation. I hear the word *Armageddon*. I feel the earth tremble: earthquakes, tidal waves, and tornadoes. These are some of my early associations with the term *eschatology*. I learned them from my devout Roman

Catholic paternal grandmother and from my mother, who was influenced by her Seventh Day Adventist grandmother. Eschatology scared the hell out of me.

There is a popular perception that eschatological discourse is an advance report of the end-time or that it provides a blueprint for the end-time. I say that it has dimensions of the end-time and the future (the not yet), but it is not an advance report of the future nor an anticipatory description. In order to understand better what eschatology is, we need to understand what Peter Phan calls the "hermeneutics of eschatological statements." If protology is an "aetiological account from the present situation of sin and salvation back into the origins and not a historical report of what transpired at the beginning," Phan, following Karl Rahner, makes the point that neither is eschatology an

> advance report of the end-time events about which many Christians are curious and search for information in the Bible. Rather... eschatology is an aetiological account from the present situation of sin and grace forward into its future stage of final fulfillment and not an anticipatory description of what will happen at the end of time and beyond. Eschatology is anthropology conjugated in the future tense on the basis of Christology.[1]

Dermot Lane, along with Phan and Rahner, underscores this crucial dimension of present human experience when he speaks of eschatology as "an approach to the future based on our understanding of present human experience" which "is influenced and illuminated by the Christ-event."[2] The future that eschatology speaks about comes out of the experience and reflection of the present, especially as the people are energized by the power of grace.

It has been the traditional practice of systematic theology to put eschatology at the end of any theological treatise or attach it as a theological appendix. This relegation is not surprising when eschatology is construed as the doctrine of the last things. But it does not have to be placed at the end of doctrinal theology, for what has been traditionally considered as the last is also first in the sense that eschatological sensibility is the power that makes us live truly in the present. Jürgen Moltmann argues that eschatology "is not one element *of* Christianity, but it is the medium of Christian faith as such, the key in which everything in it is set, the glow that suffuses everything here in the dawn of an expected new day."[3]

In recent years there has been a heightening interest in eschatology, especially on the part of theological voices interpreting it from the experience of the marginalized. This resurgence of interest in eschatology comes out of the experience of massive suffering brought about by oppressive structures and the awareness of ecological destruction such as landslides, flashfloods, drought, extinction of some species, and atmospheric change. Traditionally a turf monopolized by fundamentalist Christian groups, subaltern scholarship has recovered the message of eschatology. In fact, subaltern scholarship has reclaimed eschatology as a discourse of those who have suffered most in life, but who have refused to be caged by the past and the present, or to be trapped by an inevitably cruel future.

We can observe this recovery and reinterpretation of the eschatological message when we take a closer look at political and liberation theologies. Moltmann, for example, has made eschatology the centerpiece in his theology of hope.[4] Likewise, though much work needs to be done, the eschatological message is gaining presence in the works of liberation theologians. For example, liberation-oriented biblical scholarship has explored the revolutionary potential of apocalyptic materials.

Feminist theologians have also recovered and reinterpreted the eschatological message in support of the struggle of women. They consider eschatology an important dimension in the reconstruction of anthropology.[5] Rosemary Radford Ruether anchors eschatology in the plight of women and criticizes the notion of immortality as an attempt to extend "posthumous egoism."[6] Along a similar vein, Catherine Keller tries to establish the connection between struggles for social justice and ecological eschatology or ecoeschatology over against "econumbness," which finds expression in such forms as the secular technological utopian-apocalypticism (which seeks the conquest of another planet), the realist-triumphalist business-as-usual attitude of status-quo politics, or the Christian fundamentalist idea of rapture to the heavenly abode.[7]

Scholars who have studied the emergence of apocalyptic-millenarian movements and writings support my contention that eschatological discourse has its root among those who have experienced marginalization in society. These scholars agree that basic to the emergence of apocalyptic-millenarian movements and writings is the sense of crisis and anomie, the perception of relative deprivation and powerlessness,[8] the failure to gain access to what Sheldon Isenberg calls "redemptive media,"[9] and the experience of being cut off from society and classified as "weeds," "dirt," and "impure."[10] In the case of the Apocalypse of John (Revelation), there is agreement among scholars that it emerged out of the experience of the persecuted, the outcasts, and the powerless. It is not an expression of people who were wallowing in wealth and pleasure under a favorable regime. It emerged out of the experience of people whose expectations did not match with existing realities; people who were living on the brink of despair; people who believed in the ultimate and sovereign power of an ultimately good God, but experienced in their daily lives the oppression of idolatrous power.[11] Elisabeth Schüssler Fiorenza calls this desperate situation that breeds apocalyptic or eschatological thought a "rhetorical situation"—a situation marked by exigency and urgency; a situation where the individual or the community is confronted with a life and death decision, that is, a decision without compromise.[12]

Out of the wounded, bruised, mangled, and anemic bodies of history's victims eschatological sensibility has sprouted. Moltmann reminds us that the theodicy question (suffering) is the womb from which eschatological images of the future arise.[13] Eschatology is an offspring of those who have suffered most in life but have not been numbed or calloused by their suffering. Suffering is the womb of eschatological sensibility. Those who are enjoying themselves under the present arrangement are not capable of real eschatological imagination, for they are only predisposed to maintaining or extending the present.

Suffering, not the search for immortality, is the womb from which the notion of resurrection was born, asserts Ruether.[14] For her, the Hebraic idea of resurrection was intended not to support immortality, but to bridge the gap between the present suffering and the future vindication of those who have suffered unjustly. Detached from the question of the suffering of the downtrodden and their longing for vindication, eschatology becomes skewed to support the quest of individuals who want to extend their personalities into eternity or support their posthumous egoism. Detached from its base in the suffering of the neglected, eschatology becomes an ideological tool of those who want to control not only the earth but even the heavenly abode.

These contemporary accounts of eschatology offer a corrective to a kind of interpretation that has made eschatology captive to the sowers of Armageddon fever. These accounts have liberated eschatology from being an appendix of the Christian doctrine, from being a concern that deals only with the afterlife and is indifferent to the present existence, from obsessive individual interest, from the dualism of the physical and the spiritual, and from being an opiate or an escape to another world. In short, contemporary accounts from subaltern groups have made eschatology a vital topic in theological reconstruction.

### The New Human Being: Living in the Power of Eschatology

Having sketched the background of the character of eschatological discourse and set the context of suffering and struggle as the seedbed of its emergence, I am now ready to illustrate its bearings for anthropology. What are the manifestations of a new human being who has experienced the power of eschatology? What human countenance does eschatological sensibility shape?

#### Living the Power of Resurrection in the Midst of Daily Crucifixions

If suffering that longs for vindication is the soil out of which eschatological sensibility emerged, it makes sense to argue that there is no direct route to resurrection without crucifixion. Having the privilege of living in two worlds (the Philippines and the United States of America), I have noticed that Easter Sunday is more widely observed in the U.S. than

Good Friday. Easter Sunday is well marked not only by church members, but also by the wider secular public. This relatively widespread public observance of Easter is striking for someone, like myself, who hails from another country in which Good Friday is that day when the church's attendance swells beyond its walls, even more than Christmas worship or mass. This worship takes the whole afternoon, with seven sermons for the traditional seven last words of Jesus.

Why is Easter more widely celebrated than Good Friday in the U.S.? Have people in the U.S. experienced the message of resurrection in their lives more intensely than poor Third World peoples? Perhaps they have more reason to celebrate Easter than Good Friday. Without denying that the power of resurrection is real in the lives of people in the U.S., I want to suggest that it is common for a triumphant people to be tempted to short-cut or, if possible, bypass crucifixion in order to arrive quickly in the joyful and comforting arms of Easter celebration. It is a constant temptation for a therapeutic quick fix, aspirin culture to leap quickly over Good Friday to Easter Sunday.

I, too, would like for Easter Sunday to reign soon and wipe away the pain of crucifixion, but the healing and liberating power of Easter is real only when we have grasped the ugliness of the tomb and confronted the idols of death. No victory really worth having is cheaply won. No real hope is born out of lousy optimism, for optimism is not the wellspring of hope. There is no "cheap grace" on the way to resurrection.

The road to our Easter celebration is littered with daily crucifixions. To think of the crucifixion of Jesus in an absolutely unique and surrealistic fashion is to rob it of its power. It is the banality of the crucifixion of Jesus that draws suffering people into it. It is also this banality of daily crucifixions that makes a claim on the way we live as individuals and members of the body of Christ, the Church. We need to realize that our comforts are subsidized by the cheap labor of crucified people all over the world.

It is precisely in the banality of the daily crucifixions, when crucifixions are ordinary, when society is colonized by the culture of death, and when psychic numbing has engulfed the land, that the power of the risen Jesus must be witnessed. It is here that the power of the resurrection must blossom. Resurrection, following the lines of Christine Smith, "is that which happens to us on the other side of various kinds of death."[15] Christians hope for that grand resurrection beyond the daily crucifixions and deaths, but I am talking about the resurrection that happens to us in our earthly existence: This resurrection happens to us, not outside or beyond in an imagined sweet paradise, but in the midst of a world threatened and tyrannized by death. The words of Scott Couper, a missionary with Global Ministries (United Church of Christ, U.S.A., and Christian Church [Disciples of Christ]) in Durban, South Africa, testify to this experience of resurrection in the midst of the "various kinds of deaths":

As members of a local church HIV/AIDS ministry, we do despair. What keeps this ministry going even when we despair? We are constantly reminded by those we serve that our efforts to help are *everything* to them! What the ministry ultimately achieves is the demonstration of profound and unconditional love; and it is love that conquers all, *even the inevitable deaths.*[16]

Resurrection must be proclaimed and lived in a world tyrannized by death. Not only is the road to our celebration of the resurrection littered with daily crucifixions, but the new human being experiences resurrections in the very heart of crucifixions. I have to be lucidly emphatic on this: There is nothing salvific in the cross itself; there is nothing salvific in being put to a ghastly death. It is salvific only insofar as it is a death in confrontation with the powers of death. Yes, death against death! The new human being knows that there are moments in history when the only avenue to affirming life is to confront death with death.

### Waging in Hope: Ultimate Defiance and Hopeful Realism

Cynical realism, hedonistic carnivalism, and fatalism are logical responses to the pervasiveness of the forces of closure or the culture of death. If I continue to long and struggle for a "better tomorrow," it is not because I stick to the comfortable notion of linear progress nor because of assurances of "eventual victory" in this world.[17] There is more to learn from Michel Foucault's perceptive analysis of the cunning of power, but I have chosen to name my stance "hopeful realism," rather than what he calls "hyper- and pessimistic activism."[18] I am certainly not optimistic at the events that have begun this millennium, but I have decided to wager in hope.

Suffering–extreme suffering–can easily lead to despair and fatalism. Fatalism, or any form of resignation, is a common disease among people who have been subjugated and exploited for a long time. No amount of oratory can liberate them from fatalism and inspire hope. No amount of easy sermonizing can infuse their minds with new dynamism after decades of experiencing betrayal of their hopes and dreams. Pushed to the margins and disempowered, these people see the future not with the eyes of a hope that is open to new possibilities, but simply as a continuation of the present (dis)order. Those who have resigned themselves, such as those who have accepted their plight as natural or the will of God and those who have engaged in hedonistic play, are not really capable of hoping because they see the future simply as a continuation of the present.

Thinking of the future as nothing more than a continuation of the present serves a therapeutic function. To think of the future as nothing more than an extended time that has not yet come provides a form of security, though it is a false one. Many have enjoyed the comfort of a closed future–which is not a future–because it has relieved them of the freedom and responsibility of forging a better tomorrow. The future, by virtue of being a future, is open. However, people in submerged conditions do not see this future as containing the possibility for something new and better. Domesticated, they would rather remain in Egyptian captivity than journey into the wilderness where new possibilities (as well as risks) await. Refusal to face the open future serves as a form of refuge for these people, because everything that is associated with the open future–freedom, decision, and responsibility–is already relegated to somebody else, to those who dominate them.

While suffering can easily lead to fatalism and despair, it can also be a springboard for hope. As long as people continue to cry, there is a ray of hope, for crying is an expression that things are not all right. As long as people lament, there is a ray of hope, for it is an expression that the people have not accepted their plight as natural or the will of God. Eschatological sensibility is borne out of suffering that has refused to be silenced and numbed. We need to combat the chilly apathy that is engulfing our society, if our hopes are to remain alive.

Living without hope is living in hell; it is to experience death long before one's physical cessation. It is no accident that when Dante, in his *Inferno*, wanted his readers to understand the depths of evil, he pictured the gates of hell with these words written over them: "Abandon hope, all ye who enter here."[19] Long ago the church father Chrysostom said: "What plunges us into disaster is not so much our sins as our despair."[20] Without hope, we can only be swallowed by despair.

It is hard to live in hope when we are overwhelmed with events that continue to test our hopes. But paradoxes happen, and they happen still, for when our experience seems to be at the bleakest, there hope grows and shines. We see this in communities that have dared to hope amidst terrible situations, and in individuals whose lives show that they are "prisoners of hope." We, too, can help cultivate this hope in our place and in our time. "Because we don't bring this true hope with us from birth," says Moltmann, "and because our experiences of life may perhaps make us wise but not necessarily hopeful, we have to *go out* to learn hope. We learn to love when we say yes to life. So we learn to hope when we say yes to the future."[21]

If Moltmann could say that we learn to hope when we say yes to the future, I believe it is equally fitting to say that we learn to hope when we say yes to life. When we love life we cannot help but be prisoners of hope. Loving life necessitates that we must give ourselves to the radical demands of hope. This hope demands, for the sake of life, that we must not give up hope and the courage to act on that hope.

### Waiting in Hope: Eschatological Waiting

Without hope, one cannot truly wait. Only those who hope can truly wait. Robert McAfee Brown differentiates between waiting in hope, waiting casually, waiting in doubt, and waiting in dread.[22] Those who wait in hope are not just expecting something external to themselves to come; those who wait in hope are already being grasped by its power as they wait. "[A]lthough waiting is *not* having," as Paul Tillich would put it, "it is also having." He argues:

> The fact that we wait for something shows that in some way we already possess it. Waiting anticipates that which is not yet real. If we wait in hope and patience, the power of that for which we wait is already effective within us. He who waits in ultimate sense is not far from that for which he waits. He who waits in absolute seriousness is already grasped by that for which he waits. He who waits in patience has already received the power of that for which he waits. He who waits passionately is already an active power himself, the greatest power of transformation in personal and historical life.[23]

Waiting in hope is not the kind of casual waiting we commonly think of, nor is it an aimless and idle waiting, much less a waiting in dread. The waiting that is generated by a deep sense of hope is an active waiting. Active waiting anticipates that for which one waits. It is a kind of waiting characterized by readiness and anticipation. The activity that is generated by waiting in hope does not kill time but redeems the in-between time or the time being from being just another time. Waiting in hope redeems and gives significance to the time being. For those who wait in hope, this time being is not to be written off or grimly avoided, but embraced as an occasion for faithful living. The time being is our time, a precious and momentous time, a time to be reclaimed for creative and active living.

It amazes and humbles me to be in touch with the lives of people who, when there is no other choice but to wait, have responded to the situation creatively in order to transform it. Marginalized people have waited and have been told to wait for years. Instead of being reduced to cynicism, they have produced a waiting that is transformative. There is no denying that this waiting is forced upon them, with no choice except to wait in order to survive, but they have transformed this waiting into a strength, a waiting that in turn creatively transforms the situation.

I remember around the time when South Africa had its first national election—after the collapse of the apartheid regime—a cartoon depicted a white person complaining that he had been waiting for thirty minutes in the polling place. Then a black person said: "But I have been waiting for decades for this national election."

I am aware that it is difficult to wait for a long time and stay awake. Like Jesus' disciples who could not stay awake in Gethsemane during his final hours (Mk. 14:32–38), there is a temptation to sleep while waiting. Staying awake is a struggle; struggle is staying awake. Giving voice to unfinished dreams keeps us awake while we continue to wait.

### Living in Eschatological Imagination and Vision

Suffering and marginalization have also propelled eschatological imagination and vision. When marginalized groups speak of unfinished dreams, they are not simply denouncing that which is not right, but announcing or opening up our imaginations to alternative possibilities that are simply not given by the logic of the present. These two dimensions are inextricably interwoven. The denunciation of the "what is" propels the annunciation of the "what might be," and the annunciation of the "what might be" propels the denunciation of the "what is." Eschatological imagination is, following Dermot Lane, "a protest against the premature closure of our understanding of the present and a plea for openness towards the future."[24]

To the dismay of those who expect grand solutions, I do not have a grand utopian blueprint of an alternative tomorrow. If utopia means an ideal community to which we can point where a new world is already realized, then I do not have a utopian vision. But we can have an "atopia," following Sallie McFague, which is "an imagined world both prophetic and alluring from which we can judge what is wrong with the paradigm that has created the present crisis on our planet."[25]

This atopian or eschatological imagination does not arise simply by the wave of a magic wand or with the help of some supernatural genie in the lamp. Nor does it arise simply by sitting and imagining a better world in some meditation center. The cultural creativity that R. B. J. Walker speaks about applies to eschatological imagination. "The challenge of cultural creativity is not only a matter of creating visions of a better world," says Walker,

> but of reconstructing the conditions under which the future may be imagined. Cultural creativity does not occur in abstraction. It arises from concrete everyday practices, from people able to make connections with each other and engaging in dialogue about the meaning of their experiences.[26]

The experience of liminality, or of the in-betweenness of ethnic and racial minorities in the U.S., has generated eschatological imagination and vision.[27] The minorities' experience of living in different worlds has convinced them that people can live differently, and the exploration of this different way of living is our common search and struggle. Eschatological imagination names their unfinished dreams and articulates their longings for an alternative tomorrow.

The longings of racial and ethnic communities for a new and better world are informed by their particular experiences and perspectives, but particularity is not identical with exclusivism. In fact, the awareness that people of color have of their particular perspective and their experience of being excluded propels them to enlarge their dreams and visions. If

America, for people of color, is still an unfinished dream, it is also an unfinished dream for white America–and for all Americans!

### God Is not Finished with Us Yet: History Is Open

But why hope when there is more reason to be cynical? Is hope simply a sheer act of will and nothing more? From whence can I muster hope when I am immersed in a sea of despair? Where is the wellspring of my hope? What is enabling me to wager in hope when there are more reasons to despair?

At this point I am reminded of the 1937 debate between Walter Benjamin and Frank Horkheimer, both of Frankfurt School of Philosophy. Horkheimer, out of his historical materialist position, said that any notion of an unclosed past and an open future was idealistic. He argued that "[w]hat happened to those human beings who have perished does not have any part in the future. They will never be called forth to be blessed in eternity."[28] Horkheimer operated on the presupposition of a closed history.

In contrast to Horkheimer, Benjamin wanted to work out a notion of history that did not ignore our unity in history with the past generations, especially those who had been crucified by the idolatrous forces. Benjamin refused to see history as closed and finished. For him the work of the past was not closed, not even to a historical materialist. He believed that we can keep past history open.

Responding to Horkheimer, Benjamin said that the corrective for the idea that history is closed "lies in the reflection that history is...a form of emphatic memory (*Eingedenken*). What science has 'settled,' emphatic memory can modify."[29] Furthermore, emphatic memory gives us an experience that "prohibits us from conceiving history completely non-theologically," or it "forbids us to regard history completely without theology."[30] Emphatic memory helps us to read history theologically.

I am in agreement with the main direction of Benjamin's ideas, but I would like to reverse his order. Reading history theologically demands emphatic memory. One cannot do authentic theology without embracing the spirit of emphatic memory, especially if the sufferings of the victims are not to be in vain. Emphatic memory opens up the past and reconnects the living with the dead. The history of suffering is not closed; it is open to us through emphatic memory or through remembrance. Through our emphatic memories we open the past to establish our solidarity with those who have gone before us. This is what Christian Lenhardt calls "anamnestic solidarity."[31] But we do so because we believe that the future is open. When emphatic memory or remembrance opens up the past and our solidarity with the dead, it also opens up the future. The past is opened not only for its own sake but also in relation to the future. Those who have gone before us have a future, and this future is tied to our acts of remembrance and solidarity.

But, as people of faith and as theologians, we do not stop with the declaration that history is open. History is open, but the belief that history is open cannot survive the onslaught of the forces of death unless it is rooted in the more fundamental belief that God is not finished yet with history. More pointedly, history is open because God is not finished with history. To use a religious idiom of the black church in North America: "God ain't finished with us yet!"[32] To say this is to say "no" to those who want to give a closure to history. It is an ontological belief that history is open because God's act of creation is continuing still. It is a refusal to let the forces of closure have the final word. Of course, we can allow the forces of closure to have the final word. But we can choose, and I say we must choose, not to let these forces control the way we live our lives.

The paradigmatic resurrection event in the Christian scriptures signifies God's "no" to those who want to close history and give the final word over to the forces of death. The fate of the victims is not sealed in the graveyard and those who have suffered have not suffered in vain. For persons empowered by the liberating power of eschatology, no one has died in vain for a noble cause. It is for this reason that the apocalyptist can write, "And I heard a voice from heaven saying, 'Write this: Blessed are the dead who from now on die in the Lord.' 'Yes,' says the Spirit, "they will rest from their labors, for their deeds follow them'" (Revelation 14:13).

Bishop Oscar Romero contemporizes for us the message of resurrection in the midst of death. His words convey his deep trust that no one has died in vain in the name of life:

> My life has been threatened many times. I have to confess that, as a Christian, I don't believe in death without resurrection. If they kill me *I will rise again in the Salvadoran people.* I'm not boasting, or saying this out of pride, but rather humbly as I can...Martyrdom is a grace of God that I do not feel worthy of. But if God accepts the sacrifice of my life, my hope is that my blood will be like a seed of liberty and a sign that our hopes will soon become a reality.[33]

### Retrieval of Dangerous Memories: Turning Monuments into Movements

The saints have not died in vain, for the resurrection is God's "no" to the forces of death. But there is a challenge to which we who are still living must respond. Through our emphatic memory, as Benjamin suggested, we let those who are already dead have a claim on us and find resurrection in the community of the living. What are we being called to do?

It may seem that hoping is associated only with the future and memory with the past. This is not exactly true. In fact, those who are impassioned by eschatological imagination are also those who are deeply immersed in the memories of the past, specifically painful memories that wounded the community. Those who hope and envision a better world are also those who have not forgotten or have not lost the sense of memory. Thus, Fumitaka Matsuoka can speak of "visionary memory," a vision that is propelled by the retrieval of painful memories.[34]

The point I raise here resonates with the ideas of Benjamin I noted earlier, but there is a specific edge to the act of remembrance that gives it sharpness. For Benjamin, opening up and rereading the past involves a reading of history against the grain. This means that we need to reread the past from the perspectives of the victims, uncovering what contemporary theologians call dangerous memories.

Rereading the past against the grain allows the dangerous memories of the dead to have a claim on us, the living. In his work *Unmasking the Powers*, Walter Wink tells a story about Major Claude Eatherly, the pilot of the plane that dropped the atomic bomb on Hiroshima.[35] Wink was a pastor in Texas when the local press carried the story about Major Eatherly. Eatherly had been involved in a series of petty crimes with the sole purpose of getting arrested. The newspaper readily dismissed him as suffering from "personal guilt complex" and, on the "expert" witness of a psychiatrist, he was confined to a mental institution on the grounds of "lunacy."

The certified "expert" psychiatrist called Eatherly's behavior lunacy or a personal guilt complex, but he carried in his heart the bomb that killed thousands of people in Hiroshima. The dead of Hiroshima made a claim on Major Eatherly. Eatherly, according to Wink, "had been trying to make the nation face the immorality of this act in which he had played a small but significant part. Failing that, he had sought, by increasingly bizarre behavior, to see that at least *he* was punished, thereby forcing the guilty to punish him."[36] Wink cited a communication between Eatherly and German philosopher Günther Anders in which Eatherly said: "The truth is that society cannot accept the fact of my guilt without at the same time recognizing its own far deeper guilt." Anders replied, "One can only conclude: happy the times in which the insane speak out this way, wretched the times in which only the insane speak out this way." As the U.S. government declared Eatherly a lunatic, others came to his defense. Bertrand Russell had this to say: "The world was prepared to honor him for his part in the massacre, but, when he repented, it turned against him, seeing in his act of repentance its own condemnation."[37]

The powers-that-be of any society will do everything within their might and means to make marginalized communities lose their painful memories because this is an effective way of controlling them. But the dangerous memories must not be forgotten; they must be exhumed. Through a poem that gives voice to her mother's experience, Janice Mirikitani exhumes the painful past that former Japanese American internment camp victims suffered. When told by the hearing commissioner that her time was up, her mother (through Mirikitani's prophetic poetry) protested:

So when you tell me my time is up,
I tell you this:
Pride has kept my lips
pinned by nails,
my rage coffined.
But I exhume my past
to claim this time.[38]

To exhume the past: This is the challenge that Mirikitani poses for us, for no visionary memory forgets the pains of the past. To forgive and move forward is not to forget. Rather, it is to re-member the dis-membered; it is to make whole those who have experienced brokenness. The buried is exhumed not simply for its own sake, for there is no joy in merely exhuming the unfinished dreams of previous generations. The buried is exhumed because it is necessary in the forging of a new and better tomorrow.

Retrieval of dangerous memories is, however, only a moment in the process of forging a new and better tomorrow. The painful moments of the past and the proud monuments of the past must find resurrection in the movements of today. We must be grateful to the monuments of the past, especially for those who have paved the way for us, but true gratitude is expressed when we transform the monuments of the past into movements of today—movements of transformation and movements that weave together our scattered voices and visions.

Turning past monuments into peoples' movements is our way of making the victims and the "dis-appeared" into martyrs or witnesses.[39] We proclaim liturgically the turning of the tortured bodies and the "dis-appeared" into martyrs in the eucharistic meal, but it is in the peoples' movements that the memory of the "dis-appeared" is made bodily present. Like Carlos Bulosan, who took the task of making the poor peasants of northern Philippines "live in [his] words," so it is our task to make the monuments of the past live in our contemporary movements.

The story of Ligaya Domingo and her father Silme Domingo—both labor organizers—illustrates true gratitude to the labors of the past, the shift from anguish into anger, and the turning of monuments into movements.[40] Ligaya Domingo was only five years old when her father (Silme) and a fellow activist were shot to death by Ferdinand Marcos' henchmen in Seattle on June 21, 1981. Silme became the target of the Marcos regime's ire for his responsibility in making the International Longshoremen and Warehousemen's Union (ILWU) take an unprecedented international focus on the Philippines.

Twenty years after the incident, Ligaya is following in the steps of her father. In an interview, Ligaya says that her father is still a persistent presence in her life: "Sometimes I think about what he would want me to do, and how he would see me in what I'm doing…Sometimes I really get sad about it." Memory is very much alive in Ligaya's life.

In speaking about her labor involvement, Ligaya said that her father taught her an important lesson: "It's that you cannot simply give up the fight." But there were moments when her tone, as organizers can easily understand, revealed weariness and fatigue. "One thing that's frustrating for me," she said, "is that even when we see victories, they're small, they're really small." As an example: "We had a strike at West Seattle Psychiatric Hospital last year, and after 138 days we got the contract that we wanted. But you know, that's just one victory in a cloud of a million other things to fight for."[41]

As Ligaya was speaking about the enormity of the things to fight for and how small a single victory is, her words came out "between laugh and sigh." "Between laugh and sigh" is an expression of a Filipina upbringing, perhaps part of the survival mechanisms of people who have to surmount hardships of various sorts. "Between laugh and sigh" also captures a deep moment in the life of a person who is committed to a better tomorrow in the face of the stubborn forces of closure. What Ligaya has done is small when we think of the millions of issues to fight for, but she has done something significant. She has turned the monuments of her father's labor and sacrifice into a movement.

### Living as if the Future Were Present and the Reclamation of a Space of Freedom

Let me recount a story, "The Woodcarver," from *The Way of Chuang Tzu*. I believe this story is helpful in making us understand the ideas I want to convey under the present subtopic.

> Khing, the master carver, made a bell stand
> Of precious wood. When it was finished,
> All who saw it were astounded. They said it must be
> The work of spirits.
> The Prince of Lu said to the master carver:
> "What is your secret?"
> Khing replied: "I am only a workman:
> I have no secret. There is only this:
> When I began to think about the work you commanded
> I guarded my spirit, did not expend it
> On trifles, that were not to the point.
> I fasted in order to set
> My heart at rest.
> After three days of fasting, I had forgotten gain and success.
> After five days
> I had forgotten praise or criticism.
> After seven days
> I had forgotten my body

With all its limbs.
"By this time all thought of your Highness
And of the court had faded away.
All that might distract me from the work
Had vanished.
I was collected in the single thought
Of the bell stand.
"Then I went to the forest
To see the trees in their own natural state.
When the right tree appeared before my eyes,
The bell stand also appeared in it, clearly, beyond doubt.
All I had to do was to put forth my hand
And begin.
"If I had not met this particular tree
There would have been
No bell stand at all.
"What happened?"
My own collected thought
Encountered the hidden potential in the wood;
From this live encounter came the work
Which you ascribe to the spirits."[42]

There are various dimensions to this story, but I am going to highlight a few for my purposes here. In the story of "The Woodcarver," Khing was obviously under external pressure to produce a bell stand to the satisfaction of the Prince of Lu. He produced the bell stand not simply for art's sake, but because he had to do it. We all know such situations in real life. There are demands that we simply must meet. But Khing was able to find freedom within a given situation, which helped him move into expressing art for art's sake. Such freedom is not granted by an external authority; Khing had to reclaim it for himself. It is this freedom that enabled him to respond in a different way and to live differently.

Eschatological sensibility, as I underscored earlier, does not allow us to escape from the hard facts of this life, but even under a set of external constraints and circumstances we can choose how to respond. We can respond differently if we have learned to live as if the future were present or as if the vision informed by our eschatological imagination were already a present reality. We can nourish and maintain our creative imaginations even under external constraints, if we reclaim that "inner" freedom that is in us.

Khing, the woodcarver, reclaimed the "inner" freedom that was in himself, which the Prince of Lu attributed to the spirits. While Khing, as the story portrays, attributed his ability to the inner freedom that he reclaimed, we, who read the account through our Christian lenses, need not see this inner freedom that Khing spoke about as denial of the spirit or as antithetical to the presence of the spirit. Spirit is that inner freedom that enables us to imagine and live differently. Spirit is not only the breath that gives us life, it is breadth that gives us breathing space. It is the democratic space that peoples' movements speak about. Contrary to the common understanding about spirit, Moltmann contends that "the eternal life of God's Spirit is not different life from this life here;" rather, "it is the power that makes this life here different."[43]

Living as if the future were present provides the orientation, but it is the spirit that enables us to live as if the future were, indeed, present. Reclamation of inner freedom happens only when we get focused on something and move away from the hubbub of life. Living as if the future were present provides such a focus and enables us, with the aid of the spirit, to be transformed from within and to resist conformity from without, even to resist using the master's tools to dismantle the master's house.

Another story supports that of the woodcarver. This time a conversation between Sung Kye Yi, the first king of the Yi dynasty (1392–1910) in Korea, and Monk Moohahk, an advisor to the king, is instructive. On one occasion, Sung Kye Yi teasingly tried to put down Moohahk. "To me, you look like a pig," said the king. But the monk gently replied, "To me, you look like Buddha." "Why are you saying that?" asked the astonished king. "If you have a pig inside, you will see pigs in others, and if you have Buddha inside, you will see Buddha in others," Moohahk modestly explained.[44]

The inner freedom that empowered Moohahk to resist conformity from without resonates with Khing's experience. Going back to the story of "The Woodcarver," Khing's inner freedom empowered him to live differently. Not only did he experience freedom from external authority, he also experienced freedom from an obsession with results. Of course, results are important, and never in this world are we freed from a concern to produce results, but we can only live differently and be imaginative if we do not make ourselves a prisoner of results and if we put results within a proper perspective. When we are driven by results, we are more likely to continue with what we have been used to doing and not take the risk of other, unproven creative approaches.

But more than this, the preoccupation with results, no matter how noble the goal, can be destructive both to the agents of the action and the world that is being acted upon. An expectation of results that is not placed within the wider perspective of the exercise of creative freedom leads to the destruction of the world that is acted upon, as in the destruction of people and the environment in the name of progress and achievement, and the alienation of the agents of the action as well. Peoples' movements are not exempt from this danger when, in the name of the cause that the movement is fighting for, people are sacrificed and their creative freedom violated for the sake of the final outcome–the dreamed of society. Similarly, Nancy Victorin-Vangerud argues that when our theology "merely idealizes the telos of struggle, and not the struggle itself, we undermine our efforts toward the ideal."[45]

Because eschatological sensibility is not a prisoner of outcomes and success, it continues to flourish even when tangible success is not within reach. When success is not within reach, the final matter that counts is faithfulness. This faithfulness is exemplified by the people who endured the plague in Albert Camus' novel *The Plague*. They did not lose hope and eschatological imagination even if they were not completely successful in exterminating or escaping from the epidemic. But one thing they did, says McFague: "[T]hey…decided to live differently while they did live, to live as if life mattered while they had it, to live with integrity in light of the brutal reality that defined their world."[46]

### The Journey Is Home: The Future Is in the Journey, the Struggle Is Liberation

Too often we think of the process as a means to an end, or of the journey as only a means to reaching the destination. Too often we think of action not as an experience to be lived for its own sake, but as a means to a greater end. If that end is not achieved we consider ourselves failures. But there is something terribly amiss with this notion: It fails to realize that the process itself is constitutive of the goal, as the journey is constitutive of the destination. To put it differently, the destination is already in the journey. Or, to use the words of Nelle Morton, "the journey is home."[47]

Eschatological sensibility offers us the insight of finding a home in our journey. Finding home in the journey, says Henry Nouwen, is being "at home while still on the way."[48] Not only must the future be lived and celebrated in the present, we must find a home in our long and arduous journey. The new humanity that we strive for and look forward to is not simply out there in the future waiting for our arrival, it is present in the journey itself. While we look forward and anticipate the fullness of our liberation, the struggle itself is an experience of liberation. Even survival is an experience of liberation. Only those who struggle experience liberation; only those who journey find home in the journey. "My journey is not over yet," says Andrew Sung Park, "but I am at home; for home is everywhere God is and I am. And home is not only the place to relax, but also the place to struggle, challenge, and grow."[49] As one activist put it: "I guess our home is in the struggle."[50]

The idea of finding home in the struggle resonates with Fernando Segovia's notion of "alien" but becoming "strangers no longer." Speaking from a Hispanic perspective, there is no doubt, says Segovia, that we will continue to remain as aliens, but "we have ceased to behave as aliens, keeping our place and struggling for survival in silence; instead, we have embraced our place as aliens, found our voice as aliens, and lifted that voice up as aliens."[51]

This experience of feeling at home while still on the way or finding a home in the struggle is a profound spiritual experience: It is an expression of an encounter with the divine or of God's indwelling. When a person experiences God's indwelling, she or he finds a home. When God fills the heart (*cor* and *coeur*), the whole being finds home.

Celebrations along some points in the journey are nourishing, but, more than this, the journey is home. Yes, the journey must be celebrated as a home, because in our historical existence the future we desire is always given to us in the form of a promise. We do not have the foresight to predict the end of our journey. Much as we ache to know, that information is not accessible to us. What we are called to is to do the best that we can, to live fully in our time, and to openly trust in that ultimate life-giving power that lures us toward a desirable future.

Finding a home in our journey is liberating; it is healing. It liberates us from the dead weight of the past and prevents us from making our goal or destination into a procrustean bed. When our destination becomes a procrustean bed preventing us from seeing that this destination is already imbedded in the journey—as the flower in the bud, the spring in the freezing winter, or the butterfly in the chrysalis—we experience a great loss. It is the loss of not seeing greatness in the banal, the eternal in the momentary, and the universe in a grain of sand.

When we find a home in our journey we are liberated from our small cocoons and enabled to see ourselves and the larger world around us in a significantly fuller light. We are liberated, following William Blake's lines,

> To see a World in a Grain of Sand
> And a Heaven in a Wild Flower,
> Hold Infinity in the palm of your hand
> And Eternity in an hour.[52]

Rather than making us oblivious to the minute and common daily moments of living, eschatological imagination enables us to find a home in our journey. It piques our senses so that we may smell the fragrance of flowers and the aroma of delicious meals, hear the chirping bird and the cry of the starving people, feel the caress of our loved ones and the gentle breeze that comes our way, take delight in the radiant face that comes in the chuckle of a little child, laugh at ourselves when we discover our own ignorance, and marvel at serendipitous events.

As I watch my kids grow, eschatological imagination has taught me that I cannot ignore the small events of our togetherness, for the small things that I celebrate with them during our fleeting days may be my only significant chance to convey to them how much I love them. These small things are, indeed, the big things. While away for a week in the summer of 1998, I got a note from my family to remind me of this important message: "Enjoy the little things…for one day you may realize that these little things are the big things in Life."

Eschatological sensibility does not take us away from our earthiness, our bodiliness, and our senses. Instead, it enables us to feel and think through our bodies. Eschatological sensibility makes us thoroughly embodied subjects. It is consistent with embodied knowing, because embodied knowing evokes eschatological sensibility. Eschatological sensibility provides us with the eagle's wings to soar and the power to transcend, but only in an immanental and thoroughly embodied way. To transcend does not mean to be oblivious to particularities, but to see through the myriad of particularities.

My understanding of the theological imaginative task is imbued with the notion that the journey is home. The task of imaginative theological reconstruction does not promise us the final port or home of arrival, and I would say that no single theological work can lead us to that final port. But this work seeks to point out a direction and calls us to take cognizance that our journey into the dreamed-for "not yet" is at the same time our home.

## Conclusion: The Search for the Human Goes On

It is difficult to capture and freeze in time and space the new anthropology that we are reimagining and striving for, because it is not something that is just waiting for our discovery, nor something we can simply mine from ancient or modern texts. There were breakthrough events and breakthrough figures in the past, but the human freed from naturism, classism, sexism, and racism is still something that we have not experienced fully. The new humanity that we speak about does not only involve the task of recovery but also of reconstruction. Like women's experience of awakening into a new consciousness that, in Elizabeth Janeway's words, is moving "between myth and morning," we also wait and seek this new humanity, even as we have experienced the foretaste of its coming in the form of promise.[53]

Being human is not simply waiting to be discovered; it is more properly a process of becoming human. And this process of becoming human involves dreaming and acting as if the dreamed for humanity were already a present reality. This is the new humanity we celebrate, a future that is truly alive because it impacts the way we think, dwell, and act in the present, both individually and communally.

A realistic hope for our planet and for our society today does not lie in some miraculous interventions—whether supernatural or techno-capitalist— but in the groaning and greening socially conscious and active people who have resolved to make a difference in various locations and stations in life. No utopian realism, post-utopian cynicism, pessimistic determinism, business-as-usual realism, piecemeal pragmatism, nor couch potato optimism can take us out of sick bay. Cynicism and dogged certainty are both dangerous. No group of "think tanks" nor any fresh concoctions from intellectual mandarins and adroit gurus can provide us with an easy recipe for healing. No bumper sticker or sound bite solutions can suffice; not a single voice. It is a fallacy that without a single light to guide us we are lost; this fallacy needs to be exposed. We are in this search for a new humanity for the long haul, always aching and aiming for the promise while gathering nourishing provisions along the way, and celebrating moments of life-giving openings whenever and wherever we can.

Let us remember: We are not called to do everything, nor are we called to finish the task, but we are called to do something—to sew our piece into the quilt of our common struggle to forge a new humanity. "If [we] save one life, [we] save the whole world," says the Talmud.[54]

But wait a minute. There is another wisdom to which we must listen, a wisdom that comes from the fourfold vow of Bodhisattva in the Mahayana Buddhist tradition: "Living beings are innumerable: I vow to save them all. Illusive desires and lusts are inexhaustible: I vow to extinguish them all. Gates to dharma are numberless: I vow to learn and master them all. The way of enlightenment is peerless: I vow to realize it."[55]

How can we reconcile the seemingly contradictory points of the Talmudic wisdom and the wisdom from the fourfold vow of Bodhisattva? With the Talmud I say that saving one life is saving the whole, for a single life is not simply a number in the web of life. But with the fourfold vow I say that the demand on us has no limit. We cannot do everything, yet we must work relentlessly at that which we can do and celebrate our accomplishments along the way. But we must always strive for that which we are challenged to do and that which is greater than what we can do.

Many of us will perish "between myth and morning," but I have chosen to believe that no effort for the sake of greater well-being is wasted and no drop of blood, sweat, and tears is forgotten, for they will find resurrection in the memory of the living and in the memory of our never failing, always abiding wellspring of life—God.

## Notes

[1]Peter Phan, "Contemporary Context and Issues in Eschatology," *Theological Studies* 55 (1994): 515.

[2]Dermot Lane, *Keeping Hope Alive: Stirrings in Christian Theology* (Mahwah, N.J.: Paulist Press, 1996), 14.

[3]Jürgen Moltmann, *The Theology of Hope* (New York: Harper & Row, 1967), 16. Also cited in Lane, *Keeping Hope Alive*, 4.

[4]See Moltmann, *The Theology of Hope;* and *God for a Secular Society: The Public Relevance of Theology* (Minneapolis: Fortress Press, 1999). Also *God Will Be All in All: The Eschatology of Jürgen Moltmann*, ed. Richard Bauckham (Edinburgh: T. & T. Clark, 1999).

[5]See Ann O'Hara Graff, *In the Embrace of God: Feminist Approaches to Theological Anthropology* (Maryknoll, N.Y.: Orbis Books, 1995).

⁶Rosemary Radford Ruether, *Sexism and God-Talk: Toward a Feminist Theology* (Boston: Beacon Press, 1983), 235–58.

⁷Catherine Keller, "Eschatology, Ecology, and a Green Ecumenacy," in *Reconstructing Christian Theology*, ed. Rebecca Chopp and Mark Lewis Taylor (Minneapolis: Fortress Press, 1994), 326–345. Sallie McFague devotes a chapter that reinterprets eschatology in relation to anthropology in her work, *The Body of God: An Ecological Theology* (Minneapolis: Fortress Press, 1993).

⁸John J. Gager, *Kingdom and Community: The Social World of Early Christianity* (Englewood Cliffs, New Jersey: Prentice Hall, 1975). Also refer to his essay, "The Attainment of Millennial Bliss Through Myth: The Book of Revelation" in *Visionaries and Their Apocalypses*, ed. Paul D. Hanson (Philadelphia: Fortress Press, 1983), 146–55.

⁹Sheldon Isenberg, "Power Through Temple and Torah in Graeco-Roman Palestine," in *Christianity, Judaism and Other Greco-Roman Cults: Studies for Morton Smith at Sixty*, vols. 1–4, ed., J. Neusner (Leiden: E. J. Brill, 1975), 27.

¹⁰Jerome H. Neyrey, "The Idea of Purity in Mark's Gospel," *Semeia 35* (1986): 91–128.

¹¹Elisabeth Schüssler Fiorenza, *Invitation to the Book of Revelation: A Commentary on the Apocalypse with Complete Text from The Jerusalem Bible* (New York: Image Books, 1981), 17. See also John G. Gager, "The Attainment of Millennial Bliss Through Myth: The Book of Revelation," in *Visionaries and Their Apocalypses*, 148.

¹²Elisabeth Schüssler Fiorenza, *The Book of Revelation: Justice and Judgment* (Philadelphia: Fortress Press, 1985), 192–99.

¹³Jürgen Moltmann, *Religion, Revolution, and the Future* (New York: Charles Scribner's Sons, 1969), 45.

¹⁴Ruether, *Sexism and God-Talk*, 243.

¹⁵Christine Smith, *Risking the Terror: Resurrection in This Life* (Cleveland: The Pilgrim Press, 2001), 2.

¹⁶Scott Couper, *Global Ministries News* 2/2(Winter 2002): 5.

¹⁷Sharon Welch, *Sweet Dreams in America: Making Ethics and Spirituality Work* (New York: Routledge, 1999), xi, xvi.

¹⁸Michel Foucault, "On Genealogy of Ethics: An Overview of Work in Progress," in *Foucault Reader*, ed. Paul Rabinow (New York: Pantheon Books, 1984), 343.

¹⁹Dante's *Inferno*, cited in Douglas John Hall, *Why Christian? For Those on the Edge of Faith* (Minneapolis: Fortress Press, 1998), 103.

²⁰Chrysostom, cited in Jürgen Moltmann, *The Source of Life: The Holy Spirit and the Theology of Life* (Minneapolis: Fortress Press, 1997), 39.

²¹Moltmann, *Source of Life*, 39.

²²Robert McAfee Brown, *Persuade Us to Rejoice: The Liberating Power of Fiction* (Louisville: Westminster/John Knox Press, 1992), 41–52.

²³Paul Tillich, *The Shaking of the Foundations* (London: SCM Press, 1949), 151.

²⁴Lane, *Keeping Hope Alive*, 2.

²⁵McFague, *The Body of God*, 198–99.

²⁶R. B. J. Walker, *One World, Many Worlds: Struggles for a Just World Peace* (London: Zed Books; Boulder, Colo.: Lynne Rienner, 1988), 169.

²⁷See Jung Young Lee, *Marginality: The Key to Multicultural Theology* (Minneapolis: Fortress Press, 1995), 152–53.

²⁸For English readers, see H. Peukert, *Science, Action, and Fundamental Theology: Towards a Theology of Communicative Action* (Cambridge, Mass.: MIT Press, 1984), 206; also, refer to Lane, *Keeping Hope Alive*, 119–23, 200–10.

²⁹Peukert, *Science, Action, and Fundamental Theology*, 207.

³⁰Ibid., 207. Also, see Lane, *Keeping Hope Alive*, 202, quoting Rolf Tiedemann, "Historical Materialism…," *The Philosophical Forum* 15 (Fall-Winter 1983–1984), 79.

³¹Christian Lenhardt, "Anamnestic Solidarity: The Proletariat and its *Manes*," *Telos* 25 (1975): 133–55, cited by Peukert, *Science, Action, and Fundamental Theology*, 208.

³²Enoch Oglesby, *Born in the Fire: Case Studies in Christian Ethics and Globalization* (New York: The Pilgrim Press, 1990), viii.

³³Plácido Erdozaín, *Archbishop Romero: Martyr of Salvador* (Maryknoll, N.Y.: Orbis Books, 1980), 75.

³⁴Fumitaka Matsuoka, *Out of Silence: Emerging Themes in Asian American Churches* (Cleveland: United Church Press, 1995), 117.

[35]Walter Wink, *Unmasking the Powers: Invisible Forces That Determine Human Existence* (Philadelphia: Fortress Press, 1986).

[36]Ibid., 48.

[37]Ibid., 49. Wink citing quotations from Lionel Rubinoff, *The Pornography of Power* (Chicago: Quadrangle Books, 1968), 36–42.

[38]Janice Mirikitani, *Shedding Silence: Poetry and Prose* (Berkeley, Calif.: Celestial Arts, 1987), 35.

[39]See William Cavanaugh, *Torture and Eucharist* (Oxford: Blackwell Publishers, 1998).

[40]Jennifer Soriano, "Organizer's Daughter: Labor Organizer Ligaya Domingo," *Filipinas* (March 2000), 28–29, 31–32.

[41]Ibid., 32.

[42]Cited in Parker Palmer, *The Active Life: Wisdom for Work, Creativity, and Caring* (New York: HarperCollins, 1991), 55–56.

[43]Moltmann, *Source of Life*, 22.

[44]"Pigs in the Eyes of a Pig: Moohahk," *Modern Buddhism* (December 1995), 47, cited in Andrew Sung Park, *Racial Conflict and Healing: An Asian-American Theological Perspective* (Maryknoll, N.Y.: Orbis Books, 1996), 138.

[45]Nancy Victorin-Vangerud, *The Raging Hearth: Spirit in the Household of God* (St. Louis: Chalice Press, 2000), 185–86.

[46]McFague, *Body of God*, 208.

[47]Nelle Morton, *The Journey Is Home* (Boston: Beacon Press, 1985).

[48]Henri J. M. Nouwen, *Reaching Out: The Three Movements of the Spiritual Life* (New York: Doubleday, 1975), 147–48.

[49]Andrew Sung Park, "Church and Theology: My Theological Journey," in *Journeys at the Margin: Toward an Autobiographical Theology in Asian-American Perspective*, ed. Peter Phan and Jung Young Lee (Collegeville, Minn.: Liturgical Press, 1999), 172.

[50]Liddy Nacpil, cited by Steven de Castro, in *The State of Asian America: Activism and Resistance in the 1990s*, ed. Karen Aguilar-San Juan (Boston: South End Press, 1994), 317.

[51]Fernando F. Segovia, "Aliens in the Promised Land: The Manifest Destiny of U.S. Hispanic American Theology," in *Hispanic/Latino Theology: Challenge and Promise*, ed. Ada Maria Isasi-Díaz and Fernando F. Segovia (Minneapolis: Fortress Press, 1996), 30.

[52]"Auguries of Innocence," in *The Complete Poetry and Prose of William Blake*, ed. David Erdman (New York: Doubleday Anchor, 1988), 489.

[53]Elizabeth Dodson Gray, *Patriarchy as a Conceptual Trap* (Wellesley, Mass.: Roundtable Press, 1982), 129.

[54]Talmudic saying, cited in Tom Montgomery-Fate, *Beyond the White Noise: Mission in a Multicultural World* (St. Louis: Chalice Press, 1997).

[55]Fourfold vow of Bodhisattva in the Mahayana Buddhist tradition cited in Michael Amaladoss, *Life in Freedom: Liberation Theologies in Asia* (Maryknoll, N.Y.: Orbis Books, 1997), 84.

# Proper Name Index

# Subject Index